DUO!

THE BEST SCENES
FOR MATURE ACTORS

The Applause Acting Series

DUO!

THE BEST SCENES
FOR MATURE ACTORS

EDITED BY STEPHEN FIFE

APPLAUSE
THEATRE & CINEMA BOOKS
An Imprint of Hal Leonard Corporation
New York

792.028

Published in 2015 by Applause Theatre & Cinema Books

An Imprint of Hal Leonard Corporation
7777 West Bluemound Road
Milwaukee, WI 53213

Trade Book Division Editorial Offices
33 Plymouth St., Montclair, NJ 07042

Printed in the United States of America

Book design by Kristina Rolander

Play Sources, Permissions, and Acknowledgments can be found on pages 427–434, which constitute an extension of this copyright page.

Library of Congress Cataloging-in-Publication Data

Duo! : the best scenes for mature actors / edited by Stephen Fife.
    pages cm -- (The Applause acting series)
1. Acting. 2. Dialogues, English. 3. Older people--Drama. 4. American drama--21st century. 5. English drama--21st century. I. Fife, Stephen, editor.
  PN2080.D857 2014
  792.02'8--dc23
                    2014022112

ISBN 978-1-4803-6020-4

www.applausebooks.com

CONTENTS

Introduction   xi

PART I: SCENES FOR A MAN AND A WOMAN

THE PRICE
by Arthur Miller   3

DEATH AND THE MAIDEN
by Ariel Dorfman   9

THE MAN FROM NEBRASKA
by Tracy Letts   13

GOD OF VENGEANCE
by Sholem Asch, adapted by Stephen Fife   17

THE SPEED OF DARKNESS
by Steve Tesich   21

THE SOUND OF A VOICE
by David Henry Hwang   24

SEX WITH THE CENSOR
by Theresa Rebeck   28

LONG DAY'S JOURNEY INTO NIGHT
by Eugene O'Neill   35

THE FATHER
by August Strindberg   39

SHTICK
by Henry Meyerson   43

BREAK OF DAY
by Stephen Fife   47

THE HOUSE OF SLEEPING BEAUTIES
by David Henry Hwang   50

SEASCAPE
by Edward Albee   54

DEATH OF A SALESMAN
by Arthur Miller   59

LATER LIFE
by A. R. Gurney   67

AUGUST: OSAGE COUNTY
by Tracy Letts   72

THE SISTERS ROSENSWEIG
by Wendy Wasserstein   76

BALLAD OF YACHIYO
by Philip Kan Gotanda   81

FENCES
by August Wilson   84

WALK
by Theresa Rebeck   88

THE SPEED OF DARKNESS
by Steve Tesich   96

THE LAST TIME WE SAW HER
by Jane Anderson   100

LATER LIFE
by A. R. Gurney   112

FIGHTING OVER BEVERLEY
by Israel Horovitz   120

GOOD PEOPLE
by David Lindsay-Abaire   128

IN THE EYE OF THE HURRICANE
by Eduardo Machado   138

LONG DAY'S JOURNEY INTO NIGHT
by Eugene O'Neill   142

OTHER PEOPLE'S MONEY
by Jerry Sterner   145

I DON'T HAVE TO SHOW YOU
NO STINKING BADGES!
by Luis Valdez   150

THE SISTERS ROSENSWEIG
by Wendy Wasserstein   162

THE MATCHMAKER
by Thornton Wilder   170

BREAK OF DAY
by Stephen Fife   173

HIDDEN PARTS
by Lynne Alvarez   176

THE KEY
by Joyce Carol Oates   183

THE OIL WELL
by Horton Foote   193

TIME STANDS STILL
by Donald Margulies   198

PAINTING CHURCHES
by Tina Howe   205

GOOD PEOPLE
by David Lindsay-Abaire   211

THE MATCHMAKER
by Thornton Wilder   218

COUNTING THE WAYS
by Edward Albee   225

THE HOUSE OF BLUE LEAVES
by John Guare   230

THE TALE OF THE ALLERGIST'S WIFE
by Charles Busch   235

THE HOUSE OF RAMON IGLESIA
by José Rivera   239

A DELICATE BALANCE
by Edward Albee   243

PART II: SCENES FOR TWO WOMEN

THE OLD SETTLER
by John Henry Redwood   253

MARVIN'S ROOM
by Scott McPherson   261

SHTICK
by Henry Meyerson   267

THINNER THAN WATER
by Melissa Ross   272

DINNER WITH FRIENDS
by Donald Margulies   276

'NIGHT, MOTHER
by Marsha Norman   287

FIGHTING OVER BEVERLEY
by Israel Horovitz   295

THE GNADIGES FRAULEIN
by Tennessee Williams   301

THE OLD SETTLER
by John Henry Redwood   309

MARVIN'S ROOM
by Scott McPherson   317

PART III: SCENES FOR TWO MEN

DEATH AND THE MAIDEN
by Ariel Dorfman   325

THE SPEED OF DARKNESS
by Steve Tesich   329

AFTER CRYSTAL NIGHT
by John Herman Shaner   333

A WAY WITH WORDS
by Frank D. Gilroy   336

EYES FOR CONSUELA
by Sam Shepard   340

THE KENTUCKY CYCLE
by Robert Schenkkan   344

THE PRICE
by Arthur Miller   350

COME AGAIN, ANOTHER DAY
by Cary Pepper   361

AN ENEMY OF THE PEOPLE
by Henrik Ibsen, adapted by Arthur Miller   373

EYES FOR CONSUELA
by Sam Shepard   378

I'M NOT RAPPAPORT
by Herb Gardner   381

DINNER WITH FRIENDS
by Donald Margulies   388

THE VALUE OF NAMES
by Jeffrey Sweet   396

THAT CHAMPIONSHIP SEASON
by Jason Miller   404

THE OIL WELL
by Horton Foote   410

"MASTER HAROLD" . . . AND THE BOYS
by Athol Fugard   414

I'M NOT RAPPAPORT
by Herb Gardner   421

Play Sources, Permissions, and Acknowledgments   427

INTRODUCTION

Not long ago, I mentioned to an actor friend of mine that I was editing both this book and a monologue book for mature actors for Applause.

"Oh yeah, right, because we over-forty-year-olds are such an *underserved* community," he wise-cracked, expecting me to share in his bemusement.

I knew what he meant. Most of the great roles in dramatic literature are for actors over forty—and those that aren't, like Hamlet, are often played by actors over forty. Most of the artistic directors, producers, and other decision makers are also over forty. And, frankly, if an actor makes it to forty and is still in the profession, then he or she has probably gone to so many acting classes, interviews, and auditions—and is still doing so—that it must engender a feeling of having seen and done it all, so what more is there to add?

On the other hand, most of the attention in the profession is paid to young actors, new faces, the next big thing. We're all familiar with the media clamor over the next young celebrity whose face is suddenly plastered on every magazine cover and whose work is hailed as "raw" or "stunning" or "groundbreaking" (my personal favorite). The fact that this young performer is really just starting out, just learning the craft (and yes, it is a craft as well as a form of artistic expression) is suddenly lost in the deluge of accolades. The brilliant work of over-forty-year-old actors is often lost in this hype-driven welter, overlooked or taken for granted, unless that actor happens to be named Clooney or Pitt or Streep.

This same attitude has carried over to monologue books, scene books, and books about the craft of acting, which are mostly aimed at young performers, who, as aspirers to excellence or fame (or both), want to learn the secrets to success in their chosen profession, as well as what material they should choose to practice and hone their technique. But what about the mature actor—a veteran of life, art, and the vicissitudes of the entertainment industry—who wants to keep honing his or her craft as well? Contrary to what my wise-cracking friend said, there are not a lot of books out there that cater to this group's needs, a circumstance that Applause is hoping to rectify with this volume and the companion monologue book.

My goal in both of these books has been to compile challenging material that would appeal to the actors' imaginations. (I started out as an actor myself—not a particularly good one perhaps, but it did give me an understanding of action and character and the actor's point of view that I would not have gained otherwise.) I have tried also to seek out monologues and scenes from published plays that are (for the most part) not all that well known. My hope is that actors and drama aficionados will be inspired to seek out these plays for further examination, along with other works by the same playwrights.

While the Applause *The Best Monologues for Mature Actors* mixes classical pieces in with monologues from nineteenth- and twentieth-century plays and more modern fare, these scenes are mostly drawn from contemporary plays. Funny thing about that—it's not so easy to find two mature actors speaking to one another in today's plays. This is especially true, for some reason, in the plays of contemporary women writers, at least when the playwrights themselves are under forty. I would like to have included more work from playwrights such as Sarah Ruhl, Annie Baker, Anne Washburn, and Amy Herzog, whose plays truly have been groundbreaking (no ironic quotations needed). I simply wasn't able to find many noteworthy scenes from their published plays that featured two actors over forty years old speaking with each other.

The fact is, though, that the contemporary Western world offers people over forty—especially women—a greater variety of employment and social roles than at any other time. This is the result of the many social movements and upheavals of the twentieth century spilling over into our own time. And these changes were reflected as well in the theater's changing priorities. Where American drama was once dominated by the triumvirate of great white male playwrights—Eugene O'Neill, Tennessee Williams, and Arthur Miller (each of whom challenged the status quo)—the identity politics of the 1990s (gay, Irish, Puerto Rican, etc.) broke down any sense of social absolutes and decentralized any sense of a societal purpose. The rise of technology—specifically cell phones and a free Internet—has further placed power in people's hands to take control of their lives. At the same time, financial inequality has never been more harrowing and severe, with a few moguls exerting an undue influence over the world's economies.

What this has done is to create a dramatic climate in which the individual has never been more powerful *and* more powerless in determining his or her own destiny. The scenes in this book reflect that state of affairs: near-infinite possibilities in a world in which nothing may matter. So the Midwestern businessman in Tracy Letts's *The Man from Nebraska* wakes up one night to discover that he no longer believes in God—but what can he find to replace Him with? Or, conversely, in my own play *Break of Day,* the parents of Vincent van Gogh (a small-town minister and his wife) try to protect their well-ordered world from the disturbing force of their artist son, who has come home to live with them. But as they will find—as so many other characters do in these scenes—there are few safe places anymore in which to hide out from the disorienting effects of a turbulent, uncertain, ever-changing, and contradictory world.

That said, it is my sincere hope that actors of all stripes will find a safe place in this book in which to explore their talent, develop their potential, and challenge their limitations. Much thanks to Applause for the opportunity to put this collection together, and to Carol Flannery for her editorial suggestions. Never stop learning—that's the best policy, no matter what age you are. Here's wishing you well with that.

—STEPHEN FIFE
APRIL 2015

PART I

SCENES FOR A
MAN AND A WOMAN

CHARACTERS
VICTOR FRANZ *(late 50s), a retired police sergeant;* ESTHER *(early 50s), his wife.*

SCENE
The attic of a Manhattan brownstone soon to be torn down.

TIME
The 1950s.

    [VICTOR *and* ESTHER *enter. The attic space is filled with fine furniture and keepsakes.*]

ESTHER: [*Shakes her head as she looks around.*] Huh.

VICTOR: What?

ESTHER: Time.

VICTOR: I know.

ESTHER: There's something different about it.

VICTOR: No, it's all the way it was. I had my desk on that side and my cot. The rest is the same.

ESTHER: Maybe it's that it always used to seem so pretentious to me, and kind of bourgeois. But it does have a certain character. I think some of it's in style again. It's surprising.

VICTOR: Well, you want to take anything?

ESTHER: I don't know if I want it around. It's all so massive . . . where would we put any of it? That chest is lovely.

[*She goes to it.*]

VICTOR: That was mine. The one over there was Walter's. They're a pair.

ESTHER: Oh ya! Did you get hold of him?

VICTOR: I called again this morning—he was in consultation.

ESTHER: Was he in the office?

VICTOR: Ya. The nurse went and talked to him for a minute—it doesn't matter. As long as he's notified so I can go ahead.

[*She picks up a lamp.*]

That's probably real porcelain. Maybe it'd go in the bedroom.

ESTHER: [*Puts the lamp down.*] Why don't I meet you somewhere? The whole thing depresses me.

VICTOR: Why? It won't take long. Relax. Come on, sit down, the dealer'll be here any minute.

ESTHER: [*Sits on a couch.*] There's just something so damned rotten about it. I can't help it; it always was. The whole thing is infuriating.

VICTOR: Well, don't get worked up. We'll sell it and that'll be the end of it. I picked up the tickets, by the way.

ESTHER: Oh good. Boy, I hope it's a good picture.

VICTOR: Better be. Great, not good. Two-fifty apiece.

ESTHER: I don't care! I want to go somewhere!

[*Pause, she looks around.*]

God, what's it all about? When I was coming up the stairs just now, and all the doors hanging open . . . It doesn't seem possible . . .

VICTOR: They tear down old buildings every day in the week, kid.

ESTHER: I know, but it makes you feel a hundred years old. I hate empty rooms. What was that screwball's name?—rented the front parlor, remember?—required saxophones.

VICTOR: [*Smiles.*] Oh—Saltzman. With the one eye went out that way.

ESTHER: [*Gets up, goes to the harp.*] Well, where's your dealer?

VICTOR: [*Glances at his watch.*] It's twenty to six. He should be here soon.

[*She plucks the harp.*]

That should be worth something.

ESTHER: I think a lot of it is. But you're going to have to bargain, you know. You can't just take what they say . . .

VICTOR: I can bargain, don't worry, I'm not giving it away . . .

ESTHER: Because they expect to bargain.

VICTOR: Don't get depressed already, will you? I intend to bargain. I know the score with these guys.

[*He looks at his watch again.*]

Look at that, will you? Five-thirty sharp, he tells me. People say anything.

[*He opens a drawer in a chest, takes out an ice skate.*]

Look at that, they're still good.

[*He tests the edge with his fingernail.*]

They're even sharp. We ought to skate again sometime.

[*Pause.*]

Esther, I said I would bargain! . . . You see?—you don't know how to drink; it only depresses you.

ESTHER: Well, it's the kind of depression I enjoy!

VICTOR: Hot diggity dog.

ESTHER: I have an idea.

VICTOR: What?

ESTHER: Why don't you leave me? Just send me enough for coffee and cigarettes.

VICTOR: Then you'd never have to get out of bed.

ESTHER: I'd get out. Once in a while.

VICTOR: I got a better idea. Why don't you go off for a couple of weeks with your doctor? Seriously. It might change your viewpoint.

ESTHER: I wish I could.

VICTOR: Well, do it. He's got a suit. You could even take the dog—especially the dog.

[*She laughs.*]

It's not funny. Every time you go out for one of those walks in the rain I hold my breath what's going to come back with you.

ESTHER: [*Laughs.*] Oh, go on, you love her.

VICTOR: I love her! You get plastered, you bring home strange animals, and I "love" them. I do not love that goddamned dog!

[*She laughs with affection, as well as with a certain defiance.*]

ESTHER: Well, I want her!

VICTOR: [*Pause.*] It won't be solved by a dog, Esther. You're an intelligent, capable woman, and you can't lay around all day. Even something part-time, it would give you a place to go.

ESTHER: I don't need a place to go. I'm not quite used to Richard not being there, that's all.

VICTOR: He's gone, kid. He's a grown man; you've got to do something with yourself.

ESTHER: I can't go to the same place day after day. I never could and I never will. Did you ask to speak to your brother?

VICTOR: I asked the nurse, yes. He couldn't break away.

ESTHER: That son of a bitch. It's sickening.

VICTOR: Well, what are you going to do? He never had that kind of feeling.

ESTHER: What feeling? To come to the phone after sixteen years? It's common decency.

[*Pause.*]

You're furious, aren't you?

VICTOR: Only at myself. Calling him again and again all week like an idiot . . . To hell with him, I'll handle it alone. It's just as well.

ESTHER: What about his share? I don't want to be a pest—but I think there could be some money here, Vic. You're going to raise that with him, aren't you?

VICTOR: I've been thinking about it. He's got a right to his half, why should he give up anything?

ESTHER: I thought you'd decided to put it to him?

VICTOR: I've changed my mind. I don't really feel he owes me anything. I can't put on an act.

ESTHER: How many Cadillacs can he drive?

VICTOR: That's why he's got Cadillacs. People who love money don't give it away.

DEATH AND THE MAIDEN
BY ARIEL DORFMAN

CHARACTERS
PAULINA SALAS *(40) was arrested and tortured by her country's dictatorship fifteen years earlier;* GERARDO ESCOBAR *(45) is a lawyer married to* PAULINA *who wants to be part of the coalition replacing the now-ousted dictator.*

SCENE
The Escobars' beach house in Chile (or any country that is attempting a democracy after a period of dictatorship).

TIME
The present.

[PAULINA *has tied up Roberto, who she believes to be the man who tortured her fifteen years earlier.* GERARDO *has asked her to discuss this course of action in an adjoining room.*]

GERARDO: What are you trying to do? What are you trying to do, woman, with these insane acts?

PAULINA: I already told you—put him on trial.

GERARDO: Put him on trial, what does that mean, put him on trial? We can't use their methods. We're different. To seek vengeance in this fashion is not—

PAULINA: This is not vengeance. I'm giving him all the guarantees he never gave me. Not one, him and his—colleagues.

GERARDO: And his—colleagues—are you going to kidnap them and bring them here and tie them up and . . .

PAULINA: I'd have to know their names for that, wouldn't I?

GERARDO: And then you're going to . . .

PAULINA: Kill them? Kill him? As he didn't kill me, I think it wouldn't be fair to—

GERARDO: It's good to know that, Paulina, because you would have to kill me too. I'm warning you that if you intended to kill him, you're going to have to kill me first.

PAULINA: Would you mind calming down? I haven't the slightest intention of killing him. And certainly not you . . . But as usual you don't believe me.

GERARDO: But then, what are you going to do to him? With him? You're going to—what? What are you going to—and all this because fifteen years ago someone . . .

PAULINA: Someone what? . . . what did they do to me, Gerardo. Say it.

[*Brief pause.*]

You never wanted to say it. Say it now. They . . .

GERARDO: If you didn't say it, how was I going to?

PAULINA: Say it now.

GERARDO: I only know what you told me that first night, when . . .

PAULINA: They . . .

GERARDO: They . . .

PAULINA: Tell me, tell me.

GERARDO: They—tortured you. Now you say it.

PAULINA: They tortured me. And what else? What else did they do to me, Gerardo?

GERARDO: [*Goes to her, takes her in his arms.*] They raped you.

PAULINA: How many times?

GERARDO: More than once.

PAULINA: How many times?

GERARDO: You never said. I didn't count, you said.

PAULINA: It's not true.

GERARDO: What's not true?

PAULINA: That I didn't count. I always kept count. I know how many times.

[*Brief pause.*]

And that night, Gerardo, when I came to you, when I told you, what did you swear you'd do to them when you found them? "Someday, my love, we're going to put those bastards on trial. Your eyes will be able to rove"—I remember the exact phrase, because it seemed so poetic—your eyes will be able to rove over each one of their faces while they listen to your story. We'll do it, you'll see that we will." So now, darling, tell me who do I go to now?

GERARDO: That was fifteen years ago.

PAULINA: Tell me who's supposed to listen to my accusations against this doctor, who, Gerardo? Your Commission?

GERARDO: My Commission? What Commission? Thanks to you, we may not even be able to investigate all the other crimes that— and I'm going to have to resign.

PAULINA: Always so melodramatic. Your brow gets all furrowed up with wrinkles that make you look ten years older. And then people will see your photograph in the newspaper and won't believe that you're the youngest member of the Commission.

GERARDO: Are you deaf? I just told you that I'm going to have to resign.

PAULINA: I don't see why.

GERARDO: You don't see why, but all the rest of the country will see why, especially those who don't want any investigation of the past will see why. A member of the president's Commission, who should be showing exemplary signs of moderation and equanimity—

PAULINA: We're going to suffocate from so much equanimity!

GERARDO: —and objectivity, that this very person has found an innocent human being to be bound and tormented in his house— do you know how the newspapers that served the dictatorship, do you know how they'll use this episode to undermine and perhaps even destroy the Commission?

THE MAN FROM NEBRASKA

BY TRACY LETTS

CHARACTERS
KEN *(40s), a Midwestern businessman;* NANCY *(40s), his wife.*

SCENE
The master bathroom in the couple's home.

TIME
Late night.

[KEN *stands before the bathroom mirror, his T-shirt soggy with sweat. He shakes insuppressibly, weeps, sobs. He tries to regulate his breathing, sinks to one knee.*]

NANCY: [*Approaches from the darkness of the bedroom.*] Ken . . . ?

KEN: Go back to bed, honey.

NANCY: Are you all right?

KEN: Yes, I'm fine.

NANCY: Are you sure?

[*She approaches the doorway; He closes the door.*]

KEN: I'm sure. Go back to bed.

NANCY: You don't sound good.

KEN: Please . . .

NANCY: Are you sick?

[*Silence.*]

Ken? Open the door, you're scaring me. I'm scared. I'm coming in.

[*He raises his hand as if to bar the door, but then he allows* NANCY *to enter.*]

What's the matter? You look awful. Listen to me: are you having a heart attack?

[KEN *shakes his head.*]

A stroke? Are you sick, honey? Talk to me.

[*He can't answer, weeps. She approaches him with comforting arms.*]

KEN: [*Retreats.*] No, stay away.

NANCY: All right.

KEN: Please. Don't crowd me.

NANCY: I won't.

KEN: Don't crowd me.

NANCY: I'm not.

[*Pause.*]

Breathe.

KEN: Right.

NANCY: Are you in pain? Are you in physical pain?

[*He shakes his head.*]

Did you have a nightmare?

KEN: Kind of. No.

NANCY: Tell me what to do.

KEN: I don't believe in God.

NANCY: Okay. I don't understand.

KEN: I don't believe in God.

NANCY: What does that mean?

KEN: I don't think . . . there's a God. I don't believe in Him anymore.

NANCY: What do you believe in?

KEN: I don't know.

NANCY: What do you think you—?

KEN: Maybe we're just . . . science. Like they say. Accidental science.

NANCY: All right—

KEN: That doesn't matter. I don't know what I believe in. It doesn't matter. But I don't think there's a man in heaven, a God in heaven. I don't believe there is a heaven. We die, and . . . we're done, no more, just . . .

NANCY: All right—

KEN: Nobody listens when I pray. We're not rewarded for what we do right—

NANCY: Ken—

KEN: Or punished for what we do wrong—

NANCY: All right.

KEN: Nancy. I don't understand the stars.

NANCY: What does that mean?

KEN: The stars. In the sky. Don't make sense. To me. I don't understand them.

NANCY: Did something happen? To make you feel this way?

KEN: I don't know—

NANCY: To make you change—

KEN: I don't know, I just . . .

NANCY: Have you done something wrong?

KEN: No. No. I mean, yes. No, I just realized, I had a . . .

NANCY: A nightmare—

KEN: No—

NANCY: A vision—

KEN: No, NO! A, a, a, a flash . . . flashes, for days now, a . . . clear moment. I don't know, my head is clear! I can't talk about this, Nancy, I don't know what it means—

NANCY: All right—

KEN: I can't, I don't have . . . these aren't . . . thoughts. This isn't a decision.

NANCY: Okay, I understand.

[*Silence.*]

Tell me what to do.

GOD OF VENGEANCE
BY SHOLEM ASCH,
ADAPTED BY STEPHEN FIFE

CHARACTERS
YANKEL CHAPCHOVICH *(50s), proprietor of a small brothel;*
SORE *(pron. Sor-ra),* YANKEL*'s wife, a former prostitute (late 40s).*

SCENE
A large provincial town in Poland, not far from Warsaw. The action unfolds in the home of Yankel Chapchovich, which consists of two levels: the upstairs living quarters of Yankel and his family, and the downstairs brothel. The scene takes place in the upstairs dining room.

TIME
An early evening in March 1905.

[YANKEL *wants his sixteen-year-old daughter Rivkele to marry a rabbi's son, so he orders a Torah scroll to be made for his household—which is forbidden by Jewish law because of his profession.* YANKEL *and* SORE *are waiting for the rabbi to arrive and hopefully give his approval.* YANKEL *has made a payoff to one of the rabbi's assistants, something the rabbi's not aware of.*]

SORE: It doesn't seem right. There should be music and dancing when the Rebbe arrives.

YANKEL: You expect "decent" people to come? You must have forgotten who we are.

SORE: Who we are? Who are you? Are you a robber, a thief? No. You have a business. You don't force it on anyone, do you? Just try giving away some of your money, you'll see how much they take.

YANKEL: Oh, they'll take alright, then they'll toss you right back in the dirt. "Let him stand by the synagogue door, let him come in the door—but no further."

[*Pause.*]

Do you think they'd ever ask me to bless the reading from Torah?

SORE: Do you really think they're better than you are? This is how the world is today: if you have money, then even a "respectable man" like that Reb Elye will come to see you, he'll do you the very big favor of taking your money. He couldn't care less where it comes from—if you stole it or did something dirty—just as long as you've got it, the cash.

YANKEL: Watch out who you slander, you hear me? Don't try pushing in where you're not wanted, or they'll push you right back, six feet under!

[*Pause.*]

You have a house? Then you stay there. You have food on the table? Then eat. But don't try nosing in where you're not invited. Every dog must know his own ditch.

[*He moves away.*]

I wish we'd never started this Torah business. It will come to no good.

SORE: And you call yourself a man! Even I can say: The past is over, it's gone— fffft! We have nothing to be ashamed of. The rest of the world is no better.

[*Pause.*]

If you have money, who cares about anything else? Right? Am I right?

[*She moves closer.*]

Of course, once we've made enough, we can close up shop, and no one will be any wiser. Who cares about what used to be?

YANKEL: Do you really think so? Oh, if only I could start over, I would buy a stable of horses and go sell them abroad like my father, God rest his soul. And no one would laugh at me there, no one would stare at me like a thief . . .

SORE: The only thing, Yankel . . .

YANKEL: What?

SORE: I hear that it's hard to turn any profit selling horses . . .

YANKEL: We wouldn't need much.

SORE: The overhead, Yankel, the overhead . . . Whereas here you have money in hand, you can see it . . .

[*Pause. She works.*]

And thank God we have a daughter who is as sweet, genteel, well behaved—I wouldn't trade her for any other girl in this town! You'll see, she'll get married to a respectable man, have respectable children, and not have anything to do with our life . . .

YANKEL: Yes, and you'll show her the way, won't you?

[*Pause.*]

Letting Manke come up from downstairs. Why don't you ask her to eat at our table and sleep with us too?

SORE: Just listen to him! I brought Manke up once to show Rivkele how to embroider. What's wrong with that? Our child's a girl, after all, we have to think about her marriage trousseau. And who else does she have to be friends with? You never let her go out.

[*Pause.*]

But if it makes you unhappy, then Manke won't come.

YANKEL: Unhappy? Unhappy? From now on, I will not have my home mixed with downstairs. Do you hear me? They must be kept apart, separate, the way kosher food is kept separate from *treyf,* the way "pure" is kept apart from "polluted." Do you understand? Down there is a brothel, a house, while up here a young virgin lives, who will someday make a pure bride. There must be no mixing, none!

[*They hear footsteps on the outside staircase.*]

SORE: Shhh! Someone's coming. It must be Reb Elye.

[*She pushes her stray hairs under her wig and takes off her apron.* YANKEL *adjusts his clothing.*]

To think how you were shouting just now! What if he heard?

THE SPEED OF DARKNESS

BY STEVE TESICH

CHARACTERS

JOE *(40s) is a successful businessman and hero of the Vietnam War with a big secret;* ANNE *(40) is his wife and the mother of Mary, a high school senior.*

SCENE

South Dakota, the living room of Joe and Anne's home.

TIME

Late at night—the late 1980s.

[JOE *and* ANNE *are waiting for their seventeen-year-old daughter to come home, long past her curfew.*]

ANNE: I'm sure she's all right.

JOE: A mind is a terrible thing to have after midnight. To have both a mind and a teenage daughter is one too many.

ANNE: I remember staying out late on dates when I was her age, bored out of my mind with some guy in a Chevy, but knowing that my parents were worrying and couldn't sleep made it all worthwhile.

JOE: I'm putting her back on curfew. That's that. I don't care that she's almost eighteen. I don't care that this is her last year of school. I don't care what the other kids her age are allowed to do. You understand?

ANNE: Don't get tough with me, Joe. I don't need a curfew. I'm home. Get tough with her.

JOE: I've been tough with her.

[ANNE *looks at him.*]

Well, I have.

ANNE: I didn't say anything.

JOE: No, but you raised your eyebrows. You have the noisiest eyebrows, Anne. When you raise them, it's like venetian blinds going up. You warm enough in that?

ANNE: Yes.

JOE: There's nothing more stupid than being a parent. I remember thinking when she was three months old, "Joe," I said to myself, "time's going to fly by like that if you're not careful." It was so nice holding her in my arms, I didn't want it to fly by. But then, stupidity took over. I'm crawling around on the floor, teaching her to crawl. When she does it, I applaud like mad. And then crawling's not good enough anymore. I'm trying to get her to walk. Ride a bike. Drive a car. All I've done since she was born was to teach and encourage the child I love to grow up and leave me.

ANNE: That's what good parents are supposed to do.

JOE: That's why we're stupid. You ever think about moving?

ANNE: Moving?

JOE: Yeah.

ANNE: What do you mean moving?

JOE: Moving. Going somewhere else to live.

ANNE: You're not being serious, are you?

JOE: I don't know. I was just wondering. It's just with Mary going off to college and all. What's to keep us here?

ANNE: Our friends. My church. Your business. A lot of things.

JOE: You used to talk about living in a big city. Culture and all.

ANNE: That was a long time ago. I have you. I don't need culture. C'mon. Let's go back to bed. Take it from somebody who knows. The only way to get even with her for staying out so late is to be sound asleep when she comes home. C'mon.

[*They exit together.*]

THE SOUND OF A VOICE

BY DAVID HENRY HWANG

CHARACTERS
MAN *(40), Japanese, a transient;* WOMAN *(50), Japanese, lives alone. NOTE: There is a supernatural element to the play, in that the* WOMAN *may be a witch, and the* MAN *may know this.*

SCENE
The woman's cabin in the woods.

TIME
The present.

[*The* MAN *sits at the* WOMAN*'s table. She enters from the kitchen, carrying a tray with food. There is a vase of lovely flowers on the table. The* MAN *steals one and hides it from her view.*]

WOMAN: Please. Eat. It will give me great pleasure.

MAN: This—this is magnificent.

WOMAN: Eat.

MAN: Thank you.

[*He motions for the* WOMAN *to join him.*]

WOMAN: No, thank you.

MAN: This is wonderful. The best I've tasted.

WOMAN: You are reckless in your flattery, sir. But anything you say, I will enjoy hearing. It's not even the words. It's the sound of a voice, the way it moves through the air.

MAN: How long has it been since you've had a visitor?

[*Pause.*]

WOMAN: I don't know.

MAN: Oh?

WOMAN: I lose track. Perhaps five months ago, perhaps ten years, perhaps yesterday. I don't consider time when there is no voice in the air. It's pointless. Time begins with the entrance of a visitor and ends with his exit.

MAN: And in between? You don't keep track of the days? You can't help but notice—

WOMAN: Of course I notice.

MAN: Oh.

WOMAN: I notice, but I don't keep track.

[*Pause.*]

May I bring out more?

MAN: More? No. No. This was wonderful.

WOMAN: I have more.

MAN: Really—the best I've had.

WOMAN: You must be tired. Did you sleep in the forest last night?

MAN: Yes.

WOMAN: Or did you not sleep at all?

MAN: I slept.

WOMAN: Where?

MAN: By a waterfall. The sound of the water put me to sleep. It rumbled like the sounds of a city. You see, I can't sleep in too much silence. It scares me. It makes me feel that I have no control over what is about to happen.

WOMAN: I feel the same way.

MAN: But you live here—alone?

WOMAN: Yes.

MAN: It's so quiet here. How can you sleep?

WOMAN: Tonight, I'll sleep. I'll lie down in the next room, and hear your breathing through the wall, and fall asleep shamelessly. There will be no silence.

MAN: You're very kind to let me stay here.

WOMAN: This is yours.

[*She unrolls a mat.*]

MAN: Did you make it yourself?

WOMAN: Yes. There is a place to wash outside.

MAN: Thank you.

WOMAN: Good night.

MAN: Good night.

[*He starts to leave.*]

WOMAN: May I know your name?

MAN: No. I mean, I would rather not say. If I gave you a name, it would only be made up. Why should I deceive you? You are too kind for that.

WOMAN: Then what should I call you? Perhaps—"Man Who Fears Silence"?

MAN: How about, "Man Who Fears Women"?

WOMAN: That name is much too common.

MAN: And you?

WOMAN: Hanako.

MAN: That's your name?

WOMAN: It's what you may call me.

MAN: Good night, Hanako. You are very kind.

WOMAN: You are very smart. Good night.

SEX WITH THE CENSOR

BY THERESA REBECK

CHARACTERS

WOMAN *(40), a prostitute;* MAN *(40), a censor.*

SCENE

A bare room. A small cot covered with a bedspread has been set to one side. Also a chair.

TIME

The present.

[*A provocatively dressed* WOMAN *sits on a bed. A* MAN *wearing a suit stands across the room, by a chair.*]

WOMAN: So how do you like it? Sitting, standing, or are you a traditional kind of guy?

MAN: What?

WOMAN: Tell you what; we'll improvise.

[*She stands and crosses to him.*]

Just see what happens, huh?

[*She reaches for his jacket, as if to remove it. He backs away.*]

MAN: Don't do that.

WOMAN: Oh. Sorry. Some guys . . .

MAN: I don't want you to do that.

WOMAN: Whatever.

[*She turns and takes off her skirt. Underneath she wears black stockings and panties.*]

No shit, most guys like, you know, to be undressed. I think it reminds them of their mother, although I don't know why you'd want to be thinking about your mother at a time like this. I mean, I know about the whole psychology thing, Oedipus, whatever—we do, we talk about that stuff—but I have to say I never believed most of it. That guys want to fuck their mothers. That just, frankly, that makes no sense to me. I mean, if it's true, you guys are even crazier than I thought, you know what I mean? I mean, no offense or anything.

MAN: Stop talking.

WOMAN: [*Unbuttons blouse.*] Oh sorry. I know I kind of run on. Especially late in the day; I get tired and anything that comes into my head comes right out of my mouth. I don't know. A lot of guys like it, which is lucky for me because I just, I don't really know when it's happening—

MAN: Don't do that.

WOMAN: Excuse me?

MAN: Don't take your shirt off.

WOMAN: Oh. Okay.

[*She starts to button up again.*]

MAN: No. Leave it like that. I want to see that I can't see.

WOMAN: What?

MAN: If you button it, I can't see. I want to see that I can't see.

WOMAN: Oh. Sure.

[*She stands for a moment in the unbuttoned shirt and stockings. He stares at her.*]

So . . . are we ready to get going here? I mean, I don't mean to rush things, but it's been my experience that it kind of helps to hit the ground running, you know, just let her rip, and since you're not particularly interested in small talk, we probably should just get to it, huh?

[*Pause.*]

So are we, what? You need a hand with this clothes thing here?

MAN: No.

WOMAN: No.

[*Pause. They stare at each other.*]

Okay, sure, you're shy, I'm sensitive to that. We'll just take this real slow.

[*She reaches for his jacket carefully.*]

MAN: Don't touch me.

WOMAN: Honey, that's not going to be entirely possible under the circumstances here—

[*She tries to take the jacket off him. He shoves her, hard.*]

Hey, don't get rough with me, asshole. That's not the deal, all right?

MAN: I told you, I don't want you to touch me. We don't do that.

WOMAN: Well, what do we do?

MAN: [*Looks at her, pulls the chair over, sits on it.*] Stand here.

[*He points in front of him. She crosses warily and stands there.*]

WOMAN: So what, you just want to look, is that it? Fine. Whatever. But it's the same price, okay? We're not sailing into discount land because you're in some sort of fucking mood here, okay?

MAN: Don't say that.

WOMAN: I'm just telling you the rules.

MAN: No, I tell you the rules.

WOMAN: Listen—

MAN: I don't want you to use that word. You've used it twice. I don't want to hear that word.

WOMAN: What word?

MAN: You know the word.

WOMAN: What word? You mean fuck?

MAN: I don't want to hear it.

WOMAN: Sorry. I mean, I just, I thought that's what we were here for.

MAN: I DON'T WANT TO HEAR IT.

WOMAN: Okay, fine, I won't say anything. I'll just stand here. You can pay me to stand here; that's fine by me. Fucking weirdo. Sorry.

MAN: [*Sits, staring. Pause.*] Tell me what you want.

WOMAN: Tell you what I—you want me to tell you what I want?

MAN: Yes.

WOMAN: Okay, I want to wrap this up and go home and see my kid. It's been a long day—

MAN: No.

WOMAN: No.

MAN: No.

WOMAN: That's not what I want.

MAN: No.

WOMAN: Okay, then you tell me what I do want because I mean, I am in the dark here, all right? Usually, I have to say, usually there is not a lot of confusion about how to proceed, but—

MAN: Stop talking.

WOMAN: Stop talking. Right, I forgot.

MAN: Tell me what you want.

[*Pause.*]

WOMAN: [*Looks at him.*] Let's try this. I want you.

MAN: Yes.

WOMAN: Yes. That's a yes. Here we go. I want you . . . inside of me.

MAN: Yes.

WOMAN: Two yesses. This is a trend. I want to suck your cock.

MAN: No.

WOMAN: No. That's not what I want. Okay, fine, I—fuck, I don't know what the fuck—

MAN: NO.

WOMAN: No, sorry, I didn't mean to use that word, I meant, I mean, I meant *darn*. Darn.

MAN: Yes.

WOMAN: Yes. Darn. Sorry, I'm a little slow, darn it.

[*Pause.*]

I want you . . . in my mouth?

[*He does not respond.*]

I want you . . . to touch you.

MAN: No.

WOMAN: But I can't.

MAN: Yes.

WOMAN: I want you to look at me . . . and not see me.

MAN: Yes.

WOMAN: Yes. I want to stand in front of you naked, with clothes on.

MAN: Yes.

WOMAN: I get this. You want to have sex without sex.

MAN: Yes. Tell me what you want.

[*Pause. The* WOMAN *stares at him for a long moment, then turns and picks up her shoes.*]

WOMAN: No, I won't do it. This is sick, this is really—

MAN: Do you want the money or not?

[*Pause.*]

WOMAN: Yeah, I want the money.

MAN: Then tell me what you want.

WOMAN: [*Sets her shoes down, looks at him.*] I want . . . I want you in me outside of me.

MAN: Yes.

WOMAN: I want you to touch me . . . without feeling me. I want words with no voice. Sex with no heart. Love without bones.

MAN: [*Overlaps her.*] Yes. Yes.

WOMAN: Skin without skin. I want blind eyes.

MAN: Yes.

WOMAN: I want you to stare me dead. I want you to lick me dry. I want you to take my words. Wipe me clean. Make me nothing. Let me be nothing for you. Let me be nothing. Let me be nothing.

MAN: Yes. Yes. Yes!

[*He climaxes without touching himself. Long pause.*]

You disgust me.

WOMAN: Yeah, I know. That'll be two hundred dollars. Sir.

LONG DAY'S JOURNEY INTO NIGHT
BY EUGENE O'NEILL

CHARACTERS

JAMES TYRONE *(65) is the patriarch of the Tyrone clan and one of the greatest American actors of the late nineteenth century who sacrificed his greatness for popularity and riches;* MARY TYRONE *(55) is his wife and mother of their two sons, Jamie and Edmund— she has been battling a morphine addiction related to her second pregnancy for several years.*

SCENE

The living room of the Tyrones' summer home near New London, Connecticut.

TIME

Around 1:30 in the afternoon of an August day in 1912.

[*It is just after lunch.* JAMES *is smoking a cigar.* MARY *is full of nervous energy.*]

JAMES: We're in for another night of fog, I'm afraid.

MARY: Oh, well, I won't mind it tonight.

JAMES: No, I don't imagine you will, Mary.

MARY: [*After a pause.*] I don't see Jamie going down to the hedge. Where did he go?

JAMES: He's going with Edmund to the Doctor's. He went up to change his clothes. I'd better do the same or I'll be late for my appointment at the Club.

[*He makes a move to leave, but she reaches out and grasps his arm.*]

MARY: [*Pleads.*] Don't go yet, dear. I don't want to be alone.

[*Pause.*]

I mean, you have plenty of time. You know you boast you can dress in one-tenth the time it takes the boys.

[*Pause.*]

There is something I wanted to say. What is it? I've forgotten. I'm glad Jamie is going uptown. You didn't give him any money, I hope.

JAMES: I did not.

MARY: He'd only spend it on drink, and you know what a vile, poisonous tongue he has when he's drunk. Not that I would mind anything he said tonight, but he always manages to drive you into a rage, especially if you're drunk, as you will be.

JAMES: I won't. I never get drunk.

MARY: Oh, I'm sure you'll hold it well. You always have. It's hard for a stranger to tell, but after thirty-five years of marriage—

JAMES: I've never missed a performance in my life. That's the proof!

[*Pause.*]

If I did get drunk, it is not you who should blame me. No man has ever had a better reason.

MARY: Reason? What reason? You always drink too much when you go to the Club, don't you? Particularly when you meet McGuire.

He sees to that. Don't think I'm finding fault, dear. You must do as you please. I won't mind.

JAMES: I know you won't.

[*He turns toward the front parlor.*]

I've got to get dressed.

MARY: [*Pleads, grasping his arm again.*] No, please wait a little while, dear. At least, until one of the boys comes down. You will all be leaving me so soon.

JAMES: It's you who are leaving us, Mary.

MARY: I? That's a silly thing to say, James. How could I leave? There is nowhere I could go. Who would I go to see? I have no friends.

JAMES: It's your own fault—

[*He stops and sighs helplessly.*]

There's surely one thing you can do this afternoon that will be good for you, Mary. Take a drive in the automobile. Get away from the house. Get a little sun and fresh air. I bought the automobile for you. You know I don't like the damned things. I'd rather walk any day, or take a trolley.

[*Pause.*]

I had it here waiting for you when you came back from the sanatorium. I hoped it would give you pleasure and distract your mind. You used to ride in it every day, but you've hardly used it at all lately. I paid a lot of money I couldn't afford, and there's the chauffeur I have to board and lodge and pay high wages whether he drives you or not.

[*Pause.*]

Waste! The same old waste that will land me in the poorhouse in my old age! What good did it do you? I might as well have thrown the money out the window.

MARY: Yes, it was a waste of money, James. You shouldn't have bought a secondhand automobile. You were swindled again, as you always are, because you insist on secondhand bargains in everything.

JAMES: It's one of the best makes! Everyone says it's better than any of the new ones!

MARY: It was another waste to hire Smythe, who was only a helper in the garage and had never been a chauffeur. Oh, I realize his wages are less than a real chauffeur's, but he more than makes up for that, I'm sure, by the graft he gets from the garage on repair bills. Something is always wrong. Smythe sees to that, I'm afraid.

JAMES: I don't believe it! He may not be a fancy millionaire's flunky but he's honest. You're as bad as Jamie, suspecting everyone!

MARY: You mustn't be offended, dear. I wasn't offended when you gave me the automobile. I knew you didn't mean to humiliate me. I knew that was the way you had to do everything. I was grateful and touched. I knew buying the car was a hard thing for you to do, and it proved how much you loved me, in your way, especially when you couldn't really believe it would do me any good.

JAMES: Mary!

[*He suddenly hugs her to him.*]

Dear Mary! For the love of God, for my sake and the boys' sake and your own, won't you stop now?

THE FATHER

BY AUGUST STRINDBERG

CHARACTERS
THE CAPTAIN *(50s) is the captain of a cavalry regiment in a Swedish country town;* LAURA *(40) is his wife and the mother of their daughter, Bertha.*

SCENE
The living room of the Captain's quarters in a regimental establishment in a Swedish country town.

TIME
Day. The late 1880s.

[*A battle of wills is taking place for control of this household between* THE CAPTAIN *and his wife,* LAURA. *The immediate issue is the fate of their teenage daughter, Bertha—*THE CAPTAIN *feels his influence over her waning and wants her to move away from her mother and stay with friends of his in the local town, while* LAURA *opposes any such move.* THE CAPTAIN *has just ordered Bertha to leave the room as* LAURA *has entered it.*]

LAURA: You didn't want her to speak because you were afraid she would side with me.

CAPTAIN: I know she would like to get away from this house, but I also know that your power over her is great enough to change her mind at will.

LAURA: Oh, do I have that much power.

CAPTAIN: Yes, you have a fiendish, infernal way of getting what you want. Like all unscrupulous people, you have no compunction about the means you use. How, for example, did you get rid of Doctor Norling—and what did you have to do with getting the new doctor here?

LAURA: Well, what did I do?

CAPTAIN: You kept insulting Doctor Norling until he finally left, and then you used your brother to procure votes for your Doctor Ostermark.

LAURA: Well, that was quite simple and perfectly legal. So—you plan to have Bertha leave home, do you?

CAPTAIN: Yes.

LAURA: Then I imagine I shall have to try to prevent it.

CAPTAIN: You can't.

LAURA: Can't I? Do you think I would let my daughter be among unprincipled people—people who would teach her that everything she has learned from her mother is nothing but worthless drivel? Do you? Why, she would despise me for the rest of my life.

CAPTAIN: Would you have me allow ignorant and self-opinionated women convince her that her father is a charlatan?

LAURA: I wouldn't let that upset me.

CAPTAIN: And why not?

LAURA: Because a mother is closer to her child—more so since it's been discovered that no one can be absolutely certain who is the father of a child.

CAPTAIN: What bearing has that on this case?

LAURA: You don't know whether you are Bertha's father!

CAPTAIN: Don't I?

LAURA: How can you know what no one else knows?

CAPTAIN: Are you joking?

LAURA: No, I am simply employing your teachings. Besides, how do you know that I have not been unfaithful to you?

CAPTAIN: I can believe many things of you, but not that. Besides, if you had been unfaithful to me, you would not be talking about it now.

LAURA: Suppose I was prepared to tolerate anything: to be an outcast, to be despised—all for the sake of possessing and keeping my influence over my child—and that I told you the truth just now when I said that Bertha is my child but not yours! Suppose—

CAPTAIN: That's enough!

LAURA: Just suppose! Then your power would be over!

CAPTAIN: If you could prove that I wasn't the father, then yes.

LAURA: That shouldn't be difficult. Would you like me to?

CAPTAIN: Stop it!

LAURA: All I'd have to do would be to give the name of the real father, the details—such as time and place—and, by the way, when was Bertha born? In the third year of our marriage . . . ?

CAPTAIN: You had better stop now or I'll . . .

LAURA: Or what? Yes, let's stop now. But think carefully on what you do and what you decide. And above all, don't make yourself look ridiculous . . .

CAPTAIN: How about you?

LAURA: Oh no—I've arranged the whole thing much too well.

CAPTAIN: That's what makes it so difficult to fight you.

LAURA: Why do you enter into combat with a superior enemy?

CAPTAIN: Superior?

LAURA: Yes, it's curious . . . I have never been able to look at a man without feeling myself his superior.

CAPTAIN: Well, you shall at last meet your superior—and you will never forget it.

LAURA: That should be interesting.

SHTICK
BY HENRY MEYERSON

CHARACTERS
MURRAY *(60) is an aging comedian who just got home from the hospital after suffering a stroke while performing;* GLADYS *(55) is the younger sister of* MURRAY*'s wife, Helen, who recently confessed to her sister that she had an affair with* MURRAY.

SCENE
The living room of Murray and Helen's home.

TIME
The present.

[MURRAY *sits in a wheelchair, looking very alone. There is a knock at the door.* MURRAY *wheels over and opens it.* GLADYS *enters.*]

GLADYS: Hi, Murray.

MURRAY: Oh Jesus.

GLADYS: Aren't you glad to see me?

MURRAY: Have you come to finish me off?

GLADYS: I didn't realize the stroke caused you to be so suspicious.

MURRAY: It has nothing to do with the stroke. I know danger when I see it. You've done some job on me, Gladys.

GLADYS: She told you?

MURRAY: In spades. We just had this big blow out and then she left. You just missed her.

GLADYS: I know. I waited outside until she left.

MURRAY: You couldn't miss her. She had steam coming out of her ears.

GLADYS: It'll blow over, Murray.

MURRAY: I guess she'll be back. She didn't pack a bag. I think she went out to buy a gun.

GLADYS: I've been hanging around for weeks for this opportunity. She never leaves you alone.

MURRAY: She said she knows what happens when she does. And look. She's right. She leaves and you show up. She's brilliant, don't you think?

GLADYS: That's what I've always said.

MURRAY: You better leave. If she comes back and finds us, we'll be on the front page of tomorrow's *Post*.

GLADYS: I came to see how you were doing.

MURRAY: My doctor thinks I'm going to live. He doesn't know Helen.

GLADYS: Don't be upset.

MURRAY: Upset? Why would I be upset? What makes you think I'm upset?

GLADYS: Good, because . . .

MURRAY: I need a gun, because I can't strangle you with one hand.

GLADYS: In the long run you'll see what I did is for the best.

MURRAY: What long run? Take a good look. I don't have a long run. The long run is behind me. I'm in the short run now, Gladys, and you've just made it shorter. When did this happen?

GLADYS: Ah, you've forgotten. It began in Jersey, Murray.

MURRAY: No, you dope. When did you tell Helen?

GLADYS: I don't like the tone of your voice.

MURRAY: Tone? What tone? This is rage, Gladys. When did you tell her?

GLADYS: While you were in the hospital.

MURRAY: Given your great need for tact and honesty I'll bet it was when I was in a coma.

GLADYS: I thought that was the best time.

MURRAY: Why? You figured I was going to die?

GLADYS: You always knew me like an open book.

MURRAY: That suddenly is written in Greek.

GLADYS: I don't understand what you are so angry about. Shouldn't adults behave like adults?

MURRAY: Yes, if they're sane. Now I understand what Helen has been so upset about.

GLADYS: I know she didn't take it well, but at least she didn't threaten to kill me.

MURRAY: Not you, Gladys. She wants to kill *me*.

GLADYS: Don't be silly.

MURRAY: Don't be naïve.

GLADYS: Despite all of this, you seem to be doing okay.

MURRAY: Doctor Shapiro, that putz, thinks I'm depressed. Helen believes him.

GLADYS: You have every right to be depressed. Look what you've gone through.

MURRAY: Somehow, at this point in our lives, I don't think she cares to understand that.

GLADYS: Helen was there for you every single day, Murray.

MURRAY: I know, but lately she seems a little bitter.

GLADYS: She's been through a lot, too.

MURRAY: You were always so understanding. One of your virtues.

GLADYS: I try. How do I look?

MURRAY: Don't change the subject.

GLADYS: How do I look?

MURRAY: You know you always were good to look at, Gladys. I guess you still are.

GLADYS: Guess?

MURRAY: Okay, you are.

GLADYS: What?

MURRAY: You are still good to look at.

BREAK OF DAY
BY STEPHEN FIFE

CHARACTERS
PASTOR THEODORUS VAN GOGH *(60) is the preacher for a small village community near Zundert in the Netherlands;* ANNA VAN GOGH *(55), his wife, is in charge of running the presbytery. They have five children, the oldest being the painter Vincent van Gogh.*

SCENE
The study in the Van Gogh presbytery, northern Netherlands.

TIME
Evening. 1883.

[PASTOR THEO *comes from a long line of clergymen in the Dutch Lutheran church, but he is the least successful reverend. He and* ANNA *are currently hosting* ANNA's *niece, Kay Vos, whose young husband just died suddenly. Kay is the daughter of Reverend Stricker, the most important clergyman in Amsterdam.* PASTOR THEO *views her good report to her father as the key to being transferred to a larger congregation; but her long rambles through the woods with his son Vincent worry him. Now* PASTOR THEO *is at his writing table.* ANNA *enters, holding a piece of paper.*]

ANNA: Here's the list of pupils in the Bible Study class, dear. The only one I'm not sure about is Margaret Stoffels. Her mother insists she's enrolled, but she didn't show up for the first meeting, and I've lost any patience—

PASTOR THEO: Anna?

ANNA: Yes, dear?

PASTOR THEO: Convince Kay to go back home early.

ANNA: Why?

PASTOR THEO: Tell her it's not good for her child to stay away longer.

ANNA: But she seems to be doing so well here . . . She and Vincent have gotten so close again.

PASTOR THEO: Yes.

ANNA: Isn't that what you wanted?

PASTOR THEO: It's nothing against Vincent, dear. I just keep thinking about something Kay said . . . about handing Vincent his sketchpad.

ANNA: Yes?

PASTOR THEO: They're in the middle of the woods . . . Why wouldn't he be carrying his own sketchpad?

ANNA: I'm sure there are many reasons. He might have been looking at something on the ground, or climbing a tree, or—

PASTOR THEO: I'm sure you're right, dear. I'm sure it's nothing. Will you do as I asked?

ANNA: But it will look as if you don't trust him.

PASTOR THEO: Anna, please. If there was another disaster, I would never get Stricker to help me.

ANNA: Isn't that a chance we have to take? Isn't our family's happiness worth it?

PASTOR THEO: But I cannot be stuck here forever! Not when everyone else in the family has moved on to a place of importance but me, and now—I'm sure God intended something else for me than just this . . .

ANNA: Fine. I'll tell Kay to leave right away.

[*Pause.*]

PASTOR THEO: Maybe you're right. Christ tells us to believe in Redemption, that it's never too late.

ANNA: Why don't you tell him that, dear?

PASTOR THEO: But how could I . . . ?

ANNA: Just tell him.

THE HOUSE OF SLEEPING BEAUTIES

BY DAVID HENRY HWANG

CHARACTERS

KAWABATA *(70s), the famous Japanese writer;* WOMAN *(60s), the madam of a very unique Japanese brothel.*

SCENE

A room in the Japanese brothel.

TIME

The present.

> [KAWABATA, *a renowned Japanese novelist, has gone to an unusual brothel that caters to old men in order to do research for a novel. He meets with the* WOMAN *who runs the brothel. She serves him tea, then reaches into a desk drawer and pulls out a box containing twenty-five smooth tiles. While she speaks, she stacks the tiles in five layers of five each, such that the tiles of each layer are perpendicular to those in the layer below it.*]

WOMAN: So we can get to know each other. As I said, I must protect my girls from men who do not behave.

KAWABATA: You talk as if men should be put on leashes.

WOMAN: No, leashes aren't necessary at all.

[*She has finished building the tower of tiles.*]

There. We'll take turns removing tiles from the tower until it collapses. Understand?

KAWABATA: Is this a game you ask all your customers to play?

WOMAN: Guests. You can't touch the top layer, though, and you can only use one hand.

KAWABATA: But what's the object? Who wins, who loses?

WOMAN: There are no winners or losers. There is only the tower— intact or collapsed. Just one hand—like this.

[*She removes a piece.*]

KAWABATA: My turn? What am I trying to do?

WOMAN: Judge the tiles. Wriggle that one, for instance, yes, that one you're touching—between your fingers. Is the weight of the stack on it? If so, don't force it. Leave it and look for another one that's looser. If you try to force the tiles to be what they're not, the whole thing will come crashing down.

KAWABATA: A test of skills? There—

[*He removes a piece.*]

Your turn.

WOMAN: See? Simple.

KAWABATA: What kind of a test—? You're just an old woman. What kind of a contest is this?

WOMAN: Let's talk about you, sir. We want to make you happy.

[*They continue to take turns removing tiles from the tower through the next section.*]

KAWABATA: Happy? No, you don't understand. You can't—

WOMAN: Our guests sleep much better here. It's the warmth, they say.

KAWABATA: I don't have any trouble sleeping.

WOMAN: Don't you?

KAWABATA: Sometimes . . . sometimes I choose not to go to bed. But when I do, I sleep.

WOMAN: Our guests are never afraid to go to sleep.

KAWABATA: It's not that I'm afraid.

WOMAN: The darkness does not threaten them.

[Pause.]

KAWABATA: Old Eguchi—he says that the girls . . . that they are naked.

WOMAN: Yes.

KAWABATA: He says they are very beautiful, but I hardly . . .

WOMAN: For you, I would pick an especially pretty one.

KAWABATA: For me—? Don't start—

WOMAN: How old was your wife when you first met her?

KAWABATA: My wife? Oh, I don't know. She must have been—oh, maybe nineteen.

WOMAN: Nineteen. That is a beautiful age. I would pick one who is nineteen.

KAWABATA: Don't be ridiculous. She'd see me and—

WOMAN: But you forget, sir—our girls won't see anything.

KAWABATA: I suppose you have some way of guaranteeing this. I suppose it's never happened that some girl has opened her eyes—

WOMAN: No. Never.

KAWABATA: [*Having trouble with a tile.*] Look at this.

[*He holds out his hand, laughs.*]

Shaking. Would you mind putting some more wood in the furnace?

WOMAN: Of course.

[*She rises to do so while speaking.*]

I know what girl I would pick for you. She is half Japanese, half Caucasian. She has the most delicate hair—brown in one light, black in another. As she sleeps, she wriggles her left foot, like a cage, against the mattress, as if to draw out even the last bits of warmth.

[*She returns to the table, sits. As she does,* KAWABATA *causes the tower to fall.*]

KAWABATA: Ai! You shook it.

WOMAN: No.

SEASCAPE
BY EDWARD ALBEE

CHARACTERS
NANCY *and* CHARLIE *(60s) are on the verge of retirement and having some problems with making that transition.*

SCENE
A beach.

TIME
Lunchtime. The present.

[NANCY *and* CHARLIE *on a sand dune. Bright sun. They are dressed informally. There is a blanket and a picnic basket. Lunch is done;* NANCY *is finishing putting things away. There is a pause and then a jet plane is heard from stage right to stage left—growing, becoming deafeningly loud, diminishing.*]

NANCY: Such noise they make.

CHARLIE: They'll crash into the dunes one day. I don't know what good they do.

NANCY: Still . . . Oh, Charlie, it's so nice! Can't we stay here forever? Please!

CHARLIE: Unh—unh.

NANCY: That is not why. That is merely no.

CHARLIE: Because.

NANCY: Nor is that.

CHARLIE: Because . . . because you don't really mean it.

NANCY: I do!

CHARLIE: Here?

NANCY: Yes!

CHARLIE: Right here on the beach. Build a . . . a tent, or a lean-to.

NANCY: No, silly, not this very spot! But *here,* by the shore.

CHARLIE: You wouldn't like it.

NANCY: I would! I'd love it here! I'd love it right where we are, for that matter.

CHARLIE: Not after a while you wouldn't.

NANCY: Yes, I *would.* I love the water, and I love the air, and the sand and the dunes and the beach grass, and the sunshine on all of it and the white clouds way off, and the sunsets and the noise the shells make in the water and, oh, I love every bit of it, Charlie.

CHARLIE: You wouldn't. Not after a while.

NANCY: Why wouldn't I? I don't even mind the flies and the little . . . sand fleas, I guess they are.

CHARLIE: It gets cold.

NANCY: When?

CHARLIE: In the winter. In the fall even. In the spring.

NANCY: [*Laughs.*] Well, I don't mean this one, literally . . . not all the time. I mean go from beach to beach . . . live by the water. Seaside nomads, that's what we'd be.

CHARLIE: For Christ's sake, Nancy!

NANCY: I mean it! Lord above! There's nothing binding us, you *hate* the city.

CHARLIE: No.

NANCY: It would be so lovely. Think of all the beaches we could see.

CHARLIE: No, now . . .

NANCY: Southern California, and the Gulf, and Florida . . . and up to Maine, and what's-her-name's—Martha's—Vineyard, and all those places that the fancy people go: the Riviera and that beach in Rio de Janeiro, what is that?

CHARLIE: The Copacabana.

NANCY: Yes, and Pago Pago, and . . . Hawaii! Think, Charlie! We could go around the world and never leave the beach, just move from one hot sand strip to another: all the birds and fish and seaside flowers, and all the wondrous people that we'd meet. Oh, say you'd like to do it, Charlie.

CHARLIE: No.

NANCY: Just *say* you'd like to.

CHARLIE: If I did you'd say I meant it; you'd hold me to it.

NANCY: No I wouldn't. Besides, you have to be pushed into everything.

CHARLIE: Um-hum. But I'm not going to be pushed into . . . into *this*—this new business.

NANCY: One great seashore after another; pounding waves and quiet coves; white sand, and red—and black, somewhere, I remember reading; palms, and pine trees, cliffs and reefs, and miles of jungle, sand dunes . . .

CHARLIE: No.

NANCY: . . . and all the people! Every . . . language . . . every . . . race.

CHARLIE: Unh-unh.

NANCY: Of course, I'd never push you.

CHARLIE: You? Never!

NANCY: Well, maybe a hint here; hint there.

CHARLIE: Don't even do that, hunh?

NANCY: That's all it takes: figure out what you'd really like—what you want without knowing, what would secretly please you, put it in your mind, then make all the plans. *You* do it; *you* like it.

CHARLIE: Nancy, I don't want to travel from beach to beach, cliff to sand dune, see the races, count the flies. Anything. I don't want to do . . . anything.

NANCY: I see. Well.

CHARLIE: I'm happy . . . doing . . . nothing.

NANCY: [*Makes to gather some of their things.*] Well then, we'd best get started. Up! Let's get back!

CHARLIE: [*Not moving.*] I just . . . want . . . to . . . do . . . nothing.

NANCY: [*Gathering.*] Well, you're certainly not going to do that.

[*Takes something from him, a pillow, perhaps.*]

Hurry now; let's get things together.

CHARLIE: What . . . Nancy, what on earth are you . . .

NANCY: We are *not* going to be around forever, Charlie, and you may *not* do nothing. If you don't want to do what *I* want to do—which doesn't matter—then we will do what *you* want to do, but we will not do nothing. We will do *something*. So, tell me what it is you want to do and . . .

CHARLIE: I *said*. Now give me back my . . .

NANCY: You said, "I just want to do nothing; I'm happy doing nothing." Yes? But is that what we've . . . come all this way for? Had the children? Spent all this time together? All the sharing? For nothing? To lie back down in the crib again? The same at the end as at the beginning?

DEATH OF A SALESMAN
BY ARTHUR MILLER

CHARACTERS
WILLY LOMAN *(60) is losing hold on his traveling salesman job and on his sanity; his wife,* LINDA *(mid-50s), is doing her best to provide the emotional support that* WILLY *so badly needs.*

SCENE
The Loman family home in New York City.

TIME
Late at night.

LINDA: [*Hearing* WILLY *outside the bedroom, calls with some trepidation*] Willy!

WILLY: It's all right. I came back.

LINDA: Why? What happened?

[*Slight pause.*]

Did something happen, Willy?

WILLY: No, nothing happened.

LINDA: You didn't smash the car, did you?

WILLY: [*With casual irritation.*] I said nothing happened. Didn't you hear me?

LINDA: Don't you feel well?

WILLY: I'm tired to the death.

[*He sits on the bed beside her, a little numb.*]

I couldn't make it. I just couldn't make it, Linda.

LINDA: Where were you all day? You look terrible.

WILLY: I got as far as a little above Yonkers. I stopped for a cup of coffee. Maybe it was the coffee.

LINDA: What?

WILLY: I suddenly couldn't drive any more. The car kept going off onto the shoulder, y'know?

LINDA: Oh. Maybe it was the steering again. I don't think Angelo knows the Studebaker.

WILLY: No, it's me, it's me. Suddenly I realize I'm goin' sixty miles an hour and I don't remember the last five minutes. I'm—I can't seem to—keep my mind to it.

LINDA: Maybe it's your glasses. You never went for your new glasses.

WILLY: No, I see everything. I came back ten miles an hour. It took me nearly four hours from Yonkers.

LINDA: Well, you'll just have to take rest, Willy, you can't continue this way.

WILLY: I just got back from Florida.

LINDA: But you didn't rest your mind. Your mind is overactive, and the mind is what counts, dear.

WILLY: I'll start out in the morning. Maybe I'll feel better in the morning.

[*She is taking off his shoes.*]

These goddamn arch supports are killing me.

LINDA: Take an aspirin. Should I get you an aspirin? It'll soothe you.

WILLY: I was driving along, you understand? And I was fine. I was even observing the scenery. You can imagine me, me looking at scenery, on the road every week of my life. But it's so beautiful up there, Linda, the trees are so thick, and the sun is so warm. I opened the windshield and just let the warm air bathe over me. And then all of a sudden I'm goin' off the road! I'm tellin' ya, I absolutely forgot I was driving! If I'd've gone the other way over the white line I might've killed somebody. So I went on again— and five minutes later I'm dreamin' again, and I nearly—

[*He presses two fingers against his eyes.*]

I have such thoughts, I have such strange thoughts.

LINDA: Willy, dear. Talk to them again. There's no reason why you can't work in New York.

WILLY: They don't need me in New York. I'm the New England man. I'm vital in New England.

LINDA: But you're sixty years old. They can't expect you to keep traveling every week.

WILLY: I'll have to send a wire to Portland. I'm supposed to see Brown and Morrison tomorrow morning at ten o'clock to show the line. Goddammit, I could sell them!

[*He starts putting on his jacket.*]

LINDA: [*Taking the jacket from him.*] Why don't you go down to the place tomorrow and tell Howard you've simply got to work in New York? You're too accommodating, dear.

WILLY: If old man Wagner was alive I'd a' been in charge of New York now! That man was a prince, he was a masterful man. But that boy of his, that Howard, he don't appreciate. When I went north the first time, the Wagner Company didn't know where New England was!

LINDA: Why don't you tell those things to Howard, dear?

WILLY: I will, I definitely will. Is there any cheese?

LINDA: I will make you a sandwich.

WILLY: No, go to sleep. I'll take some milk. I'll be up right away. The boys in?

LINDA: They're sleeping. Happy took Biff on a date tonight.

WILLY: That so?

LINDA: It was so nice to see them shaving together, one behind the other, in the bathroom. And going out together. You notice? The whole house smells of shaving lotion.

WILLY: Figure it out. Work a lifetime to pay off a house. You finally own it, and there's nobody to live in it.

LINDA: Well, dear, life is a casting off. It's always that way.

WILLY: No, no, some people—some people accomplish something. Did Biff say anything after I went this morning?

LINDA: You shouldn't have criticized him, Willy, especially after he just got off the train. You mustn't lose your temper with him.

WILLY: When the hell did I lose my temper? I simply asked him if he was making any money. Is that a criticism?

LINDA: But, dear, how could he make any money?

WILLY: There's such an undercurrent in him. He became a moody man. Did he apologize when I left this morning?

LINDA: He was crestfallen, Willy. You know how he admires you. I think if he finds himself, then you'll both be happier and not fight anymore.

WILLY: How can he find himself on a farm? Is that a life? A farmhand? In the beginning, when he was young, I thought, well, a young man, it's good for him to tramp around, take a lot of different jobs. But it's more than ten years now and he has yet to make thirty-five dollars a week!

LINDA: He's finding himself, Willy.

WILLY: Not finding yourself at the age of thirty-four is a disgrace.

LINDA: Shh!

WILLY: The trouble is he's lazy, goddammit!

LINDA: Willy, please!

WILLY: Biff is a lazy bum!

LINDA: They're sleeping. Get something to eat. Go on down.

WILLY: Why did he come home? I would like to know what brought him home.

LINDA: I don't know. I think he's still lost, Willy. I think he's very lost.

WILLY: Biff Loman is lost. In the greatest country in the world a young man with such—personal attractiveness, gets lost. And such a hard worker. There's one thing about Biff—he's not lazy.

LINDA: Never.

WILLY: I'll see him in the morning; I'll have a nice talk with him. I'll get him a job selling. He could be big in no time. My God! Remember how they used to follow him around in high school? When he smiled at one of them their faces lit up. When he walked down the street . . .

LINDA: [*Trying to bring him out of it.*] Willy, dear, I got a new kind of American-type cheese today. It's whipped.

WILLY: Why do you get American when I like Swiss?

LINDA: I just thought you'd like a change—

WILLY: I don't want a change! I want Swiss cheese. Why am I always being contradicted?

LINDA: [*With a covering laugh.*] I thought it would be a surprise.

WILLY: Why don't you open a window in here, for God's sake?

LINDA: They're all open, dear.

WILLY: The way they boxed us in here. Bricks and windows, windows and bricks.

LINDA: We should've bought the land next door.

WILLY: The street is lined with cars. There's not a breath of fresh air in the neighborhood. The grass don't grow anymore, you can't raise a carrot in the backyard. They should've had a law against apartment houses. Remember those two beautiful elms out there? When I and Biff hung the swing between them?

LINDA: Yeah, like a million miles from the city.

WILLY: They should've arrested the builder for cutting those down. They massacred the neighborhood. More and more I think of those days, Linda. This time of year it was lilac and wisteria. And then the peonies would come out, and the daffodils. What fragrance in this room!

LINDA: Well, after all, people had to move somewhere.

WILLY: No, there's more people now.

LINDA: I don't think there's more people. I think—

WILLY: There's more people! That's what's ruining this country! Population is getting out of control. The competition is maddening! Smell the stink from that apartment house! And another one on the other side . . . How can they whip cheese?

LINDA: Go down, try it. And be quiet.

WILLY: [*Turning to* LINDA, *guiltily.*] You're not worried about me, are you, sweetheart?

LINDA: What's the matter?

WILLY: Listen!

LINDA: You've got too much on the ball to worry about.

WILLY: You're my foundation and my support, Linda.

LINDA: Just try to relax, dear. You make mountains out of molehills.

WILLY: I won't fight with him anymore. If he wants to go back to Texas, let him go.

LINDA: He'll find his way.

WILLY: Sure. Certain men just don't get started till later in life. Like Thomas Edison, I think. Or B. F. Goodrich. One of them was deaf.

[*He starts for the bedroom doorway..*]

I'll put my money on Biff.

LINDA: And, Willy—if it's warm Sunday, we'll drive in the country. And we'll open the windshield, and take lunch.

WILLY: No, the windshields don't open on the new cars.

LINDA: But you opened it today.

WILLY: Me? I didn't.

[*He stops.*]

Now isn't that peculiar! Isn't that remarkable—

LINDA: What, darling?

WILLY: That is the most remarkable thing.

LINDA: What, dear?

WILLY: I was thinking of the Chevy. Nineteen twenty-eight . . . when I had that red Chevy—That funny? I coulda sworn I was driving that Chevy today.

LINDA: Well, that's nothing. Something must've reminded you.

WILLY: Remarkable. Ts. Remember those days? The way Biff used to simonize the car? The dealer refused to believe there was eighty thousand miles on it.

[*He shakes his head.*]

Heh! Close your eyes, I'll be right up.

[*He walks out of the bedroom.*]

LINDA: [*Calling after* WILLY.] Be careful on the stairs, dear! The cheese is on the middle shelf!

[*She turns, goes over to the bed, takes his jacket, and goes out of the bedroom.*]

LATER LIFE
BY A. R. GURNEY

CHARACTERS
RUTH *and* AUSTIN *(50s) rekindle a romance begun almost thirty years ago—but much has changed in the interval.*

SCENE
A party in Boston, overlooking the harbor.

TIME
Evening.

AUSTIN: We've met?

RUTH: We have.

AUSTIN: When?

RUTH: Think back.

AUSTIN: To when?

RUTH: Just think.

AUSTIN: I'm thinking . . .

   [*He looks at her carefully.*]

   Ruth, eh?

RUTH: Ruth.

AUSTIN: What's your last name?

RUTH: That won't help.

AUSTIN: What was your last name when we met?

RUTH: You never knew my last name.

AUSTIN: I just knew Ruth.

RUTH: That's all you knew.

[*Pause.*]

AUSTIN: Were you married?

RUTH: When?

AUSTIN: When we met.

RUTH: Oh no.

AUSTIN: Was I?

RUTH: No.

AUSTIN: Ah. Then we're talking about way back.

RUTH: Way, way back.

AUSTIN: Were we in college?

RUTH: No.

AUSTIN: School, then.

RUTH: I doubt that we would have met either at school or at college.

AUSTIN: Why not?

RUTH: Not everybody in the world went to Groton and Harvard.

AUSTIN: So I have learned in the course of my life.

[*She laughs.*]

I feel like a fool.

RUTH: Why?

AUSTIN: An attractive woman came into my life. And I don't remember.

RUTH: My hair was different then.

AUSTIN: Still. This is embarrassing.

RUTH: You want a hint?

AUSTIN: No, I should get it on my own . . .

[*Looks at her carefully.*]

There's something . . . Goddammit, I pride myself on my memory. I can remember when I was two and a half years old.

RUTH: You can not.

AUSTIN: I can. I can remember still being in my crib.

RUTH: I doubt that.

AUSTIN: No really. I can remember . . .

RUTH: What?

AUSTIN: It's a little racy.

RUTH: Tell me.

AUSTIN: I don't know you well enough.

RUTH: Oh, come on. We're both adults.

AUSTIN: I can remember being awakened in my crib by a strange sound. A kind of soft, rustling sound. And . . .

[*He stops.*]

Never mind.

RUTH: Go on. You can't stop now.

AUSTIN: It was my nurse—we had this young nurse. I specifically remember seeing her through the bars of my crib. Standing by the window. In the moonlight. Naked. Stroking her body. And I lay there watching her.

RUTH: Through the bars of your crib.

AUSTIN: Through the bars of my crib.

[*Pause.*]

RUTH: Austin.

AUSTIN: What?

RUTH: [*Melodramatically.*] I am that nurse.

AUSTIN: No.

RUTH: No. Just kidding.

[*Both laugh.*]

No, we met after college.

AUSTIN: After college, but before I was married.

RUTH: And before I was.

AUSTIN: You are presenting a rather narrow window of opportunity, madam.

RUTH: I know it.

AUSTIN: I got married soon after college.

RUTH: As I did, sir. As did I.

AUSTIN: So we are talking about a moment in our lives when we were both . . . what? Relatively free and clear.

RUTH: That's what we were. Relatively. Free and clear.

AUSTIN: Those moments are rare.

RUTH: They certainly are.

AUGUST: OSAGE COUNTY
BY TRACY LETTS

CHARACTERS
BARBARA FORDHAM *(46) is the oldest of three daughters of the famous American poet Beverly Weston;* BILL FORDHAM *(49) is* BARBARA's *husband. They have moved away from Oklahoma to Michigan. They have a daughter, Jean, who is fourteen.*

SCENE
The Weston family home in Osage County, Oklahoma.

TIME
Summer. Night.

> [*The patriarch of the Weston family, Beverly Weston, has disappeared and is feared dead. His family has gathered at the family home, hoping for news.* BARBARA *and* BILL FORDHAM *are preparing for sleep in the living room.* BARBARA *unfolds a hide-a-bed.* BILL *enters from the study, carrying a thin, hardback book.*]

BILL: Look what I found. Isn't it great?

BARBARA: We have copies.

BILL: I don't think I remember a hardback edition. I forgot there was ever a time they published poetry in hardback. Hell, I forgot there was ever a time they published poetry at all.

BARBARA: I'm not going to be able to sleep in this heat.

BILL: I wonder if this is worth something.

BARBARA: I'm sure it's not.

BILL: You never know. First edition, hardback, mint condition? Academy fellowship, uh . . . Wallace Stevens Award? That's right, isn't it?

BARBARA: Mm-hm.

BILL: This book was a big deal.

BARBARA: It wasn't that big a deal.

BILL: In those circles, it was.

BARBARA: Those are small circles.

BILL: [*Reads from the book.*] "Dedicated to my Violet." That's nice. Christ . . . I can't imagine the kind of pressure he must've felt after this came out. Probably every word he wrote after this, he had to be thinking, "What are they going to say about this? Are they going to compare it to *Meadowlark*?"

BARBARA: Did Jean go to bed?

BILL: She just turned out the light. You would think, though, at some point, you just say, "To hell with this," and you just write something anyway and who cares what they say about it? I mean, I don't know myself—

BARBARA: Will you please shut up about that fucking book?

BILL: What's the matter?

BARBARA: You are just dripping with envy over these . . . thirty poems my father wrote back in the fucking sixties, for God's sake. Don't you hear yourself?

BILL: You're mistaken. I have great admiration for these poems, not envy—

BARBARA: Reciting his list of awards—

BILL: I was merely talking about the value—

BARBARA: My father didn't write anymore for a lot of reasons, but critical opinion was not one of them, hard as that may be to believe. I know how important that stuff is to you.

BILL: What are you attacking me for? I haven't done anything.

BARBARA: I'm sure that's what you tell Sissy too, so she can comfort you, reassure you. "No, Billy, you haven't done anything."

BILL: What does that have to do— Why are you bringing that up?

BARBARA: They're all symptoms of your male menopause, whether it's you struggling with the "creative question," or screwing a girl who still wears a retainer.

BILL: All right, look. I'm here for you. Because I want to be with you, in a difficult time. But I'm not going to be held hostage in this room so you can attack me—

BARBARA: I'm sorry, I didn't mean to hold you hostage. You really should go then.

BILL: I'm not going anywhere. I flew to Oklahoma to be here with you and now you're stuck with me. And her name is Cindy.

BARBARA: I know her stupid name. At least do me the courtesy of recognizing when I'm demeaning you.

BILL: Violet has a way of putting you in attack mode, you know it?

BARBARA: She doesn't have anything to do with it.

BILL: Don't you believe it. You feel such rage for her that you can't help dishing it in my direction—

BARBARA: I swear to God, you psychoanalyze me right now, I skin you.

BILL: You may not agree with my methods, but you know I'm right.

BARBARA: Your "methods"? Thank you, Doctor, but I actually don't need any help from my mother to feel rage.

BILL: You want to argue? Is that what you need to do? Well, pick a subject, all right, and let me know what it is, so I can have a fighting chance—

BARBARA: The subject is me, you narcissistic motherfucker! I am in pain! I need help!

BILL: I've copped to being a narcissist. We're the products of a narcissistic generation.

BARBARA: You can't do it, can you? You can't talk about me for two seconds—

BILL: You called me a narcissist! And when I try to talk about you, you accuse me of psychoanalyzing you—!

BARBARA: You do understand that it hurts, to go from sharing a bed with you for twenty-three years to sleeping by myself.

BILL: I'm here, now.

BARBARA: Men always say shit like that, as if the past and the future don't exist.

BILL: Can we not make this a gender discussion?

BARBARA: Do men really believe that here and now is enough? It's just horseshit, to avoid talking about the things they're afraid to say.

THE SISTERS ROSENSWEIG

BY WENDY WASSERSTEIN

CHARACTERS

PFENI ROSENSWEIG *(40) is a world-traveling journalist;* GEOFFREY DUNCAN *(40) is an attractive and hip composer/ director of stage musicals.*

SCENE

A sitting room in Queen Anne's Gate, London.

TIME

Late afternoon, a weekend in late August 1991.

[PFENI *enters from downstairs, with her laptop computer. She sits on the window seat and works. Enter* GEOFFREY.]

GEOFFREY: I've just had my consciousness raised by the full assemblage of the Temple Beth El sisterhood. I fielded such penetrating questions from Mrs. Ida Hershkovitz as, "Mr. Duncan, I would like to know what exactly your function as director of *The Scarlet Pimpernel* was. You didn't write the story or the music and you don't act. So, from my point of view, you're being paid very good money just to sit there and do nothing."

PFENI: Poor Gorgeous.

GEOFFREY: Gorgeous loves it, darling! She's a star! The most beautiful and well-connected woman in Newton. They've asked me to the States to direct the West Newton Community Center revival of *Milk and Honey*. I suggest we do *Marat/Sade* Instead.

[*He kisses her.*]

I love that you have no bloody idea what I'm babbling about. Did Jordan ring? He said he'd be by around now.

PFENI: No, he didn't ring. Was Jordan at your talk?

GEOFFREY: I thought the ladies might want to meet him. Royal Jordan flatware is very big in the States these days.

[*Takes a sip of* PFENI's *tea and spits it out into the cup.*]

What's the matter with this tea? Uccch! Undrinkable!

PFENI: Geoffrey, that was mine!

GEOFFREY: "I would give all my fame for a pot of ale and safety."

PFENI: Geoffrey, please sit down. You're making me anxious.

GEOFFREY: [*Sings and dances.*]

Oh pretty baby, I can't sit down.

Don't you hear the band a groovin', I can't sit down.

Gotta get your motor movin'.

All right, U.S., for fifty points?

PFENI: "You Can't Sit Down," 1963. The Dovelles.

GEOFFREY: You're the brightest woman I've ever known.

PFENI: No, my sister Sara's the brightest woman you've ever known.

GEOFFREY: [*Finally sits.*] Pfeni . . .

PFENI: What is it, Geoffrey? You're beyond manic today.

GEOFFREY: Pfeni, after my speech to the Gorgeous ladies, I drove around London for hours. And then up past the Isle of Dogs and out to Greenwich. And I sat at the water's edge on the bow of the *Cutty Sark* and thought about us. Mostly about you, actually. Pfeni, I love you. I will always love you. But the truth is, I miss men. What?

PFENI: Nothing.

GEOFFREY: I want us to be the most remarkable friends. The Noel and Gertie of our day.

PFENI: I'm not in the theater, Geoffrey. I'm a journalist.

GEOFFREY: You know how wonderful I think you are. You must know that the entire time that I've been with you, I've never acted out, I've never cheated on you.

PFENI: Really, not even on the *Cutty Sark*?

GEOFFREY: Bitchiness doesn't become you, darling.

PFENI: I'm sorry.

GEOFFREY: You also don't have to be so bloody polite.

PFENI: The only place I am at home, or even close, is when I'm with you.

GEOFFREY: Pfeni, when I sat next to you at the ballet, it was a dark time in my life. Jordan had just left me, and my friends were becoming increasingly ill.

PFENI: So you thought to yourself, why not try something completely different. Why not get as far away from the hurt and the fear as possible. And there I was seated beside you; pretty, eccentric, and more than just a little bit lonely. You're right. You do have an eye for real talent.

GEOFFREY: Pfeni, don't.

PFENI: Why? Am I being self-indulgent? And maybe even just a little bitchy? Geoffrey, you're the one who said we should get married that very first night. You're the one who said what beautiful children we'd have, just this morning.

GEOFFREY: But we would have beautiful children. Pfeni, my friends need me.

PFENI: I never stopped you from being there for them.

GEOFFREY: I was frightened.

PFENI: And you're not now?

GEOFFREY: You really don't understand what it is to have absolutely no idea who you are.

PFENI: What?

GEOFFREY: I thought about this on the bow of the clipper ship. For all your wandering, you're always basically the same—you have your sisters, your point of view, and even in some casual drop-in way, your God. Pfeni, the only time I have a real sense of who I am and where I'm going is when I'm in a darkened theater and we're making it all up. Starting from scratch. But now I want a real life outside the theater, too. So maybe I will regret this choice. I know I'll miss you. But I'm an instinctive person, my luv, and speaking to those ladies, it all just clicked. Today this is who I am. I have no other choice. I miss men.

PFENI: It's all right, Geoffrey, I do too.

[*A car horn is heard.*]

Jordan.

GEOFFREY: I don't have to go.

PFENI: He's waiting for you.

GEOFFREY: We're in no rush.

PFENI: Please, Geoffrey, just go.

GEOFFREY: [*Kisses her head.*] Sugar pie, honey bunch.

BALLAD OF YACHIYO

BY PHILIP KAN GOTANDA

CHARACTERS

PAPA *and* MAMA *(50s) are worried about the future of their seventeen-year-old daughter, Yachiyo.* PAPA *has burned his daughter's poems, the parents want her to find something secure. (*MAMA *teaches the Japanese Tea Ceremony.)*

SCENE

A small hut on a cane plantation in Kauai, Hawaii.

TIME

Night. 1919.

[PAPA *and* MAMA *lit.* PAPA's *shirt is off, and* MAMA *is doing* yaito *(moxa burning) on his back to relieve the pain from his having been lifting heavy boxes.*]

PAPA: Did you tell her about the poems?

[*No response.*]

PAPA: Mama?

MAMA: She asked about them, so I told her.

PAPA: She asked about them?

MAMA: She remembers us fighting about them all the time.

PAPA: I burned them all, didn't I?

MAMA: I didn't tell you to burn them, Papa.

PAPA: You're always saying, "You don't need to write poems here. It's a waste of time. You just need to know how to work." And now you want her to learn those things.

MAMA: Because she's interested in those—

PAPA: She's not interested in tea, she's just doing it because you tell her to. *Itai, itai!*

[*Hurts.*]

You trying to set me on fire . . .

MAMA: *Yaito* is good for the muscle. I told you not to lift the crates, you should have waited for the boys. Always trying to prove yourself. The heat will help. Right here?

[*Testing the muscle.*]

PAPA: Yeah—ahhh . . .

[MAMA *puts another small ball of the salve on his back.*]

If I just soak in the *ofuro* [bath] for a while, the hot water—

MAMA: Sit still, Papa.

[*They work awhile in silence.*]

PAPA: Mama?

MAMA: Hmm?

PAPA: What if she gets into trouble? Waimea is so far away.

MAMA: She's got a good head on her shoulders. You worry about her too much, Papa.

PAPA: Old man Takamura's daughter was always peculiar. And his son-in-law, the potter. We don't know anything about him.

MAMA: [*Lighting a match.*] This is going to burn a little . . .

PAPA: I've heard rumors.

MAMA: He's not from around here. He's from Japan. A good family. His father is a famous artist, I hear. *Erai* man.

PAPA: *Itai, itai* . . .

MAMA: Be good for Yachiyo to be around those kind of people. She can learn something. Make a better life for herself.

PAPA: [*Reaches back and takes her hand.*] I still keep worrying, Mama.

FENCES

BY AUGUST WILSON

CHARACTERS

TROY MAXSON *(53) is a former Negro League baseball player who makes a living driving a garbage truck;* ROSE MAXSON *(50) is his wife and mother of their son, Cory.*

SCENE

The Maxson home in the Squirrel Hill section of Pittsburgh.

TIME

Morning, 1950s.

[*The lights come up on* ROSE *hanging up clothes. She hums and sings softly to herself.*]

ROSE: [*Sings.*] Jesus, be a fence all around me every day. Jesus, I want you to protect me as I travel on my way. Jesus, be a fence all around me every day.

[TROY *enters from the house.*]

Jesus, I want you to protect me, As I travel on my way.

[*To* TROY.]

'Morning. You ready for breakfast? I can fix it soon as I finish hanging up these clothes?

TROY: I got the coffee on. That'll be all right. I'll just drink some of that this morning.

ROSE: That 651 hit yesterday. That's the second time this month. Miss Pearl hit for a dollar . . . seems like those that need the least always get lucky. Poor folks can't get nothing.

TROY: Them numbers don't know nobody. I don't know why you fool with them. You and Lyons both.

ROSE: It's something to do.

TROY: You ain't doing nothing but throwing your money away.

ROSE: Troy, you know I don't play foolishly. I just play a nickel here and a nickel there.

TROY: That's two nickels you done thrown away.

ROSE: Now I hit sometimes . . . that makes up for it. It always comes in handy when I do hit. I don't hear you complaining then.

TROY: I ain't complaining now. I just say it's foolish. Trying to guess out of six hundred ways which way the number gonna come. If I had all the money niggers, these Negroes, throw away on numbers for one week—just one week—I'd be a rich man.

ROSE: Well, you wishing and calling it foolish ain't gonna stop folks from playing numbers. That's one thing for sure. Besides . . . some good things come from playing numbers. Look where Pope done bought him that restaurant off of numbers.

TROY: I can't stand niggers like that. Man ain't had two dimes to rub together. He walking around with his shoes all run over bumming money for cigarettes. All right. Got lucky there and hit the numbers . . .

ROSE: Troy, I know all about it.

TROY: Had good sense, I'll say that for him. He ain't throwed his money away. I seen niggers hit the numbers and go through two thousand dollars in four days. Man bought him that restaurant down there . . . fixed it up real nice . . . and then didn't want nobody to come in it! A Negro go in there and can't get no kind of service. I seen a white fellow come in there and order a bowl of stew. Pope picked all the meat out of the pot for him. Man ain't had nothing but a bowl of meat! Negro come behind him and ain't got nothing but the potatoes and carrots. Talking about what numbers do for people, you picked a wrong example. Ain't done nothing but make a worser fool out of him than he was before.

ROSE: Troy, you ought to stop worrying about what happened at work yesterday.

TROY: I ain't worried. Just told me to be down there at the Commissioner's office on Friday. Everybody think they gonna fire me. I ain't worried about them firing me. You ain't got to worry about that.

[*Pause.*]

Where's Cory? Cory in the house?

[*Calls.*]

Cory?

ROSE: He gone out.

TROY: Out, huh? He gone out 'cause he know I want him to help me with this fence. I know how he is. That boy scared of work.

He ain't done a lick of work in his life.

ROSE: He had to go to football practice. Coach wanted them to get in a little extra practice before the season start.

TROY: I got his practice . . . running out of here before he gets his chores done.

ROSE: Troy, what is wrong with you this morning? Don't nothing set right with you. Go on back in there and go to bed . . . get up on the other side.

TROY: Why something got to be wrong with me? I ain't said nothing wrong with me.

ROSE: You got something to say about everything. First it's the numbers . . . then it's the way the man runs his restaurant . . . then you done got on Cory. What's it gonna be next? Take a look up there and see if the weather suits you . . . or is it gonna be how you gonna put up the fence with the clothes hanging in the yard.

TROY: You hit the nail on the head then.

ROSE: I know you like I know the back of my hand. Go on in there and get you some coffee . . . see if that straighten you up. 'Cause you ain't right this morning.

WALK
BY THERESA REBECK

CHARACTERS
MAN *(40) is here at the beach, trying to get away from it all;* WOMAN *(40) is in a wheelchair with only a short time to live—or is that a lie? You decide.*

SCENE
By the seashore, on a bench facing the beach.

TIME
Day. The present.

[*A* MAN *sits on a bench. A* WOMAN *wheels herself on in a wheelchair.*]

WOMAN: Hi.

[*The* MAN *looks at her as she nods in greeting, nods in response.*]

MAN: Hi.

WOMAN: Is this your bench?

MAN: No, it's not my bench.

[*He smiles politely and looks out at the ocean.*]

WOMAN: I'm taking a walk. You know, it's weird, you don't take walks. I mean, who in L.A. ever takes a walk? Then one day, all of a sudden, you're in a wheelchair, with a life-threatening disease, and all you want is to, you know, take a walk. Perfect, huh?

MAN: Yeah. [*Looks at his watch.*]

Well . . .

[*He stands to go.*]

WOMAN: Oh, don't let me drive you off.

MAN: No, you're not. I was going.

WOMAN: No, you were just sitting here.

MAN: Well, now I'm going.

[*He starts to go.*]

WOMAN: [*Good-humored.*] Oh, that's lovely. I tell you I'm dying and you're like, oh, good-bye. What, are you in show business? You're in show business, aren't you? That's how come you're so sensitive.

MAN: No, no, that's not—

WOMAN: You're not in show business.

MAN: Of course, I'm in show business, but I'm not—look. I have compassion. I do. But I have a lunch.

[*He shrugs, only vaguely apologetic. She is slightly taken aback.*]

WOMAN: For your information, most people, when they find out that someone is dying, they actually try to be nice.

MAN: [*A little stung, but trying.*] I am being nice, come on. I don't even know you, right? I mean, right? And come on. I live here, I work here, Los Angeles, you know. I'm trying to be nice. It's just, trouble is not my thing, okay?

WOMAN: I'm with you there. Death isn't really my thing either and yet, I just don't know, I can't get it out of my mind.

[*Beat.*]

It's fine, go ahead. I'm sorry I bothered you. I just, I thought you were taking a walk. It seemed like a good thing to do. That's what you were doing, right? Taking a walk, looking at the ocean?

MAN: Yeah.

WOMAN: Good.

[*She smiles at him and looks away. Now he feels stupid. He waits a minute, unsure whether or not he should go.*]

MAN: Are you, you know? Going to be okay here?

WOMAN: Oh yeah, I'm fine. It's so pretty here, isn't it? The sky. I'll tell you, that's something that doesn't get old. Air. You think about things like that, once you, whatever. What's worth your time, and what's not. Like, computer games. If you only had, say, two months to live, would you spend any of that time playing computer solitaire? No. I mean the answer to that is just, no fucking way. On the other hand, you only have a couple months, you could spend a whole afternoon just looking at the ocean. Watching a bird fly in circles. It's weird, huh? You don't think about things like that. Until you're like, you know. Dying.

[*Beat.*]

MAN: Did my mother ask you to come here?

WOMAN: [*Dry.*] No.

MAN: [*Trying to be halfway nice.*] Sorry, I just—it's the sort of thing she'd do.

WOMAN: No, actually. This isn't about you.

MAN: [*Not getting that.*] So how much—what did you say, two months? That's rough.

WOMAN: Oh no, that was just a, they don't know. I mean, it's not like being on death row, here's your date with oblivion. Now that is something I would not enjoy. Not a lot of years, but you know, several, that's a blessing. Well, not a blessing. I actually would not describe what's happening to me like that. I'm sorry, I realize I'm rambling a bit, but ever since this happened to me, I tend to, whatever comes into my head comes right out of my mouth. Pretty soon I'm not going to be able to talk, that's what they— everything shuts down, bit by bit, your neurons stop working, muscle neurons, stuff people like you and I know nothing about, it all just stops working, so they don't know when, but eventually your voice goes, and they can give you one of those throat things that help for a while, or if you still have the use of your hands, you can type, until that goes too. So then you're just in there, apparently, in your head, not able to move or talk or feel or anything. But you're still in there. It sounds like a Beckett play to me, frankly, and to tell you the truth, I never really liked those things, sitting through a Beckett play. It's a nightmare. If I only had two months to live, that's one of the things I would not do.

[*Beat.*]

You know who Beckett is?

MAN: [*Testy.*] Of course I know who Beckett is. What do you think, just because I'm in the business, I don't—that's so—really, I mean, I'm being nice here.

WOMAN: Oh, you are.

MAN: So, I know who Beckett is, okay?

WOMAN: Ever seen one of his plays?

MAN: Hey, you just said they were boring.

WOMAN: They are.

MAN: So, exactly. Though, I have to say—if you don't mind—

WOMAN: No, I'm interested.

MAN: Harlan Ellison wrote this short story, it's amazing, about this sort of horrible, giant super-computer—malevolent, totally evil, that takes over the world.

WOMAN: Uh-huh.

MAN: And it's like, it kills off the entire human race, and then realizes at the last minute, that if it kills off everybody? It'll get bored. So it saves the last human beings, there are like six of them or something, and they just are like toys to this computer—

WOMAN: Like wanton flies to the gods.

MAN: Yeah, like bugs, but really, like toys.

WOMAN: Go on.

MAN: So this super-computer tortures these people for the longest time, and then one of them figures out a way to just murder all the others, to put them out of their misery? And he does it, before the super-computer can stop him. But then he's the only one left, and the computer is so enraged that it turns him into a blob. This blob, you know, that can't feel anything, or say anything, or move, but this person is still there. Because that's the super-computer's revenge.

WOMAN: [*Beat.*] Wow, that's really—

MAN: It just seemed the same. What you were saying.

WOMAN: [*Simple.*] Yeah, it's—that's weird, it's so the same.

[*Convinced.*]

My life has turned into a science-fiction movie. Now we know. God is a bad science-fiction writer.

MAN: [*Honest.*] No, come on, you can't think like that. Like, God would do something like this to you.

WOMAN: Why can't I?

MAN: I don't know.

WOMAN: [*Suddenly bitter.*] Well, you can. Okay? You get something like this, out of the blue, believe me, you start thinking about God, and what the hell he could possibly be up to. And you know, the only thing I could come up with, is that perhaps he is trying to make this big metaphoric point. 'Cause this disease, the one I have? Is actually different from Alzheimer's, where the body stays whole but the mind goes, so technically you end up with a person without a person inside. My disease, the body disintegrates but the mind stays whole, so you end up with a person and nowhere to put it! It's a metaphor, see? God is using me to make a point of the lack of spirituality in a materialistic culture. That's what it has to be. There is no explanation for a disease that would turn my body to mush, leaving me intact, because I'm not my body, I'm me, I'm in here. I'm me. I'm—

[*Beat.*]

I'm sorry. I think it's not a bad point, the Death of Spirituality in a Materialistic World. But I can't help wishing that God had come up with a different way to make it.

MAN: [*Simple, trying to comfort her.*] I don't believe in God.

WOMAN: [*Knows she's asking the hard question.*] Do you believe in anything?

MAN: Yes, of course.

WOMAN: What?

[*Beat.*]

MAN: You know, I really do have to go. That lunch.

WOMAN: You like the people you're having lunch with?

MAN: Yeah. They're fine.

WOMAN: Fine?

MAN: [*Defensive.*] The food will be very good. I am not wasting my life, okay?

WOMAN: I didn't—

MAN: You implied it, okay? Did you not just, deliberately—I mean, okay. I'm sorry you're sick, okay? But that's not my fault, and it's got nothing to do with me, and I have to go. I mean, I don't know you. Right? And just because I enjoy myself and don't want to think about death all the time—I admit, I live in Los Angeles and like it, but that doesn't make me a shallow person, okay? And I don't know you. Okay?

WOMAN: Okay.

MAN: Good.

WOMAN: Believe me. If I'm not going to waste the rest of my remaining time here on Beckett plays, or computer games, I'm certainly not going to spend it worrying about you.

MAN: [*Suddenly furious.*] HEY. I don't need anyone worrying about me! You and my mother, God—this is—God.

[*He stops himself, looks down and away. But he does not go. She considers him for a moment, then looks back out at the ocean.*]

WOMAN: You know, surprisingly, while there many things you don't want to do anymore, once you find out your days are numbered, there are some things that you didn't want to do while you had all the time in the world, that now you do want to do.

Did that make sense? You know, like you never have time to read poetry because it seems too hard, just too hard, and then, oddly enough, when you're in real trouble, the stuff suddenly makes sense. Shakespeare. Auden. Emily Dickinson. Charles Dickens, he's not actually a poet, but he's written some very good sentences. Time gets short, you don't mind spending it with them. Or that bird out there. It's pretty, isn't it?

MAN: [*Quiet.*] Where?

[*He glances up, then.*]

Oh, look—

WOMAN: Look.

[*They both watch, suddenly amazed, as something unseen happens in the sky. After a moment—.*]

WOMAN: [*Continuing.*] Oh, my.

MAN: Oh.

[*They continue to watch.*]

MAN: [*Continuing.*] Poetry?

[*The* WOMAN *looks at him, surprised, then looks away.*]

WOMAN: You should try it.

MAN: Maybe I will.

[*Beat.*]

I will.

WOMAN: Good.

[*They smile at each other for a moment, then turn back to watch the sky. Blackout.*]

THE SPEED OF DARKNESS
BY STEVE TESICH

CHARACTERS
JOE *(40s) is a successful businessman and hero of the Vietnam War with a big secret;* ANNE *(40) is his wife and the mother of Mary, a high school senior.*

SCENE
South Dakota, the living room of Joe and Anne's home.

TIME
Night—the late 1980s.

[JOE *and* ANNE *have just returned from a formal dinner where* JOE *was presented with the award as South Dakota's "Man of the Year" for his reputed heroism twenty years earlier in the Vietnam War. But* JOE *got too drunk at the ceremony and made something of a fool of himself. He also invited over Lou, his ex-war buddy, currently homeless. Now* JOE's *tuxedo jacket is on the floor, his shirt is undone, and he is drinking coffee. His wife,* ANNE, *has changed back into her everyday clothes, as well as an overcoat.*]

JOE: I thought you were asleep. Where're you going?

ANNE: Nowhere. I just got back.

JOE: Feels like I'm dreaming. Back from where?

ANNE: I took Mary over to Eddie's house for the night.

JOE: You what? You were worried about her being in her own home?

ANNE: Yes.

JOE: I see.

ANNE: I didn't know how far things would go around here.

JOE: So you had to protect her, right?

ANNE: Right.

JOE: I see. From me?

[ANNE *starts to pick up his jacket.*]

Leave it.

[*But she doesn't, so* JOE *rips it out of her hands and tosses it back on the floor.*]

I said, leave the fucking thing. Leave it. From me? You had to protect her from me?

ANNE: Yes.

JOE: What did you tell her?

ANNE: Not to confuse the violence she saw with the lack of love between us.

JOE: All those nights. All those nights I worried about her getting home safely and now home's the place to fear and I'm the menace in my Marsee's life. That hurts.

ANNE: I know.

[*Silence.*]

Where's Lou?

JOE: Asleep. You have to be a guest in this house to get any sleep, it seems. There's some coffee in the kitchen if you want it.

ANNE: No.

JOE: [*Looking at his watch.*] Where've you been all this time? It's a short ride to Eddie's house.

ANNE: Driving around. I drove past the bar where we met all those years ago.

JOE: Went out of your way a bit.

ANNE: Yes. Do you remember that night?

JOE: I'm a little too full of nights I remember.

ANNE: You were drunk. I was drunk. And when you told me your name was Joe, I was sure you were lying, but I was so . . . something . . . it didn't matter. He's lying. So what. We were a couple of used people, ready to be used again that night, and yet that very night you told me that you loved me. Do you remember what you said?

JOE: No.

ANNE: Tell me again.

JOE: Why?

ANNE: Please.

JOE: Oh, Anne.

ANNE: Please.

JOE: [*Relenting.*] It was dark. We were making love in my room. I reached up and turned on the light 'cause I wanted to see you. And I told you, "I've done this many times with many women. But I've never seen it before. The love I'm making in somebody's eyes. I see what I'm doing in your eyes, Annie. And I love you for it."

ANNE: It was the first time for both of us, that kind of love. I don't think we even knew how wrong everything had been until something went right. We were so happy to learn that our broken parts could mend, that we really didn't care how they mended. I think in our rush to love and be loved, we mended crooked. Around a lie.

JOE: There's worse things in life than that.

ANNE: I wish I'd known ahead of time that I'd meet you. I would've lived differently. There'd be nothing now to tell your daughter because she'd be yours, all yours, and I know how a man like you feels about things like that. If she can't be all yours, I can. But this lie is keeping us apart. It's grown as Mary has grown. I almost told her in the car tonight, but I didn't want to do it without you.

JOE: You should have. She might have been relieved to learn that the man she saw this evening was not her father. An early graduation present. You saw Lou. Do you know who he is? You're looking at him. Take you and Mary away from me and you have Lou.

ANNE: Nothing can do that, Joe.

JOE: Easy for you to be brave.

ANNE: Easy. To tell my daughter that I'd been with so many men that I don't even know who fathered her. To tell her that even when I knew I was carrying her inside of me, I carried on in the same way. God knows what would have happened to us both had I not met you. Don't you see? You weren't the only one saved. You saved both of us.

JOE: There's such a thing as being saved by the wrong guy. Maybe this lie is not the same lie for both of us. Maybe mine's different. Maybe mine's like a fishing hook. I might have to bleed to pull it out.

THE LAST TIME WE SAW HER
BY JANE ANDERSON

CHARACTERS
HUNTER *(early 60s), the boss, is a well-bred man of logic.* FRAN *(mid-40s), is an attractive woman wearing a tasteful middle-management business ensemble—skirt and jacket, comfortable heels, pearls, and matching earrings. She's considered extremely competent and a good performer. She tries to explain to her boss why she's having a problem at work.*

SCENE
Hunter's office.

TIME
The workday.

[*Golf memorabilia and pictures of* HUNTER'*s family are displayed on his very organized desk. He tends to talk in thoughtful, measured tones.* FRAN *is seated in front of the desk, waiting to talk to him.*]

HUNTER: [*On the phone.*] . . . Uh-huh, well then I think we should have a meeting with management, find out what's going on down there . . . exactly, no I couldn't agree more . . . sooner than later, absolutely . . . all right . . . I appreciate it.

[HUNTER *hangs up, makes a long note to himself while* FRAN *stares at her nails.* HUNTER *finally puts his pen down.* FRAN *looks up, ready to talk.*]

HUNTER: Excuse me.

[*He punches his intercom.*]

Nancy could you call Paul Christianson at the Columbus office and tell him we'd like to review his client records back through '06. And as soon as I'm done with this meeting, get Don Lillie on the phone for me. Thank you.

[HUNTER *snaps the intercom off, moves his note pad to another part of his desk, and turns to* FRAN, *indicating that she now has his complete attention.*]

HUNTER: Yes, Fran.

FRAN: Well, I'm not going to take up a lot of your time with this— or my time, for that matter, because, to be frank, I have quite a full morning ahead of me, as I'm sure you do, and so I'll be very brief about this.

HUNTER: All right.

FRAN: As you know, I've made a long-term commitment to the company and I'd like to contribute as much as I can.

HUNTER: Well, Fran, as a matter of fact we're very happy with your performance and we'll certainly look into extending your opportunities.

FRAN: Oh. Well, thank you. I appreciate that, thank you very much.

HUNTER: So.

[*A beat.*]

Is there a problem?

FRAN: No, I wouldn't consider it a problem. It's just something I would like you to be aware of so I can continue here without spending unnecessary energy on this particular issue. My primary goal, really, is to remove any obstacles to my own efficiency level.

HUNTER: That sounds fine to me.

FRAN: And again, this is not something that needs to take up your time, or be a concern or whatever—but I happen to be gay, for what that's worth, and basically I wanted you to be aware of that so that I don't have to be concerned about you finding out from another source.

HUNTER: I see.

[*A beat.*]

Well, I don't have any opinion about this particular issue one way or the other.

FRAN: No, well, that's fine.

HUNTER: It's uh . . . well, in any case these things exist and as I see it, what you do in the privacy of your home is your business and I certainly respect that.

FRAN: Thank you. Normally I wouldn't have brought this to your attention because I believe that, uh, the work is primary, but certain things have become rather problematic for me, and as I said, in order for me to maintain my own efficiency level I'm going to let certain people in the office know about me and I didn't want that information to reach you without talking to you first.

HUNTER: Well, I appreciate that.

[*A short beat.*]

FRAN: And that's really all I needed to say.

[*Another short beat.*]

HUNTER: Can I ask you why you feel you need to discuss this in your office?

FRAN: Well, it's the whole effort of secrecy that's becoming rather burdensome.

HUNTER: I see.

FRAN: For instance, my secretary who handles all of my personal calls—she's been talking to my companion, to Judith, for six years now, and she still thinks that Judith is my roommate. Frankly, I'm too old to have roommates.

HUNTER: Maybe you could tell your secretary that Judith is not your roommate but just a very good friend.

FRAN: But my secretary already knows that Judith lives with me . . .

HUNTER: Oh, I see, yes, that would still make her suspect.

FRAN: I think the whole point is that my secretary has probably guessed by now who Judith is and there's no point in lying about our relationship.

HUNTER: Then if you feel she knows, then why is there a need to discuss it with her?

FRAN: Because there is a certain discomfort when things are left unsaid, you see, it's like—well for instance, what if you couldn't tell your secretary that your wife was your wife. What if you had to make some story that, uh, your wife was your sister who was sharing the house with you until both of you could afford to live on your own?

HUNTER: Uh-huh.

FRAN: And your secretary knew that she was your wife but she treated her like your sister.

HUNTER: Well, in fact when my secretary does speak to my sister she treats her with as much courtesy as she does my wife. I expect her to treat everyone with courtesy.

FRAN: That was a bad example. It's not really about courtesy. My secretary is very polite.

HUNTER: Uh-huh.

FRAN: I just think that we waste a lot of time dancing around the subject.

HUNTER: No, I understand that.

FRAN: And my relationship with Judith—it's put a very big strain between us. We've been together for eight years now. We own a house together. She's a successful marketing executive. She doesn't appreciate it when my secretary says, "Fran, your roommate is on the line."

HUNTER: Well, again, that's something you can correct with your secretary. You know, my secretary once referred to my wife as "The Mrs."—I don't know why she did that but I found it inappropriate and I told her to please always refer to my wife as either my wife or Mrs. Hunter. So you might tell your secretary not to refer to Judith as your roommate but as Judith. Or you might even prefer that she only use her last name, which I feel is always more respectful.

FRAN: Yes, but I still think I need to discuss with my secretary who, exactly, Judith is.

HUNTER: Not necessarily, you're simply asking her not to use that particular reference.

FRAN: But you see it goes beyond that. Judith has reached a point where she doesn't want to be treated as something unmentionable anymore.

HUNTER: Yes, but that's your personal business. If my wife and I have any kind of argument or personal problem to resolve, I leave it at home. I don't discuss it with my secretary or my partners—or anyone else.

FRAN: No, I absolutely agree with that. Please understand that I'm a very private person—

HUNTER: I think the same thing applies with expressing affection in public. For instance, my youngest daughter and her boyfriend are physically very expressive with each other and there are times when I find it inappropriate. I believe in discretion no matter what particular bent you are.

FRAN: I'm not disagreeing . . .

HUNTER: You know what it is, Fran? I think that people are losing their manners. And I mean that in a larger sense. For instance in business, it used to be, if there was a dispute, there was a protocol for sitting down and talking things over. But now, people just pick up the phone—and I'm not a prude, but when someone uses foul language with me it just puts me in the wrong frame of mind.

FRAN: Uh-huh.

HUNTER: And here's another example: my oldest daughter, Melissa, works for a law firm downtown. And at lunchtime she goes to a certain coffee shop and there are some individuals who work behind the counter who are consistently rude to her. Not just rude, mind you, but outright abusive, turning their backs on her when she tries to talk to them, giving her evil looks—and by the way my daughter is one of the nicest gals you could ever meet. Melissa calls me in tears and says, "Dad, I just don't understand it." And frankly, neither do I. These particular individuals happen to be black and I don't mean to sound prejudiced, in fact I've hired a lot of black individuals and some of them were fine people— but I've noticed a general hostility coming from that particular group that's very disturbing. I want to sit down and say to them, "Look, if you really want things to change, then you're going to have to learn some manners." That kind of behavior is just plain counterproductive. Is that being racist?

FRAN: Uh, well . . .

HUNTER: Or maybe it's just being old-fashioned. I don't know. The world is going too fast for me. I wish my daughter could have grown up in a gentler time. There's no reason that she should have to fear for her life when she goes to lunch, absolutely no reason.

FRAN: [*Trying to be polite.*] No, I can understand that.

HUNTER: But my hunch is that it's perhaps different with the gays—that is the term you like to use?

FRAN: [*A beat.*] Yes.

HUNTER: I think that, as a whole, the gays are probably better educated and I'd say, quieter, more polite than the other groups. There's a young man who works over in accounting who's questionable, but he's sharp as a tack and works harder than anyone else over there. It'd be foolish for me to fire him. It'd just be plain bad business.

FRAN: Well. Yes it would.

HUNTER: [*A beat.*] So as we stand, you will be talking to your secretary and I assume this will be confidential?

FRAN: No, actually I was planning on telling everyone in my division.

HUNTER: I see. May I ask why?

FRAN: Well, because it will make things more comfortable.

HUNTER: For you or for them?

FRAN: For everyone, I hope.

HUNTER: Let me make a suggestion . . . let's recap the situation. You've been here for how long, six years?

FRAN: Yes.

HUNTER: And you're respected, well liked, your division is extremely productive—so from a professional standpoint would you say that everything is working as it should?

FRAN: Fairly well, yes.

HUNTER: Well, not fairly well, Fran, I'd even say your department is excelling.

FRAN: Oh, well, thank you.

HUNTER: So, if we were really to examine the situation, you'd have to say that whatever problem you're having is of a personal, not of a professional, nature.

FRAN: But this does affect my professional relationships.

HUNTER: Ah, but now you're saying that you have a personal problem that may have a negative effect on those who you work with.

FRAN: No, that's not what I'm saying.

HUNTER: Here's another example. We had a manager in a division over in Dayton who had an alcohol problem. It wasn't an overwhelming problem, he was never drunk when he came to work but his drinking habits were, in fact, affecting his home life. So finally, very quietly, he took two weeks off, got himself in to a program, and when he came back no one was the wiser. You see. It was no one's business that he had an alcohol problem, in fact, it would have undermined his authority if anyone knew. Do you see what I'm saying?

FRAN: I don't think this is really the same thing.

HUNTER: This is what I don't quite understand. Being that your situation is related to your sexual behavior, why would you think that appropriate to display in the workplace?

FRAN: I wouldn't be displaying any behavior—

HUNTER: It's not even appropriate for normal people to display their sexual feelings in the workplace.

FRAN: I didn't say it was appropriate, that's not what I would do.

HUNTER: Then what, exactly, is it that you would want to do?

FRAN: I simply want to let people in my office know that I'm in a relationship with a woman and that for me it's a very normal part of my life.

HUNTER: And how exactly will that improve your work performance?

[*A beat.*]

Do you see what I'm saying now?

FRAN: Yes, but that wasn't my original point.

HUNTER: Yes, I believe that you said that you were concerned with maintaining the efficiency level in your department. Isn't that what you said?

FRAN: I don't think you understand my situation, Mr. Hunter. I eat lunch alone every day because I'm terrified that people will ask about my personal life. I sit with a sandwich and a Cup O' Soup at my desk reading old copies of *Computer News*. People think I'm strange. I'm beginning to think I'm strange. I don't show up to office parties. I don't show up to picnics. I don't have drinks with our clients. When I go away for a conference, after the seminars I go straight to my room and order room service. I don't have a personality anymore. I have nothing to bring home to Judith. We eat dinner in silence. The only conversation is directed to the cat. This is not my idea of a life.

HUNTER: [*A beat.*] Fran, have you ever seen a play called *The Rainmaker?*

FRAN: Excuse me?

HUNTER: *The Rainmaker,* the movie had, ah, Burt Lancaster. Have you ever seen it? You know that scene when Lizzie says to Starbuck that she's always thought that she was plain? And Starbuck says, Lizzie, that's all nonsense, it's all in your head. You can be the most beautiful woman in the world if you believe it." Remember that scene?

FRAN: I'm not sure what you're getting at.

HUNTER: Let me ask you, was there ever a time when you were attracted to men?

FRAN: Excuse me?

HUNTER: There was never a time when you were in love with a man or had a crush on some fellow?

FRAN: No, Mr. Hunter.

HUNTER: And perhaps you were disappointed or hurt?

FRAN: No, nothing like that ever occurred.

HUNTER: Have you sought counseling on this issue?

FRAN: I've been to a psychiatrist, if that's what you're asking.

HUNTER: [*Somewhat concerned.*] Oh, you have.

FRAN: But it was for a very brief period of time. I only went twice.

HUNTER: Uh-huh. And did you discuss the possibility of having sexual feelings towards men?

FRAN: Yes I did. And there didn't seem to be any feelings to discuss.

HUNTER: So if a man in your office, for instance, said, "Fran, I find you very attractive. Can I take you out to dinner," you wouldn't accept?

FRAN: Why would I do that? I live with Judith.

HUNTER: But what I don't quite understand is that, well, when a man and a woman are together, as opposed to a woman and a woman or a man and a man, the design of the male and female body is made in such a way that it's physically pleasurable for those of the opposite sex to be together. In other words, is the experience that you have, satisfying?

FRAN: Mr. Hunter, if you're asking me how I do it, it's none of your business.

HUNTER: But don't you think, Fran, that everyone in your office will be wondering the same thing?

FRAN: As I said, it's no one's business.

HUNTER: Bingo. And that's why you don't need to tell anyone.

FRAN: Mr. Hunter, I'm about to lose my life's companion. I swear to God, she's going to leave me.

HUNTER: Are you attracted to your secretary?

FRAN: Excuse me?

HUNTER: I'm wondering if you ever look at your secretary in a romantic way. It's a natural reaction. I certainly look at mine from time to time, not that I'd ever do anything about it. I've been married to my wife for twenty-six years and I've always been faithful to her. But it's a normal and healthy thing for a man to look at other women. I was just curious to know if you have the same impulse.

FRAN: Absolutely not.

HUNTER: Ah. Well, there you go. Perhaps you aren't attracted to women after all.

FRAN: She's not my type, Mr. Hunter.

[*Getting up.*]

I don't think we need to take any more time with this. Thank you for seeing me.

HUNTER: I'm sorry this has been such a problem for you, Fran. I wish we could find a solution to this. I'll put my thinking cap on it.

[FRAN *ignores this, just wants to get out.* HUNTER *takes* FRAN's *hand and holds it in a fatherly fashion.*]

HUNTER: Believe in yourself, Franny. Don't be afraid to dream.

LATER LIFE

BY A. R. GURNEY

CHARACTERS
RUTH *and* AUSTIN *(50s) rekindle a romance begun almost thirty years ago—but much has changed in the interval.*

SCENE
A party in Boston, overlooking the harbor.

TIME
Evening.

RUTH: [*Sets her plates down.*] I brought dessert.

AUSTIN: [*Settling at the table.*] Very thoughtful.

RUTH: And coffee.

AUSTIN: Decaf, I hope.

RUTH: [*Sliding him his cup.*] What else.

[*They eat brownies or something.*]

Mmmm.

AUSTIN: A little rich, isn't it?

RUTH: Well, we deserve it. We were so healthy with the main course.

AUSTIN: Right. In Boston, they'd say we're getting our just desserts.

[RUTH *gives him a weak smile. Pause.*]

Everything all right, by the way?

RUTH: With the telephone call?

AUSTIN: Judith told us who it was.

[*Pause.*]

RUTH: He's at the . . . what is it? The Skyway Lounge, out at the airport.

AUSTIN: What? He's there?

RUTH: He's there.

AUSTIN: And?

RUTH: He wants me to join him.

AUSTIN: When?

RUTH: Now. Right now.

AUSTIN: But you're here.

RUTH: That's right. I'm here. Which is what I said. I said I'm having a very good time right here.

AUSTIN: What did he say to that?

RUTH: He said he could give me a better one, right there.

AUSTIN: Could he?

RUTH: He can . . . fun.

AUSTIN: Did you tell him about me?

RUTH: No.

AUSTIN: Why not?

RUTH: He might have shown up with a baseball bat.

AUSTIN: I could have dealt with that.

RUTH: Oh yes? With your squash racquet?

AUSTIN: I would have done something.

RUTH: [*Touching him.*] I know you would have, Austin.

[*She gets up.*]

I just don't want you to, that's all.

[*She looks out.*]

He's got two tickets on tonight's red-eye back west. First class. And he wants to order a bottle of champagne to drink while we wait.

AUSTIN: Champagne? At an airport bar?

RUTH: He knows I like it.

[*Pause.*]

First class, too. He knows I'm a sucker for that.

[*Pause.*]

And he'll charge everything to *my* credit card.

AUSTIN: Sounds like a nice guy.

RUTH: Oh, he . . . has his problems.

AUSTIN: Sure sounds like it.

RUTH: Of course we all do, don't we?

AUSTIN: Ouch.

RUTH: No, but I mean we do. Lord knows I do, too.

AUSTIN: Name one.

RUTH: Him.

AUSTIN: Okay.

RUTH: He's not good for me.

AUSTIN: That's an understatement.

RUTH: But he has some redeeming social virtues.

AUSTIN: Such as?

RUTH: Well . . . for one thing, he loves me.

AUSTIN: Oh, sure.

RUTH: He does . . . He's never traded me in for some young bimbo. He's never taken me for granted. He loves me . . . I walk out, I leave him, I say this is it, and what does he do? He telephones all over the country till he finds out where I am. Then he grabs a flight to Boston. Calls me here. Offers me champagne. And begs me to come back . . . He loves me.

AUSTIN: How can he love you if he hits you?

RUTH: He doesn't hit me.

AUSTIN: I hear he does.

RUTH [*More to herself.*] Judith? . . .

[*To* AUSTIN.]

Once, maybe.

AUSTIN: Once is enough.

RUTH: By mistake.

AUSTIN: Oh, Ruth.

RUTH: It was by *mistake,* Austin!

AUSTIN: Some mistake. That's a big mistake.

RUTH: Sometimes he gets . . . carried away.

AUSTIN: Yes, well, that's not love in my book.

RUTH: Oh, really?

AUSTIN: That has nothing to do with love. Rape, violence, things of that kind, I'm sorry, they elude me. They totally elude me. If that's love, then I'm afraid I know nothing about it.

[*She looks at him as if for the first time. Pause. Sounds of people singing around a piano come from within. They sing a lively song.*]

Well. How about a song at twilight?

RUTH: Maybe it's better if I just . . .

[*She makes a move to go.*]

AUSTIN [*Getting in her way.*] Ruth.

[*She stops.*]

Tell you what. We'll go to the Ritz Bar, you and I. It's a very pleasant, very quiet place. And *I'll* buy you champagne. And I promise you it will be a better brand than what your Marlboro Man comes up with, out at the airport. And I'll pay for it *myself.*

RUTH: Austin . . .

AUSTIN: No, and I'll tell you something else. After we've had champagne, we'll go to my place. If you'd like.

RUTH: Oh, Austin . . .

AUSTIN: No, now I don't want you to feel obligated in any way. But I have a very nice apartment on Beacon Street, and we can walk there, right down Arlington Street from the Ritz. And I have a guest room, Ruth. It's a nice room. With its own bath. I keep it for the kids. You can sleep there if you prefer. I'll even lend you a pair of decent pajamas.

RUTH: Decent pajamas . . .

AUSTIN: No, now wait. If, when we're there, you'd like to . . . to join me in my room, if you'd care to slip into my bed, naturally I'd like that very much. Very much indeed. But you wouldn't have to. Either way, you'd be most welcome. And if things worked out, why we might . . . we might make things more permanent . . . I mean, it's a thought, at least. And if they don't, well, hell, you should always feel free to leave any time you want.

RUTH: Oh, well . . .

AUSTIN: I mean, we obviously get along. That's obvious. We did on Capri and we do now. Hey, come to think of it, this is a second chance, isn't it? We're back to where we were, but this time we're getting a second chance.

[*Pause.*]

So. What do you say?

RUTH: [*Kissing him.*] Oh, Austin. Austin from Boston. You're such a good man.

[*She starts out. Singing continues within.*]

AUSTIN: Where are you going?

RUTH: I don't want to tell you.

AUSTIN: To him?

RUTH: I think so. Yes.

AUSTIN: Why?

RUTH: Why?

AUSTIN: Why him and not me?

RUTH: Oh, dear.

AUSTIN: How can you love that guy?

RUTH: If you don't know, I can't tell you.

AUSTIN [*Turning away from her.*] You don't think I'm attractive?

RUTH: I think you're one of the most attractive men I've ever met.

AUSTIN: Then it must be my problem.

RUTH: Yes.

AUSTIN: You think it's a crock of shit!

RUTH: No! Not at all. No! I take it very seriously. I take it more seriously than you do.

AUSTIN: You think something terrible is going to happen to me?

RUTH: I think it already has.

AUSTIN: When?

RUTH: I don't know.

AUSTIN: Where?

RUTH: I don't know that either.

AUSTIN: But you think I'm damned into outer darkness?

RUTH: I do. I really do.

AUSTIN: But you won't tell me why?

RUTH: I can't.

AUSTIN: Why not?

RUTH: It's too painful, Austin.

AUSTIN: Do you think I'll ever find out?

RUTH: Oh, I hope not.

AUSTIN: Why?

RUTH: Because you'll go through absolute hell.

AUSTIN: You mean I'll weep and wail and gnash my teeth?

RUTH: I don't think so, Austin. No. I think you'll clear your throat, and square your shoulders, and straighten your tie—and stand there quietly and take it. That's the hellish part.

[*She looks at him feelingly.*]

I've got to dash.

FIGHTING OVER BEVERLEY

BY ISRAEL HOROVITZ

CHARACTERS

BEVERLEY *and* ARCHIE *(both late 60s) were in love forty years ago in London, but* BEVERLEY *chose to marry Zelly instead. Now* ARCHIE *has shown up, hoping to convince* BEVERLEY *that she made a terrible mistake.*

SCENE

The living room of Beverley and Zelly's home in Gloucester, Massachusetts.

TIME

Midwinter, the present; 1 p.m. on a Saturday.

ARCHIE: I et both me breakfast and me lunch in town . . . before comin' here to your house.

BEVERLEY: You should've come straight here.

ARCHIE: I had a look around Gloucester.

BEVERLEY: You shouldn't've wandered around in the cold, Arthur. That was silly. You should've come straight to us.

[*Pauses.*]

You came in by train?

ARCHIE: I did . . . but, not all the way from home.

BEVERLEY: [*Laughs.*] Well, I know that! You must have flown from home.

ARCHIE: I took a boat from home.

BEVERLEY: Did you? . . . A cruise ship?

ARCHIE: A freighter . . . a container ship . . . out of Liverpool.

BEVERLEY: [*Pours out fresh cups of tea.*] There's yours.

ARCHIE: Tar, very much, lovey.

[*Sips; smacks his lips.*]

Lovely!

[ARCHIE *and* BEVERLEY *share a smile.*]

I don't fly. Not since the war. It's too upsetting. I've had my fill of sky and clouds, thank you very much.

BEVERLEY: I can understand that, Arthur. I really can. Zelly doesn't like flying after his bad luck in the War.

ARCHIE: I shouldn't think he would.

BEVERLEY: Zelly has some terrible memories!

ARCHIE: As do I! I don't even try to sleep at night. My night dreams are too upsetting. I get whatever sleep I can in the daytime. Usually, no more than an hour or two.

BEVERLEY: And that's enough? . . . Rest.

ARCHIE: Rest? Rest is something other than sleep, isn't it?

[*There is a pause.*]

You know, Bev, I'd known Zelly'd lost his leg, but, actually seeing it, actually meeting Zelly, I mean, and seeing, firsthand, that he's legless, I . . . well . . .

BEVERLEY: It's upsetting, I know, but, Zelly's adjusted to the artificial leg, totally. He takes two walks a day.

ARCHIE: Does he, then?

BEVERLEY: Two a day. One in the morning, one in the afternoon.

ARCHIE: Every morning, every afternoon?

BEVERLEY: Never misses.

ARCHIE: That's good to know, eh?

[ARCHIE *smiles at* BEVERLEY, *flirtatiously.* BEVERLEY *giggles, girlishly.*]

BEVERLEY: *Arthurrrr!*

[*Exits into kitchen with tea tray.* ARCHIE *calls after her.*]

ARCHIE: We've got things to sort out, don't we, Bev? All this chat and backchat we're doin' is bloody tiresome. Small talk, middle talk, grand talk: it's all bloody useless *talk,* isn't it? We don't have time! It's not like we're *young people!*

[BEVERLEY *re-enters.*]

Is your Zelly a good husband then?

BEVERLEY: As husbands go, Zelly's a good one, yes.

ARCHIE: [*Without warning.*] You made a terrible mistake, Beverley. I'm sure you know that you did. I mean, it's obvious, isn't it?

[*Pauses.*]

I intend to take you back with me, Beverley. He's had you for forty-five years. Enough's enough, isn't it. I may not have personally married, but, I know how these marriages work, Bev. Each one grows complaisant . . . mild . . . obliging. You get along, but there's no fight left, there's no fire, no passion, no . . . excitement. We'll be starting fresh, you and me, Bev. It'll fire you up. You'll live longer. I promise you.

BEVERLEY: Arthur, you can't be serious!

ARCHIE: Oh, I am, Bev. I've loved only you. At first I thought it was just a kind of obsession . . . because of your jilting me as you did. But, after some years, I came to realize it was true love, Bev. Nobody's ever held a candle to you! You're the one.

[BEVERLEY *is stunned.*]

BEVERLEY: I'm just . . . flabbergasted!

ARCHIE: Are you, now? Well, then, you can easily imagine how bloody flabbergasted *I* was, can't you? . . . Waitin' at the station in Knutsford, alone, ring in a ring-box in me pocket, all paid for. Smile all over me face: ear to bloody ear! I'm watchin' couples re-couplin'. kissin', huggin', passion in the air thick as mustard! I'm thinkin' ta' meself, "Bev's *so in love with me!*" . . . Ten hours later, I trudge home, totally nackered, deeply depressed, bewildered, quite honestly devastated, and I hav' ta' tell Ma'am you never showed. She is stunned. Nearly falls backwards from the shock of it. I tell her I think you've bolted with your Yank. Ma'am says ta' me, "Never!" She says, "Bev's not that sort!" Two years later, almost to the day, that woman is in her grave.

BEVERLEY: You're not implying I was in any way *responsible* for your mum's death, are you?

[*Stares at* ARCHIE. *Five count.*]

You are.

ARCHIE: This is not a matter of implication, Miss Leach. These are hard cold facts of life!

BEVERLEY: I was eighteen, Arthur.

ARCHIE: As was I!

BEVERLEY: I'm so sorry, Arthur. I'm sorry that I did what I did. If I were able to live my life over, I would do things differently.

ARCHIE: How so?

BEVERLEY: I wouldn't've run off, so mysteriously. I would've talked with you, eye to eye, truthfully.

ARCHIE: Would you have changed the outcome?

BEVERLEY: Meaning, would I still have married Zelly?

ARCHIE: Well . . . yes.

BEVERLEY: I don't know if I would have married Zelly, but I do certainly know I wouldn't have married *you,* Arthur.

ARCHIE [*After a pause; feelings hurt.*] I think I should be told why you've just said what you've just said.

BEVERLEY: Oh, Arthur . . . *please!* Entire *lifetimes* have passed between then and now. I would not be made to feel so profoundly *guilty.*

ARCHIE: No one can make a person feel guilt that isn't there, Bev. I hav'ta say this to you, because it's what I deeply feel to be true.

[*New tone, suddenly sweet.*]

Would you let me kiss you, Bev? I so much want to kiss you.

BEVERLEY: I'd prefer you didn't.

ARCHIE: For old time's sake.

BEVERLEY: I think not.

[*She pauses, thoughtfully.*]

The idea of a man wanting to kiss me . . . wanting me, romantically . . . is not an unattractive idea. And you're not an unattractive man, Arthur. But I don't mean to hold out any false hope, especially to you, given our . . . history. I only want to be truthful with you.

[*Without warning.*]

Close your eyes, please.

[ARCHIE *closes his eyes.* BEVERLEY *kisses him on lips, lightly.*]

ARCHIE: I love you dearly, Bev . . .

[ARCHIE *moves in for a major kiss.* BEVERLEY *backs away. He pulls her to him roughly. She pushes him away from her, angrily.*]

BEVERLEY: Certainly not!

ARCHIE: Please, Bev . . .

BEVERLEY: *This is my husband's house! Kindly respect this!*

ARCHIE: [*Yells; a rejected lover.*] *Why did you run off and marry him?*

BEVERLEY: *Because I fell in love with him!*

ARCHIE: *Why?*

BEVERLEY: Zelly was exciting to me! He was forbidden by my parents. He was exotic, he was *American!* . . . Zelly was young and beautiful. He got into a plane and he flew against the enemy. Zelly fought to save me, my family, our little town . . .

ARCHIE: *So did I, all of the above!* What's so bloody great about what he did versus what I did?

BEVERLEY: There's a tremendous difference, Arthur. Zelly was shot down whilst protecting me . . . *us!* Zelly was decorated, made a hero. Even my father called Zelly "hero."

ARCHIE: Because he was shot down?

BEVERLEY: I beg your pardon?

ARCHIE: Him: Zelly. Gettin' shot down made the hero of him?

BEVERLEY: Of course it did.

ARCHIE: *Jesus!* That is *sickening*! That just makes me *sick*.

[ARCHIE *moves to the window, turns his back to* BEVERLEY. *He clenches his hands into fists; grinds his fists together.*]

BEVERLEY: I shouldn't have said "yes" to you, Arthur. It was wrong of me to have said "yes" to you. I do apologize. I wouldn't have hurt you, not knowingly, Art, not for the world. I adored you, Artie. I just didn't ever *love you*.

ARCHIE: Then why ever did you say you'd marry me then?

BEVERLEY: Because you asked me long before I met Zelly . . . Because you persisted . . . Because you wouldn't let me say otherwise . . . Because you wouldn't let me say "no."

[*Walks to the window, looks outside; then turns to* ARCHIE *again.*]

I've just lied to you, Arthur. I was *thrilled* when you proposed marriage to me. But, you, personally, did not thrill me. Zelly, personally, did.

ARCHIE: And does he, Zelly, still thrill you, now?

BEVERLEY: Thrill me, now? . . . No.

ARCHIE: Then, leave him, Bev! He's had his time! He's had his chance! Let me have mine! I know I can thrill you. Maybe I couldn't when I was nineteen, but I can thrill you *now* . . . and he can't now. You said so, yourself! . . . We can't let the most exciting times of our lives slip so far into the past. That's death! We've got to have plans for the future! *Thrillin'* plans! We've got to find outrageous thrills! We got to have life left! Beverley, please, trust me! . . . I understand that Zelly did all the right kind of talkin' ta' you back then. But back then's done and gone, and it's *me* who's bloody talkin' to you *now,* my love! I'm talkin' and I'm sayin' I got my health, I've got a fair spot of wealth, and I've got all the time in the world to prove the tremendous lot of love I feel for you, Beverley Leach. You're the only woman I've ever bloody loved, Beverley. And, oh, God, I do still love you. What I lack in grace and charm, I make up for in the depth of my love for you, lass. What I lack in the way I look, I make up for in the way I look at *you*! . . . Let me prove myself to you, Bev. The worst that can happen is that you'll explode yourself out of this bloody *tedium*!

GOOD PEOPLE
BY DAVID LINDSAY-ABAIRE

CHARACTERS
MARGARET WALSH *(50) went to the same public high school in Boston as* MIKE *(50). Now* MIKE *has become the successful Doctor Michael Dillon, while* MARGARET *has hit a dead end in her life.*

SCENE
Dr. Michael Dillon's office in Boston.

TIME
Afternoon. The present.

[*A couple of family photos on a shelf behind his desk.* MIKE, *about fifty, handsome, is working at his desk. After a couple beats* MARGARET, *also fifty, peeks in.*]

MARGARET: Mike?

MIKE: [*Comes to the door.*] There you are!

MARGARET: How you doin'?

MIKE: Come on in!

[*She comes in. He gives her a hug.*]

Holy Jesus. Margie Walsh.

MARGARET: Hi, Mike.

MIKE: From prehistoric times.

MARGARET: Just about.

[*He's a little too amiable. She's a bit uncomfortable.*]

MIKE: Sorry you had to wait out there, I was on the line with the caterer.

MARGARET: It's okay.

MIKE: My wife's throwing this party, so there are all these questions about the menu.

MARGARET: I hope it's okay that I came in without an appointment or anything.

MIKE: It's fine. I had some cancellations, which never happens, so—

MARGARET: Yeah, they said.

MIKE: You got lucky.

MARGARET: Is the party for you?

MIKE: The party?

MARGARET: You said your wife was throwing a party.

MIKE: Oh, yeah, it's my birthday this weekend—

MARGARET: March 22nd.

MIKE: [*Beat.*] That's right. Anyway, she lives for that stuff. Any excuse to throw a party.

MARGARET: That's nice.

MIKE: I'm really sorry you had to wait.

MARGARET: I wouldn't have come down, but I called a few times on Monday, and then again yesterday, but they wouldn't put me through.

MIKE: They do that if I'm with patients.

MARGARET: I didn't want to be a pest about it.

MIKE: It's totally fine. How you doin'?

MARGARET: I'm okay.

MIKE: Still in Southie?

MARGARET: Yeah, down on Tudor Street.

MIKE: The Lower End.

MARGARET: Lower End.

MIKE: Same as always.

MARGARET: I guess.

MIKE: This is crazy. Look at you.

MARGARET: I'm fat.

MIKE: You are not.

MARGARET: Well, I'm not seventeen.

MIKE: No, nobody's seventeen. How's Gobie?

MARGARET: Oh, he's, uh, down in Virginia somewhere.

MIKE: Oh yeah?

MARGARET: Or Georgia, I guess. Somewhere down there. Last I heard.

MIKE: Well, say hi to him from me.

MARGARET: Okay. We haven't heard from him in a while.

MIKE: Did you ever marry him?

MARGARET: Oh God, no.

MIKE: You were together a while, though.

MARGARET: Not really.

MIKE: Well, tell him I say hello.

[*Laughing.*]

I think he owes me a few bucks.

MARGARET: We don't really— He could be dead for all I know.

MIKE: [*Laughing.*] That deadbeat was always— What'd you say?

MARGARET: I said he could be dead for all I know.

MIKE: Oh.

MARGARET: We've lost touch.

MIKE: That's too bad.

MARGARET: Not really.

MIKE: Oh, okay.

[*Silence.*]

MARGARET: So Jeannie said she ran into you. At the luncheon thing.

MIKE: Yeah, she's the same, huh?

MARGARET: Yeah.

MIKE: Mouthy from Southie.

MARGARET: [*Little chuckle.*] Yeah.

MIKE: I would've known her anywhere.

MARGARET: I heard you were a doctor, but I didn't know if it was true or not.

MIKE: It's true.

MARGARET: That is awesome.

MIKE: Oh, thanks.

MARGARET: I never would've guessed that.

MIKE: No?

MARGARET: I mean, I knew you were smart. Everybody knew that, but I would never have pictured you delivering babies.

MIKE: I don't actually deliver the babies.

MARGARET: You don't?

MIKE: I mean, I *have* in the past but— I'm a reproductive endocrinologist.

MARGARET: I don't know what you just said, but I just got a little excited.

MIKE: [*Chuckles.*] Okay.

MARGARET: Was that even English?

MIKE: I do fertility stuff.

MARGARET: You should've just said that.

MIKE: And I help with high-risk pregnancies.

MARGARET: I only went to Southie High after all. You can't be using those five-dollar words on me.

MIKE: Sorry.

MARGARET: I'm just playin' with you.

MIKE: You asked what I did.

MARGARET: I know, I was kidding.

MIKE: Okay. I mean, I went to Southie High, too.

MARGARET: Yeah, and U-Penn, and wherever else.

MIKE: Right.

MARGARET: I didn't go to U-Penn.

MIKE: No, I know.

MARGARET: [*Chuckles.*] I didn't go to U-Anywhere.

[*Pause.*]

A doctor, though. I think that's awesome.

MIKE: Thank you.

MARGARET: You're the only doctor I know. In real life, I mean.

MIKE: Real life?

MARGARET: Not somebody I *go* to, in other words. You know what I mean.

MIKE: Yeah. Personally.

MARGARET: *Personally.* Exactly.

[*Silence.*]

MIKE: So, are you pregnant, or—

MARGARET: *No.* God. Am I *pregnant*?

MIKE: I'm just pulling your leg.

MARGARET: Oh. I thought you were really asking me.

MIKE: Although, we've had some older moms in here. You'd be surprised. Almost fifty, some of them.

MARGARET: I'm not pregnant.

MIKE: No, I know.

MARGARET: [*Beat.*] So you got the messages then?

MIKE: Yeah, the receptionist played them for me.

MARGARET: Then you know why I—

MIKE: Yes, I was just—

MARGARET: I didn't mean to bug you about it.

MIKE: No, I should've called you back. This is the first slow day we've had.

MARGARET: It's just, my landlady's tapping her foot for the rent, so—

MIKE: No, I know.

MARGARET: I wouldn't have come, but I didn't know if you were getting the messages.

MIKE: No, I got them.

MARGARET: So Jeannie said I should just come down here.

MIKE: The trouble is, Margie, I don't have anything open right now.

MARGARET: [*Beat.*] No, I figured.

MIKE: And you saw, we don't have a lot of people out there.

MARGARET: No, I know.

MIKE: Just a couple girls answering the phones.

MARGARET: Right.

MIKE: Have you even worked one of those systems? You have to know how to—

MARGARET: I wouldn't *have* to be answering the phones. I just mentioned the phones because I didn't know what you might have.

MIKE: I see.

MARGARET: I could do whatever. Janitorial stuff or—

MIKE: We have a service that does that. A cleaning service. They come at night.

MARGARET: Oh, I couldn't do nights, I don't think. Not with my Joyce.

MIKE: [*Beat.*] I have nothing to do with the cleaning folks anyway. They hire their own people.

MARGARET: That's okay, I couldn't do nights. I just didn't know what the jobs are in a doctor's office. I don't know if there's filing or whatever?

MIKE: That's what I'm saying, I don't have anything.

MARGARET: Right.

MIKE: I'm sorry, I should've called you back.

MARGARET: I knew it was a long shot. I only came down because Jean said she ran into you. I told her it was stupid.

MIKE: Have you tried Gillette?

MARGARET: [*A wry chuckle.*] Yeah.

MIKE: Back in the day everybody worked down Gillette. Is that place still open?

MARGARET: Oh, yeah, they're open.

MIKE: I'm sorry, Margie.

MARGARET: That's okay.

MIKE: If I hear about anything, I'll definitely call you. I have your number now.

[*This is probably the time she should leave. But she doesn't.*]

MARGARET: [*Regarding a photo over his shoulder.*] Is that your family?

MIKE: Yeah.

MARGARET: Can I see?

MIKE: [*Slightest pause.*] Sure.

MARGARET: You don't want to show me?

MIKE: [*Hands her the photo.*] Of course. I don't care if—

MARGARET: [*A little laugh.*] I'm not gonna *stalk* them.

MIKE: It's just an old photo, that's all. That's in D.C. We were there for a while, so . . .

MARGARET: [*Pause as she takes in the photo.*] Your wife is beautiful.

MIKE: Thank you.

MARGARET: And young.

MIKE: Oh. Not really. Like, I said it's an old picture.

MARGARET: How old?

MIKE: I don't know. Three years.

MARGARET: So, it's not that old. She's still young.

MIKE: Younger than me, yeah. A little bit.

MARGARET: [*A little chuckle.*] "A little bit." Okay.

MIKE: I waited awhile. To settle down.

MARGARET: Well, she's beautiful. Your daughter too.

MIKE: Thank you. She's six now.

MARGARET: Your wife?

MIKE: You're funny.

MARGARET: [*Hands the photo back.*] She is beautiful though. They both are. Everybody's beautiful.

IN THE EYE OF
THE HURRICANE

BY EDUARDO MACHADO

CHARACTERS

MANUELA *(58) and* MARIO *(52) are sister and brother in a well-to-do Havana family, whose bus company business is in the process of being nationalized by Fidel Castro. Meanwhile, the family itself is in crisis, as their mother's health is declining from diabetes.*

SCENE

A private area at a shrimp-and-avocado lunch in the backyard of the family home in a small Cuban town.

TIME

Afternoon. 1960.

MANUELA: You're crying, Mario.

MARIO: Leave me alone.

MANUELA: What is it?

MARIO: I got a cold.

MANUELA: How did you get it?

MARIO: I don't know, how does one get anything . . .

MANUELA: By working for it.

[MARIO *laughs.*]

MARIO: Really, is that how?

MANUELA: Don't be sarcastic.

MARIO: You seem to know so much, sister.

MANUELA: What are you implying?

MARIO: Nothing, I'm stuffed up, out of . . .

MANUELA: Out of what?

MARIO: Place, out of place.

MANUELA: Well . . .

MARIO: It's Mama.

MANUELA: Yes.

MARIO: Her illness. What's it called again?

MANUELA: Diabetes.

MARIO: Have you told her yet?

MANUELA: I'm not going to tell her.

MARIO: That sugar, all that sweet sugar water is killing her. The syrup she has for blood has gone out of control.

[*He starts to cry.*]

MANUELA: Everyone thinks that their mother will never die. I don't like seeing you sad.

MARIO: I'm crying from anger!

MANUELA: Never mind, Mario.

MARIO: Mother's illness has made me angry at you and your husband.

MANUELA: You're my brother and I've tried—

MARIO: Angry at you.

MANUELA: Tried to reach you, but—

MARIO: Your husband—

MANUELA: Stop your accusations.

MARIO: I haven't accused anybody.

MANUELA: We would have been nowhere, if Oscar hadn't come into my life. He saved all of us.

MARIO: All but Papa.

MANUELA: Please. It's not my fault that Mama has . . . It's not my fault that Papa . . .

MARIO: Right, let's not bring it up.

MANUELA: Fine.

MARIO: Fine.

[*They embrace.*]

MANUELA: Lunch will be ready soon.

[MARIO *looks out the window.*]

MARIO: Here he comes.

MANUELA: Who?

MARIO: Your husband.

[MANUELA *looks out.*]

MANUELA: Look, see him. He has a bunch of gladioluses for Mama. Look at the way he's talking to Hugo. He reassures your nephew with a touch, how he takes care of your dead brother's son. How my husband has protected us, all of us. And you resent him?

MARIO: Right.

MANUELA: Go and say hello to Mama.

MARIO: I drove to the corner and bought her a carton of Lucky Strikes.

MANUELA: Here.

[*She goes into a drawer and takes out a syringe.*]

You inject her, she thinks you have a steadier hand.

MARIO: Where's the medicine?

MANUELA: Rosa has it.

MARIO: Lucky Strikes.

MANUELA: She'll like that. Steal me a pack.

MARIO: If she lets me.

[*He exits.*]

LONG DAY'S JOURNEY INTO NIGHT

BY EUGENE O'NEILL

CHARACTERS

JAMES TYRONE *(65) is the patriarch of the Tyrone clan and on*
of the greatest American actors of the late nineteenth century wh
sacrificed his greatness for popularity and riches; MARY TYRONE
(55) is his wife and mother of their two sons, Jamie and Edmund—
she has been battling a morphine addiction related to her secon
pregnancy for several years.

SCENE

The living room of the Tyrones' summer home near New London
Connecticut.

TIME

Around 7 p.m. in the evening of an August day in 1912.

[*After dinner.* JAMES *has a glass of whiskey in his hand, but he's no*
drinking much. (NOTE: Cathleen, referred to in this scene, is the
housekeeper.)]

MARY: I'm sorry if I sounded bitter, James. I'm not. It's all so fa
away. But I did feel a little hurt when you wished you hadn't com
home. I was so relieved and happy when you came, and gratefu

to you. It's very dreary and sad to be here alone in the fog with night falling.

JAMES: I'm glad I came, Mary, when you act like your real self.

MARY: I was lonesome. I kept Cathleen with me just to have someone to talk to.

[*Pause.*]

Do you know what I was telling her, dear? About the night my father took me to your dressing room and I first fell in love with you. Do you remember?

JAMES: Can you think I'd ever forget, Mary?

MARY: No, I know you still love me, James, in spite of everything.

JAMES: Yes! As God is my judge! Always and forever!

MARY: And I love you, dear, in spite of everything.

[*Pause.*]

But I must confess, James, although I couldn't help loving you, I would never have married you if I'd known you drank so much. I remember the first night your barroom friends had to help you up to the door of our hotel room, and knocked and then ran away before I came to the door. We were still on our honeymoon, do you remember?

JAMES: I don't remember! It wasn't on our honeymoon! And I never in my life had to be helped to bed or missed a performance!

MARY: I had waited in that ugly hotel room hour after hour. I kept making excuses for you. I told myself it must be some business connected with the theater. I knew so little about the theater. Then I became terrified. I imagined all sorts of horrible accidents. I got on my knees and prayed that nothing had happened to you—and then they brought you up and left you outside the door.

[*She sighs; pause.*]

I didn't know how often that was to happen in the years to come, how many times I was to wait in ugly hotel rooms. I became quite used to it.

OTHER PEOPLE'S MONEY
BY JERRY STERNER

CHARACTERS

LARRY "The Liquidator" GARFINKLE *(mid-40s) is an overweight corporate raider who has a penchant for donuts and for failing companies like New England Wire and Cable;* BEA SULLIVAN *(mid-60s) is trying to save New England Wire and Cable (her family's business) and the lawyer representing it (her daughter Kate Sullivan) from* GARFINKLE's *clutches.*

SCENE

Garfinkle's *office, New York City.*

TIME

Afternoon. The present (1989).

[*Lights up on* GARFINKLE *in his office.* BEA *enters.*]

BEA: Good Afternoon, Mr. Garfinkle.

GARFINKLE: Oh no—the donut thrower. Wait—I got to get my catcher's mask.

BEA: I'm sorry, I didn't bring any.

GARFINKLE: Aw . . . And I was looking forward to some of your nutritious health donuts—you know—yogurt sprinkles—penicillin-filled.

BEA: . . . These offices are every bit as impressive as my daughter said they were.

GARFINKLE: . . . What do you know . . . I like your daughter. She's hot shit.

BEA: . . . I think so too . . . assuming I know what you mean.

GARFINKLE: You know what I mean. She's terrific. And she didn't get that way working for those clowns at Morgan Stanley. She must've got it from you.

BEA: That's kind of you.

GARFINKLE: Did she send you? I wouldn't put it past her.

BEA: She didn't send me. She would be upset with me if she knew. I expect this meeting will be held in confidence.

GARFINKLE: Have a seat.

[*She sits.*]

What can I do for you?

BEA: You can take the million dollars I'm about to offer you.

GARFINKLE: [*Sitting.*] . . . This is gonna be some day.

BEA: I thought that might interest you. There is a trust fund, in my name, with a million dollars, primarily in treasury notes, in it. I will turn it over to you if you call off your fight with us. We will buy back your shares at thirteen, which Kate informs me gets you even, plus you'll have a million dollars profit.

GARFINKLE: How come I never had a mother like you?

BEA: Is that acceptable?

GARFINKLE: My mother—I gotta send a check once a month. Would you like to meet her?

BEA: Is that acceptable?

GARFINKLE: How much money you make a year?

BEA: I don't see—

GARFINKLE: How much?

BEA: Forty thousand. Plus health insurance.

GARFINKLE: Why would you give up a million to save forty?

BEA: That's my affair. Is it agreeable to you?

GARFINKLE: Who are you doing it for?

BEA: Myself. I don't need the money.

GARFINKLE: I don't either.

BEA: Then why are you doing it?

GARFINKLE: That's what I do for a living. I make money.

BEA: You will have made money. If you accept my offer you will have made a million dollars. For a few weeks' effort you will have made more than most working a lifetime.

GARFINKLE: Go home. I don't want your money.

BEA: Why? Isn't it good enough for you?

GARFINKLE: It's good. It's just not enough.

BEA: I know a million dollars is not a great deal of money to you. It's all I have. If I had more, I'd offer you more. I had really hoped to appeal to whatever decent instincts you have left. I'm here to plead for my company.

GARFINKLE: Go home.

BEA: Please, Mr. Garfinkle.

GARFINKLE: I don't take money from widows and orphans. I make them money.

BEA: Before or after you put them out of business.

GARFINKLE: You're getting on my nerves. Go home.

BEA: I intend to. Before I go, I'd like to know—I'd like you to tell me—how can you live with yourself?

GARFINKLE: I have no choice. No one else will.

BEA: How? How can you destroy a company . . . its people . . . for the sake of dollars you don't even need?

GARFINKLE: Because it's there.

BEA: . . . Because it's there?

GARFINKLE: What? People climb mountains—swim oceans—walk through fire—'cause it's there. This way is better. You don't get all sweated up.

BEA: There are people there. There are dreams there—

GARFINKLE: Do you want to give a speech or do you want an answer? 'Cause the answer is not complicated. It's simple. I do it for the money. I don't need the money. I want the money. Shouldn't surprise you. Since when do needs and wants have anything to do with one another? If they did, I'd be back in the Bronx and you'd be getting Yorgy his coffee up in Grimetown. You don't need the job. You need the million dollars. But you're prepared to give up what you need—a million dollars—for what you want—a stinking job. You're fucked up, lady. You're sick. Go see a psychiatrist.

BEA: You are the sick one. Don't you know that?

GARFINKLE: Why? 'Cause I know what I want and I know how to get it? Lady, I *looooooove* money. I love money more than I love the things it can buy. You know why? Money is unconditional acceptance. It don't care whether I'm good or not, whether I snore or don't, which God I pray to—it makes me as much interest in the bank as your does. There's only three things in this world that give that kind of unconditional acceptance—dogs, donuts, and money. Only money is better. It don't make you fat and it don't shit all over the living room floor.

BEA: I hope you choke on your money and die!

[*She exits.* GARFINKLE *smiles sadly.*]

I DON'T HAVE TO SHOW YOU NO STINKING BADGES!

BY LUIS VALDEZ

CHARACTERS

BUDDY *(50s) and* CONNIE *(48) are a Chicano couple with children.* BUDDY *owns a restaurant,* CONNIE *sells real estate and has an acting career. They're trying to stay ahead of the wolf at the door and have some fun in the process.*

SCENE

Their family home in the Los Angeles area.

TIME

An early morning, early 1990s.

[*At rise: Coffee is perking in the kitchen. We hear the upbeat sounds of a '50s rock 'n' roll classic.* CONNIE VILLA, *an attractive forty-eight-year-old Chicano, is dancing. Dressed in a fluffy pink nightgown, she ambles over to the phone and makes a call, while the music on the stereo tape deck plays. Sitting on a wooden stool at the breakfast bar,* CONNIE *dials carefully. As the music ends, she is talking into the phone with a laid-back, brassy tone and worldly air.*]

CONNIE: [*On phone.*] Hello, Betty? This is Constance D'Ville— Connie Villa! How ya doin' today? . . . Great. Listen, any word on that picture? . . . Well, when was I supposed to go back for that interview? I know we talked about it yesterday, but . . . well, I was wondering . . . Did you get a chance to ask the casting director about Buddy? . . . Nothing? Nothing at all? Please, Betty. Without him, I'm sunk! Central America's out of the question . . . Yeah . . . yeah. I'll hold, sure.

[*The back door, down the hall, opens and closes. The sound of heavy breathing and footsteps.*]

Buddy? . . . Is that you, *viejo*?

BUDDY [*Enters, jogging in place.*] *Viejo*, my ass. Look at me—I'm an animal!

[BUDDY *is a hefty, well-preserved Chicano, hungover but dressed in a jogging suit and running shoes, with the balding hair and body weight of an aging prizefighter. He jogs up to* CONNIE, *tosses her the morning paper and then picks her up and spins her around while she is talking to her agent.*]

CONNIE: Wait a minute, Betty. There's an animal in the house! No, it's only Buddy.

[BUDDY *drops to the floor and does ten, grunting and counting vociferously.*]

What? . . . Oh. What about Buddy? . . . Nothing, huh? A part in what? . . . *The Hairy Ape*?

BUDDY [*Puffing.*] All right! No *que* no?

CONNIE: No, Betty, I don't think so. We don't do waiver theater. Screw the exposure. We don't work for free.

BUDDY: Twenty minutes flat, old lady!

[CONNIE *makes a face and stands, still on the phone. She wipes his sweat off the floor.* BUDDY *hops on the exercise bike.*]

CONNIE [*Into phone.*] He's right here, dripping sweat all over the floor . . . Yeah, he was out jogging. Or as we say in Spanish— "hogging."

[BUDDY *playfully grunts like a hog, heading for the kitchen.*]

Which reminds me: the residuals for the AT&T commercial, when do they start? . . . Well, okay, keep me posted. See you at the banquet tonight. *Ciao.*

[*Hangs up.*]

Betty says there might be something in a couple of days.

[BUDDY *opens the refrigerator door, we hear a beer pop open.*]

Beer, *hombre*? It's still morning.

BUDDY: Gotta replace my body fluids. Would you believe I just ran five miles?

CONNIE: No.

BUDDY: Okay. Would you believe three miles?

CONNIE: I believe you ran around the house, slowly.

BUDDY: Honest. *Hice jog hasta la* freeway and back. Ran like an Apache . . .

[CONNIE *reaches up to the cabinet for vitamins;* BUDDY *eyes her over.*]

What's for breakfast?

CONNIE: What would you like?

BUDDY: How about a little *chorizo con huevos* . . . in bed?

CONNIE: Don't start, *senor.*

BUDDY: [*Sidling up to her.*] Jogging always makes me horny.

CONNIE: Breathing makes you horny.

BUDDY: At my age I hate to let a good erection go to waste.

CONNIE: Down, boy.

[*Flicks at his feigned erection.*]

How about some butterless toast?

BUDDY: I'll stay on my liquid diet.

[*He takes a long swig on his beer and straddles one of the breakfast stools, noticing a letter on the counter. He picks it up as* CONNIE *pours orange juice and sets out the vitamins for* BUDDY.]

What's this?

CONNIE: [*Exchanges* BUDDY's *beer for a glass of juice.*] It's from Lucy. She says Bob and her are doing just fine. Bob just got tenure at the Economics Department at Arizona State, and she's about to open her own practice in pediatrics in downtown Phoenix, which is why they've decided to wait to have a baby of their own. Go ahead, read it.

BUDDY: What the hell for? You just told me all that's in it.

CONNIE: Pick up your beer cans.

[*He tosses the letter back on the counter; then he crosses to the den, taking his beer, and starts picking up other empty beer cans.*]

At least your daughter writes. Sonny, on the other hand, forget it. Not one written word since he got back east. We're lucky if he even calls once a month to ask for money. Do you think he's okay?

BUDDY: Sixteen years old and studying pre-law at Harvard? What could go wrong? A bad case of zits? The kid's a prodigy. He'll own his own law firm by the time he's twenty-five.

CONNIE: God knows, the last thing I want to be is one of those clinging *madrecitas* that won't let their kids grow up or they lose their purpose in life. *Chale,* man, not me, boy. I hung up my uterus a long time ago. I like my freedom, and I'm ready to go places.

[BUDDY *crosses up into the kitchen, carrying several empty beer cans.*]

How late did you stay up last night?

BUDDY: Late. I was listening to a little Gershwin and I fell asleep watching my favorite picture.

[*He deposits the cans into a garbage bag under the sink.*]

CONNIE: What's that, a twelve pack? I thought you looked a little hungover this morning!

BUDDY: I always look hungover in the morning!

CONNIE: After twenty-five years, you think I don't . . . ?

BUDDY: [*Laughs.*] It was just a few beers, *chingao.* Can't I have a few lousy beers—alone, by myself, in my own *pinche* den, in my own *pinche* house?

CONNIE: Not when you had a *pinche* drinking problem, just a few *pinche* years ago . . .

BUDDY: [*Drops cans into a trash bag.*] That's ancient history.

CONNIE: Especially if you drink alone.

BUDDY: Actually, I had a weird dream Sonny was here in the house, right here in the den, I was there in my chair, there was someone outside and he came in, setting up shots, like he was directing a new *Twilight Zone* or something, can you beat that?

CONNIE: Mm, hmm, Harvard School of Law, Class of '92.

BUDDY: Anyway, this morning I woke up with a new movie idea.

CONNIE: Finish taking out the garbage.

BUDDY: This one's real hot. You wanna hear it? It'll only take a second.

[BUDDY *crosses to the stereo and turns on the* Star Wars *theme.*]

CONNIE: Go on.

BUDDY: Well, the first shot shows him speeding across the giant screen in his spaceship, blasting all rockets. Right? And his little ship sorta resembles a chopped down '56 Chevy, with fuzzy dice hanging over the dashboard, while the hero sits in the cockpit, down low, see? His head barely visible. *Orale, mamacita.*

CONNIE: Like a lowrider.

BUDDY: You got it. Well, suddenly there's these laser beams shooting at his tail, see? And the screen fills up with this giant space battle cruiser in hot pursuit.

CONNIE: Sounds familiar.

BUDDY: Except that the giant battle cruiser looks like a huge sombrero! A sombrero flying saucer!

[*Laughs.*]

And it's chasing the Chicano spaceman, 'cause they're the Interplanetary Border Patrol, the Space Migra, and he's trying to escape across the border to Earth! You get it?

CONNIE: [*Crosses to the stereo and turns it off.*] Take out the garbage.

BUDDY: It's a satire.

CONNIE: It won't sell, Buddy.

BUDDY: [*Angered.*] How the hell do you know? You're trying to tell me I don't know the *pinche* business? Shit, I was personal friends with Humphrey Bogart when you were still in grammar school, lady. Bogey and me were like that!

[BUDDY *takes the garbage to service patio.*]

Won't sell, my ass. I could pick up that *pinche* phone right now and peddle this *pinche* idea to a dozen *pinche* big-time directors.

[*Offstage. Exits to garage.*]

Spielberg, Redford, Brian de Palma—they all know me!

[*We hear the trash can lid slammed on. Pause. Buddy re-enters.*]

CONNIE: [*Concerned.*] What's with all the pinches? What's eating you?

BUDDY: The Garcias' German shepherd chased me down the *pinche* block this morning.

CONNIE: [*Crosses to hall closet for cleaning equipment.*] Again, *hombre*?

BUDDY: Fifth time. And he's not the only one. The new Oriental families on the other block have pit bulls. *Pinches perros!* Why is it all the rich *gabachos* over in Beverly Hills have these little lousy Chihuahuas, and all the Mexicans and Chinks on this side of town have these big Nazi killers?

CONNIE: [*Carpet sweeping.*] We could use a guard dog ourselves, for when we go out of town. It's been years since we went to Mexico. Wouldn't it be nice to travel now that the kids are out of the house?

BUDDY: [*Looks out toward the backyard.*] Dogtown . . . Here we are in Montgomery Park, and all these people still live in Dogtown. Know what I mean? In their minds, they never left.

CONNIE: And you did?

BUDDY: Lock, stock and *perros.* I was drafted.

CONNIE: Well, personally, I like "this side of town." I'm glad we left the barrio, but I wouldn't live in Beverly Hills if they paid me. Too many Latina maids at the bus stops.

BUDDY: In Korea I even ate some *perro* once.

CONNIE: East is east, and west is west, especially in L.A. Of course, there is always north and south, south of the border—way south? Honduras would be nice. Or Belize. Or Costa Rica.

BUDDY: [*Puts his arms around her.*] We never use the goddamn pool anymore . . . Remember when we first put it in? Sonny and Lucy went crazy out there. We had some great times together.

CONNIE: [*Squirts armpits, getting away.*] That was ten, fifteen years ago, *senor,* that pool hasn't been cleaned in so long, there's something slimy growing at the bottom.

BUDDY: [*Tongue in cheek.*] I'm growing some class A Colombian seaweed.

CONNIE: Be serious.

[*He turns and faces her tensely, in a showdown of sorts.*]

BUDDY: Okay. Then let's talk about the Nicholson movie.

CONNIE: So that's what's eating you!

BUDDY: I know damn well you really want to do it.

CONNIE: [*Cautiously.*] Betty says I still have a good chance at the part of the madam.

BUDDY: [*Scoffing, spreading legs into the air.*] Another Mexican whore?

CONNIE: [*Trying to joke, sliding up next to him.*] Of course not, she's Costa Rican! Come on, at least I own the house. Buddy, it's a great part. A speaking part. I'd only be on location for three weeks. A month's shoot at the most.

BUDDY: [*Tightening.*] I got news for you. They're already shooting down there.

CONNIE: Where?

BUDDY: Everywhere! Nicaragua, El Salvador, Miami.

CONNIE: The location's in Costa Rica.

BUDDY: [*Blowing up.*] People are KILLING each other down there! Don't you understand? You'd be all alone. You wanna get killed, or even worse, raped to death?

CONNIE: [*Cleaning trophies.*] Then come with me.

BUDDY: I've got a business to run.

CONNIE: Betty can talk to them. Get you some kind of small role.

BUDDY: Small role? I read for these people, same as you. If they don't want me, I ain't gonna beg them. Fuck 'em. Who needs their two-bit TV movies anyway. Cecile B. DeMille once ate at my restaurant . . .

CONNIE: [*Pleading.*] It's a feature, Buddy . . .

BUDDY: [*Goes to fridge for beer.*] Outta town we work as a team or no dice! Remember? Nobody goes anywhere alone.

[CONNIE*'s face takes on an undaunted look.*]

CONNIE: What about the Stallone picture last year in Mexico? You went alone.

BUDDY: On restaurant business. I brought back Pedro Wong, didn't I? Where else was I to find a Chinese Mexican cook?

CONNIE: But you acted.

BUDDY: [*Goes to phone, dials.*] For Pedro's sake, I saved our business! Fried rice and refried beans, our chili relleno runneth over now. In this case, Wong was right.

[CONNIE *groans, returns his stuff to hall closet.* BUDDY'*s call connects with his restaurant; he talks to his cook. On the phone.*]

Pedro, *joe san! . . . Frijoles ju ho mee-ah! Menudo ju ho mee-ah? Tortillas gow mee-ah? Ngaw dee you jew-ng mole? Gup gaee* chicken chow yuk? *Ngaw, chee dee lai gwaw. Hay te watcho!*

[*Hangs up.*]

Besides, Sly cut my scene out of the picture, so it didn't count, sweetheart.

CONNIE: Well, maybe Jack will cut my scene out of the picture and it won't count either, sweetheart.

BUDDY: *Sabes que?* Before you start getting on a first name basis with stars, you better make damn sure you've even got a job.

CONNIE: Oh, that's cruel, Buddy. That's really cruel.

BUDDY: It's a cruel business.

CONNIE: I'm only asking for a little support and encouragement. Is that such a big deal?

BUDDY: I knew it was a mistake to let you start acting.

CONNIE: All I want is a little harmless fun in my life! Who knows, maybe I've got a talent or two I never had a chance to develop before. Is that so bad?

BUDDY: [*Like Jackie Gleason.*] Put 'em in a couple of pictures, way in the background, and suddenly everybody wants to be a star!

CONNIE: Why do you have to be such a fat ass *cabezudo?*

BUDDY: [*Pause.*] Okay . . . now you're hitting below the belt, see? Enough's enough. Get this whole crazy scheme outta your head. Get dressed and get on the phone and work on your little real estate sideline. *Ya estuvo!* No more show business today. I'm gonna drain the pool.

[BUDDY *heads for the backyard.* CONNIE *follows him.*]

CONNIE: If it weren't for my little real estate sideline, we couldn't even have the goddamn pool!

[*The phone rings.* CONNIE *and* BUDDY *look at each other, then race to it.* CONNIE *answers.*]

Hello? Oh, hi, Betty . . . Yeah?

[*Brightening.*]

Really?

BUDDY: [*Hanging on her shoulder.*] I'm serious, Connie. Don't take it.

CONNIE: [*On phone.*] I'll take it! . . . When? That soon? . . . Right . . . MGM, sound stage eighteen. Great! Got it . . . Thanks, Betty. *Ciao.*

[*Hangs up.*]

BUDDY: [*Frustrated.*] What? What?

CONNIE: *DALLAS!* Over at MGM. They want both of us.

BUDDY: [*Impressed.*] Both of us?

[BUDDY *turns to tuck shirt into pants.*]

CONNIE: [*With a caustic edge.*] Work for a whole two days, *mi amor.* Both of us—right here in town, just the way you like it. A maid and a gardener. Are you happy now?

BUDDY: [*With gardener accent.*] Well, you could have consulted me before you agreed to it.

CONNIE: [*Blowing up, furious, hits* BUDDY *in the stomach.*] Look, Buddy, if you don't want the goddamn job, call Betty! I'm taking it. Interview's on the lot in fifty minutes.

[CONNIE *starts to storm out;* BUDDY *chases her, looking like the cat who ate the canary.*]

BUDDY: [*Holding* CONNIE.] Heh, heh, wait a minute. How much is the Nicholson picture worth? You know the score? We haven't gotten this far by fooling ourselves, right? I'm the Silent Bit King and you're my Queen! No more, no less. Right?

CONNIE: [*Deadly serious, pushes* BUDDY *away.*] Buddy, I'm tired of being silent.

[CONNIE *walks out without another word.* BUDDY *holds back, then glances at the Bogart poster.*]

BUDDY: So, who am I, Charlie Chaplin?

[BUDDY *exits, walking like "The Little Tramp."*]

THE SISTERS ROSENSWEIG

BY WENDY WASSERSTEIN

CHARACTERS

MERV KANT *(58) is an American in London, the world leader in synthetic animal coverings;* SARA ROSENSWEIG *(54) is a brilliant woman, the only female head of a Hong Kong bank, who has had her problems with romantic relationships.*

SCENE

A sitting room in Queen Anne's Gate, London.

TIME

A weekend in late August 1991. 11:30 p.m.

[SARA *begins straightening the living room.*]

SARA: Aren't you going home to bed? It's very late.

MERV: Not when I can watch you clean.

SARA: You enjoy watching women clean?

MERV: I enjoy watching women who don't need to clean, clean.

SARA: Actually, I have to clean. The help is on vacation and I like a tidy household.

MERV: Just like your mother.

SARA: My mother never cleaned. When I came home from college, she made an effort and pushed all of the laundry under the bed.

MERV: But I bet she was a great cook.

SARA: She never cooked. We all went out to dinner every night at Sparky's family restaurant.

MERV: Was your mother Jewish?

SARA: For a supposedly intelligent man you have a persistently narrow perspective.

MERV: Thank you.

SARA: Excuse me.

MERV: You called me intelligent; I didn't know that you noticed.

SARA: I know you, Merv. You're just like all the other men I went to high school with. You're smart, you're a good provider, you read *The Times* every day, you started running at fifty to recapture your youth, you worry a little too much about your health, you thought about having affairs, but you never actually did it, and now that she's departed, your late wife Roslyn is a saint.

MERV: Her name was Helene. We lived in Roslyn.

SARA: And I'm sure you traveled and I'm sure your children are very nice people, and, Merv, if my sisters or I had any sense, we would all have married you too.

MERV: What about Gorgeous? I thought she did marry me. Old Henry sounds like a nice enough guy: lawyer, good father, stays home to watch the kids play lacrosse.

SARA: [*Begins dusting the mantelpiece.*] Yes, Henry's wonderful, and I'm sure you're wonderful, and Tom's wonderful. You're all wonderful.

[*Knocks over the napkin rings.*]

Goddamn it, Gorgeous!

MERV: Hey, hey, take it easy. Take it easy.

SARA: You know what really irritates me in life, Merv? When men like you tell women to take it easy because somewhere they believe that all women are innately hysterics.

MERV: Why won't you give me a break?

SARA: Why won't you please just go home!

[*She starts to cry suddenly. He puts his arm around her.*]

MERV: It's all right. I promise.

SARA: [*Laughs slightly and moves away.*] Now you're really convinced all women are hysterics. I'm sorry. Really. Tessie says I should take stress tabs.

MERV: You're fine. Let's talk about something else. How 'bout the American class system. Or, I've got a lively topic: Count Metternich and the Concert of Europe. Sadie, my lips haven't formed those words since I was a senior in high school.

SARA: Why did you call me Sadie?

MERV: You called me Mr. Kantlowitz. And Gorgeous called me Merlin the Magician. I figure anything goes in this house.

SARA: My grandfather called me Sadie. Sara was too biblical for him. He hoped I'd grow up to be a singer.

MERV: So you do sing!

SARA: When I was at Radcliffe. I was with a girls' singing group. The Cliffe Clef. I was a Cleffie!

MERV: Can I hear a little?

SARA: Merv, we're too old for this.

MERV: For what?

SARA: You're a very nice man. But you're not my type.

MERV: Sadie, you're not mine either. You're not what I'd call a warm or accessible woman.

SARA: Unlike the wonderful Roslyn.

MERV: Unlike the wonderful Roslyn. Tell me something, when did you figure out that you had all the answers?

SARA: High school. I knew what the teacher was going to ask before she asked it. I knew what was going to become of every girl in my class, and I knew, for some reason, I was different from them.

MERV: You weren't a nice Jewish girl?

SARA: Why do you always come back to that?

MERV: I have a limited repertoire. I'm not as smart as you are, Sadie. I didn't get double 800s on my College Boards.

SARA: When we took those tests, they didn't publish those results.

MERV: But I'm sure the school called your mother just to let her know. What? So I'm right.

SARA: It was no big deal.

MERV: Of course it was a big deal. I'll bet the valedictorian was nowhere as intelligent as you are.

SARA: Sonia Kirschenblatt. Went to Bryn Mawr, married an astronomy professor, lives in Princeton, works for educational testing.

MERV: Fuzzy brown hair. Poodle skirts. Started going to Greenwich Village bookstores at sixteen.

SARA: You knew her?

MERV: Her parents had at the Brighton Beach Baths. I was a cabana boy. I shtupped her the year before she went to Bryn Mawr.

SARA: So Sonia Kirschenblatt went to Bryn Mawr not a virgin.

MERV: It was no big deal.

SARA: Are you kidding? Thirty years ago it was a very big deal.

MERV: Look, thank God she didn't get pregnant or today I'd be an astronomy professor at Princeton. I like talking to you, Sadie. I wish you'd stop pushing the ashtray back and forth and maybe your shoulders could come down from your ears.

[*Starts to rub her shoulders.*]

I didn't think they could get any higher. Pretty soon they'll be on the ceiling.

SARA: Merv, do you want to "shtup" me tonight in Queen Anne's Gate, like you did Sonia Kirschenblatt that hot and lusty summer night at the Brighton Beach Baths?

MERV: We did it at Columbia in my dorm room in John Jay Hall.

SARA: They didn't allow women in Columbia dorm rooms then.

MERV: Sonia was a woman of great ingenuity. She didn't get to be valedictorian by being a half-wit.

SARA: But she wasn't so smart, either. She just worked hard.

[*Gets up from the couch.*]

Look, Merv, if you're thinking, "I know who this woman is sitting next to me. I grew up with her, with women like her, only sometime in her life she decided to run away. She moved to England, she dyed her hair, she named her daughter Tess and sent her to Westminster. She assimilated beyond her wildest dreams, and now she's lovely and wants to come home," you're being too obvious. Yes, I'm lonely, but I don't want to come home.

MERV: What about connect, Sadie?

SARA: Connect?

MERV: Connect, to another person.

SARA: How many support groups did you join when Roslyn died? I'm sorry, that was cruel.

MERV: No, but it was in surprisingly bad taste. I joined two, plus last year I went on Outward Bound to find myself on a cliff on Prince Edward Island.

SARA: And what did you learn about yourself?

MERV: That I couldn't write poetry. That I couldn't solve the Middle East with a Marx Kant peace plan. That I wasn't a particularly original thinker. And that more than anything, I wanted to be in love again.

SARA: To have someone take care of you.

MERV: Listen, my wife wasn't named Roslyn and she wasn't a saint. She drank a little, she was depressed a little, and she thought she could have been a contender if it wasn't for me. She put me through school, she brought up the children, and finally she got to take art classes at the museum four years before she died. Is that fair to a talented, intelligent woman? Sadie, I've already done having someone take care of me.

SARA: I'm sorry. I guess I'm the one's being too obvious.

MERV: Thank you.

SARA: You're welcome.

MERV: I still believe there can be happiness in life, Sara. Brief but a moment or two.

SARA: Who's to say what's happy?

MERV: Are you?

SARA: It's not so bad. I'm looking forward to Tessie going to college and selling the house for a cozy flat.

MERV: And sex?

SARA: I miss sex. I always liked sex.

MERV: What about Lord Gefilte?

SARA: You heard Tessie. His taste runs to younger women.

MERV: I think you're gorgeous.

SARA: My sister is Gorgeous.

MERV: No, you are, Sara Rosensweig.

SARA: [*Laughs.*] Jesus. No one's called me that in thirty years.

[*He kisses her somewhat passionately.*]

I could never love you, Merv. And I'm old enough now and kind enough not to let you love me. But, Merv, just for one night I could be Sonia Kirchenblatt at the Brighton Beach Baths and you a Columbia sophomore.

MERV: You think I have the energy of a Columbia sophomore?

SARA: I certainly hope so, Merv.

[*She starts to lead him up the stairs. He stops suddenly.*]

MERV: Sadie, I do have one request.

SARA: What?

MERV: Would you sing for me?

SARA: Merv, I . . .

MERV: I'll sing with you. I'm a wonderful singer. I was Mrs. Chiang Kai-Shek in the Columbia Varsity Show of 1955.

SARA: So I heard.

MERV: You don't have to do anything fancy. I would just like it very much if I could hear you sing.

SARA: Merv, I have every Sinatra song ever recorded. How 'bout we let Frank sing?

MERV: But he was never a Cliffe Clef.

SARA: Please, Merv, pick a Sinatra song and let's go upstairs.

MERV: [*Puts on "Just the Way You Look Tonight." He begins singing.*]

Lovely, don't you ever change,

Keep that breathless charm . . .

Take it, Sara . . .

SARA: [*Quietly.*] Merv, I just can't sing for you.

MERV: [*Touches her face and begins leading her upstairs, singing.*]

Just the way you look tonight.

THE MATCHMAKER
BY THORNTON WILDER

CHARACTERS

Wealthy merchant VANDERGELDER *(60) has hired matchmaker*
DOLLY LEVI *(somewhere over 50) to find him a wife. What he finds
is something other than what he expected.*

SCENE

The living room of a prosperous spinster's home in Yonkers, New York.

TIME

1880s. Afternoon.

VANDERGELDER: A lot of foolishness. Everybody falling in love with everybody. I forgave 'em, Ermengarde and that artist.

MRS. LEVI: I knew you would.

VANDERGELDER: I made Cornelius Hackl my partner.

MRS. LEVI: You won't regret it.

VANDERGELDER: Dolly, you said some mighty unpleasant things to me in the restaurant tonight . . . all that about my house . . . and everything.

MRS. LEVI: Let's not say another word about it.

VANDERGELDER: Dolly, you have a lot of faults.

MRS. LEVI: Oh, I know what you mean.

VANDERGELDER: You're bossy, scheming, inquisitive . . .

MRS. LEVI: Go on.

VANDERGELDER: But you're a wonderful woman. Dolly, marry me.

MRS. LEVI: Horace!

[*Rises.*]

Stop right there.

VANDERGELDER: I know I've been a fool about Mrs. Molloy and that other woman. But, Dolly, forgive me and marry me.

[*He goes on his knees.*]

MRS. LEVI: Horace, I don't dare. No. I don't dare.

VANDERGELDER: What do you mean?

MRS. LEVI: You know as well as I do that you're the first citizen of Yonkers. Naturally, you'd expect your wife to keep open house, to have scores of friends in and out all the time. Any wife of yours should be used to that kind of thing.

VANDERGELDER: [*After a brief struggle with himself.*] Dolly, you can live anyway you like.

MRS. LEVI: Horace, you can't deny it, your wife would have to be a *somebody.* Answer me: am I a somebody?

VENDERGELDER: You are . . . you are. Wonderful woman.

MRS. LEVI: Oh, you're partial.

[*She crosses, gives a big wink to the audience, sits on sofa.*]

[VANDERGELDER *follows her on his knees.*]

Horace, it won't be enough for you to load your wife with money and jewels, to insist that she be a benefactress to half the town.

[*He rises and still struggling with himself, coughs so as not to hear this.*]

No, she must be a somebody. Do you really think I have it in me to be a credit to you?

VANDERGELDER: Dolly, everybody knows that you could do anything you wanted to do.

MRS. LEVI: I'll try. With your help, I'll try—and by the way, I found your purse.

[*Holds it up.*]

VANDERGELDER: Where did you—! Wonderful woman!

MRS. LEVI: It just walked into my hand. I don't know how I do it. Sometimes I frighten myself. Horace, take it. Money walks out of my hands, too.

VANDERGELDER: Keep it. Keep it.

MRS. LEVI: Horace!

[*Half laughing, half weeping, and with an air of real affection for him.*]

I never thought . . . I'd ever . . . hear you say a thing like that!

BREAK OF DAY
BY STEPHEN FIFE

CHARACTERS

PASTOR THEODORUS VAN GOGH *(60) is the preacher for a small village community near Zundert in the Netherlands;* ANNA VAN GOGH *(55), his wife, is in charge of running the presbytery. They have five children, the oldest being the painter Vincent van Gogh.*

SCENE

The garden behind the Van Gogh presbytery, northern Netherlands.

TIME

Day. Spring, 1884.

[ANNA *and* PASTOR THEO *are waiting for their oldest son, Vincent, to return to the presbytery, the first time he's been back since storming off after a terrible argument with his father almost two years ago. Now* PASTOR THEO *is on his knees weeding the garden.* ANNA *stands watching him, wearing a kitchen apron over her clothes.* PASTOR THEO *wears some kind of outer garment to protect his clothing while he does the gardening.*]

ANNA: It's getting cold, Theodorus. Why don't you do this another day?

PASTOR THEO: I've let it go too long as it is.

ANNA: A few days either way . . .

PASTOR THEO: [*Pulling weeds.*] "Don't put off till tomorrow" . . . that's what my father always said.

[*Weeding.*]

Anyway, this will help me think.

ANNA: Let's try not to argue this time. Let's try to be a family, all right?

PASTOR THEO: If Vincent wants to be eccentric, so be it. I just hope the parishioners understand.

ANNA: I think they do. They accept it. And there will be no more talk of that other thing, will there? You promise me?

[*Pause:* PASTOR *nods.*]

He really wants to come back. That's what Theo says. He's really changed now.

PASTOR THEO: I suppose we'll find out soon enough . . .

[*Pause.*]

ANNA: [*Removes her apron.*] I'm going into the village now, dear. Is there anything I can get you?

PASTOR THEO: Are you sure there's time?

ANNA: He isn't due for three hours.

[PASTOR *nods, goes back to weeding.* ANNA *looks at him with concern, then goes over and kisses him on the forehead.*]

PASTOR THEO: What was that for?

ANNA: I think you're a very great man.

PASTOR THEO: Ha. Tell it to the clerical board.

ANNA: [*Shakes her head.*] I'm so glad I married you.

[ANNA *exits through the door stage right.* PASTOR THEO *continues weeding.*]

HIDDEN PARTS
BY LYNNE ALVAREZ

CHARACTERS
THOMAS ARN *(62) is a retired farmer who has violated a sacred trust.* CYNTHIA *(57) is his wife, a pianist and keeper of the family secrets. They have a son, Justin (21), an obsessive concert pianist. They have also raised an adopted daughter, Daria (15).*

SCENE
A cornfield on a farm in the Midwest, USA.

TIME
The present. It is nearly twilight.

THOMAS: [*Screams out.*] AAAAAAAAAAAAAAAAAAAAAAAAAAAA!

[CYNTHIA *quickly opens the shutters.*]

CYNTHIA: What's wrong? What is it?

THOMAS: AAAAAAAAAAAAAAAAAAAAAAAAAAAAAA!

CYNTHIA: What is it? Thomas? Are you having a heart attack?

THOMAS: "I tell you God himself has put me in the wrong. He has drawn the net around me. If I cry 'Murder' no one answers"!

CYNTHIA: Are you having a fit, dear? Maybe I should come upstairs.

THOMAS: No. No. Don't come near me! I've done a terrible thing. I can't stand it any longer. "O earth, cover not my blood and let my cry for justice find no rest. For look! My witness is in Heaven."

CYNTHIA: [*Overlapping.*] Are you quoting the Bible again? Honestly! Thomas, please. Tell me what is wrong?

THOMAS: I can't stand the hate anymore. I can't stand the loathin' and the bitterness. I can't stand the loneliness 'n the house in pieces. I want this all to heal!

CYNTHIA: I hardly know what to say. It's a pity. It really is. But I believe we're past healing, Thomas.

THOMAS: There's still hope for us.

CYNTHIA: No, Thomas.

THOMAS: Are you about to leave me too?

CYNTHIA: No.

THOMAS: Any particular reason?

CYNTHIA: I'm your wife.

THOMAS: In name only, and hell, you could change your name again.

CYNTHIA: After all these years?

THOMAS: They do it all the time, I hear.

CYNTHIA: I wouldn't recognize myself. Besides, we have a solid marriage. Not a good marriage. But solid. We have a child we've seen to manhood. We have a house and land. I fix meals and you eat them. I play the piano and you listen. We talk.

THOMAS: But that's all.

CYNTHIA: I suppose so.

THOMAS: I thought, after all these months, we'd find something beautiful again in the sameness 'n the solitude out here. But I was wrong.

CYNTHIA: You were wrong.

[*Pause.*]

I will tell you something, Thomas. I would like to see you redeem yourself. You see I had a talk with Justin.

THOMAS: I talked with the boy too.

CYNTHIA: And . . . well, you can appreciate that Justin is afraid of you.

THOMAS: The boy's always been afraid of me. Ever since he was a little one. Made me afraid to even pick him up.

CYNTHIA: Well, there you were, gritty from the fields, and always staring at him with those hawk's eyes of yours.

THOMAS: Well, damn my eyes then! I can't help it if I got hawk's eyes.

CYNTHIA: Justin is still afraid of you and you haven't helped it any, waving your gun in his face and threatening him like a bully. He's still very concerned about Daria, and you can see why!

THOMAS: I know why!

CYNTHIA: And he wants me to help him steal Daria away.

THOMAS: I knew it! I knew it!

CYNTHIA: He's only said that because he's so awfully frightened of you, Thomas Arn. But I can't do things that way. Secretly. Therefore, I am appealing to your better judgment. And now that you are talking of healing, well, I want you to let them go off together without a fuss. With your blessing.

THOMAS: Over my dead body, they will!

CYNTHIA: Justin's going to take her all over the world and offer her an education. She would feel like part of the human race again.

[*She takes out a handkerchief and dabs her eyes.*]

She'd let her hair grow and clean her face and wear beautiful clothes. Justin would buy her beautiful clothes, I know he would.

THOMAS: I can't let them.

CYNTHIA: You're completely hopeless!

THOMAS: "I tell you God Himself has put me in the wrong. He has drawn the net around me. If I cry 'Murder,' no one answers."

CYNTHIA: You quoted that once already today! Anyway, to hear you quoting the Bible is blasphemy!

[*She is crying.*]

THOMAS: I will never consent to them bein' together and that's that! I got good reason.

CYNTHIA: That's all you'll say?

THOMAS: That's it!

CYNTHIA: This hurts me terribly. I don't know why. I certainly shouldn't have any feeling left for you. But I do. I do.

[*Straightening herself.*]

However, I'm letting you know. If you so much as threaten those two beautiful young people, I'm leaving you and you'll never see me again!

[*She slams her shutter and starts playing "Moon Over Miami."*]

THOMAS: I knew it! Damn!

[*He paces.*]

Cynthia, angel . . . Cynthia. Come out.

[CYNTHIA *stops playing to listen.*]

Come out. I have something to tell you.

CYNTHIA: [*Opens the shutter.*] All right, Thomas. What do you have to say?

THOMAS: Step outside the window. I want to look at you. I want you to see my face.

[CYNTHIA *steps out and faces* THOMAS.]

CYNTHIA: God knows why. Here I am.

THOMAS: You're a beautiful woman. I'd almost forgotten.

[*She starts to leave.*]

No. No. I didn't mean to offend you. I'm just nervous. Can't even find a quote from Job to cover it. Well . . . I'll never let Justin walk away with Daria. Maybe since you're standin' there, maybe you'd better sit down on something.

CYNTHIA: Will you get on with it! You're driving me crazy!

THOMAS: All right. Justin raped Daria and I'll kill him before I let him get near her again.

CYNTHIA: What possible reason do you have for saying that?

THOMAS: I know you don't believe what I say. I don't blame you. I've lied once already and sullied my credibility. But I swear on the Holy Bible. I swear on . . . on Aldebaran 'n Arcturus. I swear on my love for you. Justin raped Daria 'n I never told you 'cause I couldn't bear to see the look on your face I'm seein' right now.

CYNTHIA: [*Steps out of sight.*] Don't look at my face then. Say what you need to.

THOMAS: I saw Justin scratched and running through the field. His face was red and his clothes was tangled. And when I walked out of the corn, I saw Daria scratched, like me, caked with dirt, and she was grabbing your hand and crying, crying so hard no tears would come, crying so very hard I had to turn away. And in that moment, you blamed me. I saw it. And I thought Justin was young and foolish. I thought he'd got outta hand. Oh, I was a stupid man. I thought rape was no more than a cow bein' bothered by a bull she didn't want. I thought Justin was your special boy and gettin' him you didn't need me no more. I thought ten million thoughts in that one second. But Justin did a terrible thing and I let him go. And I let you despise me. And I can't tolerate it. I thought I could. I thought I could tolerate almost anything. Great heat. The bitterest cold. And in my heart I thought Justin would come back and beg my forgiveness. But he didn't and I can't tolerate it! And if I so much as see Justin brush that girl's cheek, after all these months and months without you, I swear I don't know what I'll do.

[CYNTHIA *comes into the yard and faces* THOMAS *again.*]

CYNTHIA: You wouldn't kill him?

THOMAS: Now that I see you standing right before me, all I want is for you never to go away. I won't kill Justin. If Daria knows it was him 'n still loves him, I'll let them leave—if that's what you want. Whatever your choice is, I'll abide by it.

CYNTHIA: Oh, Thomas. How will I know? I recall that Justin left a week before the rape and when we called him in Chicago with the news, he sobbed so hard he could barely speak.

THOMAS: You believe what you want. I watch people. Always have. I watched our son since the day he was born 'n I know how he runs 'n I know how he cries 'n I know he was wearin' the same blue suit we bought for his concert.

[*Pause.*]

I'll tell you something, Cynthia, if that boy had been overcome by passion 'n if he had come to me cryin' 'n beggin' for mercy, my heart would have gone out to him. But he planned it 'n he stalked that little girl 'n he never said a word.

CYNTHIA: I'm going in now, Thomas.

THOMAS: Do you believe me?

CYNTHIA: Let me alone for a while. I have to gather my thoughts.

[CYNTHIA *climbs through the window and slowly closes the shutters. The lights dim.*]

THE KEY
BY JOYCE CAROL OATES

CHARACTERS

MELISSA *(late 40s) and* EDWIN *(early 50s) are both white people in crisis who have come to the West Indian island of St. Kitts looking to change their lives.* MELISSA *has fled her unhappy marriage and a brutal winter back in Minneapolis, Minnesota.* EDWIN *is a big-boned, heavyset man, clumsy and desperate for love. They have both just arrived on the island.*

SCENE

Each sits alone at adjoining tables on the terrace of an expensive resort on the island of St. Kitts.

TIME

Late afternoon.

[MELISSA *sips a green-colored, tropical cocktail while trying to read a paperback copy of* Pascal's Pensees, *a book that meant a lot to her back in college.* EDWIN *has just ordered a drink, and he tries to get the waiter's attention, to bring him some "macadonia" nuts.*]

EDWIN: [*Craning his neck, calls after a waiter who is out of earshot.*] Those nuts? In the bowls?

[*Giving up.*]

Deaf when it suits them.

MELISSA: [*Wiping eyes with napkin.*] Macadamia nuts.

EDWIN: Eh?

MELISSA: You said "macadonia."

EDWIN: Maca *what*?

MELISSA: Anyway—we don't need them.

EDWIN: Well—we're sure as hell paying for them.

MELISSA: [*Raising her glass again.*] Here's to—happiness!

EDWIN: [*Following suit.*] "Caribbean holiday"!

MELISSA: No snow, no ice, no wind, no—*that*!

EDWIN: You said it—*that!*

[*Leaning toward* MELISSA.]

I guess I didn't get your—name?

MELISSA: [*A just perceptible pause.*] Angelina.

EDWIN: Angelina—that's pretty!

MELISSA: Sometimes called Bunny.

[*Giggles.*]

EDWIN: Bunny! *That's*—

[*Not knowing what it is.*]

—Uh, that's—well, that's *something,* eh!

MELISSA: And your name?

EDWIN: Oh, I'm—

[*Blinking.*]

—Edwin.

MELISSA: [*As if a bit disappointed.*] Oh—Edwin.

EDWIN: [*Apologetically.*] I guess it isn't a—a very imaginative name. I guess it isn't a—*romantic* name.

MELISSA: It's a fine, solid name. Ed-win. *Ed-win.*

[*Pause.*]

A mature name.

EDWIN: [*Inspired.*] Sometimes called Tickle.

MELISSA: What?

EDWIN: Tickle.

MELISSA: Tickle?

EDWIN: [*As if to tickle her.*] You asked for it!

MELISSA: [*Lurching away, startled.*] Oh—I—I—

EDWIN: [*Suddenly sober, wiping mouth with napkin.*] Jeez, I'm sorry.

[*Pause, embarrassment on both sides.*]

EDWIN: Just a—a joke. Guess it was a . . . pretty poor one.

MELISSA: [*Stiff; glancing around to see if they were being observed.*] Oh, I—well.

EDWIN: Game I used to play with my—my daughter, son, when they were—uh—little.

MELISSA: I—see.

[*A pause. Calypso music quite loud. Offstage laughter.*]

EDWIN: [*Awkwardly.*] This is a—a lively place, eh? You—came here alone?

MELISSA: Yes, I came here alone. And you?

EDWIN: Yes, I—alone.

MELISSA: [*Sipping drink.*] It's lovely here—the view. The turquoise sea.

[*Both gaze out to sea, into the audience, staring, shading their eyes.*]

EDWIN: The Gulf of Mexico . . .

MELISSA: Actually it's the Caribbean.

EDWIN: Oh, I know *that*! But isn't it the Gulf of Mexico too?

MELISSA: Due south of us, where we're sitting, is Venezuela.

EDWIN: Guess I should study the tourist maps—I sure have a lot of them.

[*Sips drink.*]

I guess I asked you, Angelina—have you ever been here before?

MELISSA: [*Dreamily, as if making the effort.*] Here? Oh, no.

[*Pause.*]

Did you ask me?

EDWIN: I—thought I did.

[*Glancing at her covertly.*]

You are a—uh—a very—uh—very attractive woman—uh—to be—in a place like this—alone.

MELISSA: [*Frowning, self-conscious.*] Well—I'm—I try to be—independent.

EDWIN: Oh, you look like an independent woman! You surely do!

MELISSA: I think I may be beginning a phase of my life, a new and distinct phase of my life, like—like a—a crescent moon that's going to become a full moon, a phase where I will be—become—ever more—and more—independent.

[*A bit breathless, removes sunglasses and lays them on the table.*]

Yes, I think I am!

[*Looks at him boldly, blinking.*]

EDWIN: That's—fascinating.

[*Removes his sunglasses, sets them down, knocking them against* MELISSA's *so that both pairs of glasses topple to the floor.*]

Oh—shit! Sorry!

[EDWIN *picks the glasses up, grunting.*]

Jeez, that was clumsy of me! Is this cracked?

[*Examines her sunglasses, as she reaches to take them from him.*]

A hairline crack—

MELISSA: Oh, that's quite all right—

EDWIN: I'll pay for it—pay for new lenses.

MELISSA: [*Retrieving the glasses and dropping them into her purse; almost inaudible.*] Damn clumsy fool.

EDWIN: [*Startled.*] What?

MELISSA: [*As if not knowing she'd spoken, making an effort to smile, even to be flirtatious.*] Oh, I said, Edwin, it's quite all right—*perfectly* all right. They were old glasses anyway. Last year's.

EDWIN: Let me replace them—will you?

MELISSA: That isn't necessary.

EDWIN: Oh, but it is!

MELISSA: It was just an accident, after all.

EDWIN: It *was*, but, like—

[*At a loss how to speak.*]

—like *mal*practice—you can get sued for accidents!

MELISSA: [*Laughing, a trifle impatient.*] Well—nobody's going to sue you over a trifle.

EDWIN: [*More soberly.*] Yes, well, I *have* been sued over a trifle. More than once.

[*Sips drink, with feeling.*]

[*A pause. Outburst of laughter stage right, toward which* MELISSA *and* EDWIN *glance, as if hopefully.*]

They look like they've been bar-hopping all over the island.

MELISSA: I hope they're not guests of this hotel.

EDWIN: [*As if casually.*] Are you a guest of—this hotel?

MELISSA: [*Lowering eyes.*] I—uh—actually, I—have one of those little houses—down along there—

[*Pointing.*]

—overlooking the beach.

EDWIN: [*Delighted.*] Do you? So do I! So do I! Real nice, aren't they? Cost you an arm and a leg, but, well, that's what we're here for, eh?

MELISSA: [*Carefully.*] I'm here to—enjoy myself.

EDWIN: Great view of the Gulf—!

MELISSA: Especially, I look forward to waking up early tomorrow— hearing the surf. Waking to the surf.

EDWIN: Not *too* early, I hope!

[*Laughs awkwardly, coughs.*]

I mean—it's your—uh—vacation, isn't it?

MELISSA: [*Stiffly.*] I enjoy rising early, when I can.

EDWIN: [*Hastily.*] Oh, I do too, I do too!—when I can.

MELISSA: [*Dreamily.*] To hear the waves in the Caribbean in my sleep, my dreams . . . to sleep with my window open to the tropical moon that's like a—a—luminous, overripe fruit in the sky . . . to see the sun like an eye afire rising on the horizon of the sea . . .

[*Passionately.*]

How I've yearned for that! All my life, without knowing!

EDWIN: [*After a seemingly respectful pause, squinting out toward the sea.*] Yes—but—uh—which way are we facing?

[*As he points seaward.*]

Sort of south and west, isn't it?

MELISSA: South and *east.*

EDWIN: But, yes—isn't the sun going *down* over there?

[*Pointing.*]

MELISSA: My windows face east.

EDWIN: Well—I could be wrong.

MELISSA: *My* windows, in the cottage *I* requested, face east.

EDWIN: I s'pose we could be—uh—sort of—turned around, reversed.

[*Pause.*]

When you cross the equator, all kinds of weird things happen!

MELISSA: [*As if waving away annoying insects, but unconsciously.*] We are nowhere near the equator.

[*The calypso music has increased in volume.*]

EDWIN: [*Drawing a breath, awkwardly flirtatious.*] So—uh—you're Angelina—eh? Or is it—Bunny?

MELISSA: Depends.

EDWIN: Depends on what?

MELISSA: On the context.

EDWIN: Which context?

MELISSA: The human context.

EDWIN: Meaning—?

MELISSA: Who I'm with.

EDWIN: Oh, yes?

MELISSA: And where.

EDWIN: Oh, yes?

MELISSA: And when.

EDWIN: Ohhhhh, uh-huh.

[*Distracted by the music.*]

Jeez—that's getting loud.

MELISSA: It *is*—a bit.

EDWIN: [*Snapping his fingers, tapping a foot, not quite rhythmically.*] Tonight, they're s'posed to have a live band, a steel band. For dancing, I wonder?

MELISSA: I don't know. This is my first day.

EDWIN: *My* first day too.

[*Smiles.*]

Actually, I saw you—spotted you—in the airport. Miami.

MELISSA: [*Embarrassed.*] Oh—come on.

EDWIN: I did!

MELISSA: With all those—gorgeous—young women—on every side?

EDWIN: And I hoped—I swear this is true—I hoped you'd be flying on to Saint Kitts. In my heart of hearts, I swear.

MELISSA: [*Embarrassed, not knowing whether to be flattered or skeptical.*] Oh—you'd say that to—anyone!

EDWIN: [*Almost offended.*] Hey—I'm not a liar, I'm a guy who speaks his mind.

[*Pause, then rather daringly.*]

Heart.

[*Music up stridently.* MELISSA *presses hands over ears, winces delicately.*]

MELISSA: Oh!

EDWIN: Maybe I'd better ask them to turn it down.

MELISSA: Yes, please—Edwin—would you?

[EDWIN *remains unmoving, face creased in a frown.*]

MELISSA: Yes—would you?

EDWIN: You think they'd know better!

[*Gets to his feet, blustery, irritable.*]

Excuse me—waiter? Waiter?

[*Pause.*]

Where is everybody?

[*No response, as* EDWIN *moves off stage right.*]

Excuse me—*excuse me . . .*

[EDWIN *exits.* MELISSA *hurriedly swallows a large mouthful of her drink; fumbles inside her purse again; checks her compact mirror again; shuts the compact with a snap, drops it back into purse; gets restlessly to her feet, paces about, smoothing dress over thighs— the dress is a bit wrinkled—and fusses with straps of dress, hair, earrings.*]

MELISSA: [*Biting at thumbnail.*] I shouldn't be here—I shouldn't be here—I *should* be here!

[*Derisively.*]

What're you saving it for, Bunny, back in Twin Cities? Your heirs?

[*Retrieves purse, fumbles inside, takes out little gold pill box, shakes out two pills onto palm of hand, swallows them down with another mouthful of her drink.*]

Ah!—that will help.

[*Pause; head back, eyes shut, lifts hair as if feeling the sea breeze.*]

That *does* help!

THE OIL WELL
BY HORTON FOOTE

CHARACTERS

MRS. LOULA THORNTON *(60s) and* WILL THORNTON *(mid-60s) have been married for years, raising their kids and making a hardscrabble livelihood from their farm. But now the oilmen have come to their town and made an offer that could change everything.*

SCENE
The front porch of a ranch near Harrison, Texas.

TIME
Night. 1953.

[MRS. THORNTON *turns off the light in the room except for a lamp on the table. She goes out on the porch. She stands for a moment looking out into the yard.* WILL *comes out upstage-right. She hears him and turns to him.*]

MRS. THORNTON: Couldn't you sleep?

WILL: [*Comes out front door onto porch.*] No, ma'm.

MRS. THORNTON: Well, you'll be tired in a little while. That was a long nap you had. Come sit with me.

WILL: Yes, ma'm. Want me to bring some chairs out?

MRS. THORNTON: No. I like to sit on the steps.

[*She sits down. He sits beside her.*]

WILL: Children gone to bed?

MRS. THORNTON: Yes. They both have to work tomorrow.

WILL: So do I.

MRS. THORNTON: I know.

WILL: Things got kind of behind today and yesterday. But I'll catch up.

[*A pause.*]

MRS. THORNTON: I was thinking about the first time I ever saw this house. I remember when you brought me out in the buggy to have Sunday dinner with your family. I was scared. My, I was scared. I don't think I've ever been so scared since.

WILL: I remember.

MRS. THORNTON: I remember when I came back here as a bride.

WILL: I remember that too.

MRS. THORNTON: Forty years goes fast.

WILL: Like nothing. Like nothing at all.

MRS. THORNTON: I hope you didn't mind too much, Will.

WILL: No sense in lying to you. It broke my heart at first. But it's been broken before and I guess it'll mend. It always has.

MRS. THORNTON: Of course it has. That's what I told the children.

WILL: And we've got lots to be grateful for. Our health . . . and our children. We certainly have fine children . . . They never give us trouble.

[*A pause.*]

Loula . . .

MRS. THORNTON: Yes, Will?

WILL: Do you know what I was thinking in there?

MRS. THORNTON: What, Will?

WILL: Now I don't want you to get mad at me when I tell you, or to call me a fool . . .

MRS. THORNTON: I won't.

WILL: Now you promise?

MRS. THORNTON: I promise.

WILL: Well . . . I was thinking . . . maybe they were digging in the wrong place. That has happened, you know.

MRS. THORNTON: It has?

WILL: Lots of times. I've known out of a farm of a thousand acres for them only to find oil on ten. You've heard of that.

MRS. THORNTON: That's sure. I've heard of that.

WILL: And I heard H. T. Mavis say he was putting a well down on George Weems's place whether mine came in or not.

MRS. THORNTON: Is that so?

WILL: And H. T. Mavis is a lucky man.

MRS. THORNTON: Yes. He is. He certainly is.

WILL: And if he finds it there, it stands to reason they'll be back here. Because our place is next to Mr. George's . . . Don't that stand to reason?

MRS. THORNTON: Yes, it does.

WILL: [*He is quite excited now.*] Of course, don't you worry. I'll go on raising my cotton. But it makes me feel so much better knowing there's still a chance. Don't it you?

MRS. THORNTON: Yes, it does.

WILL: Well, I'm glad you feel that way. I was afraid you might think I was foolish. A man has to have his hopes, don't he, Loula? I couldn't live without hoping. And if the time comes when there's a law against hoping, I want them to take me out and shoot me. That's how I feel about it.

[*He stands up. He is more like the old* WILL *now as he walks left in the yard.*]

Yes, sir. I see now how it will work out. For H. T. Mavis is a lucky man. And I'm lucky to be having a place next to the one he owns the minerals on. And you know something? It wouldn't surprise me if he weren't here the first thing in the morning to try and buy our rights. Thinking now he can get them for nothing . . . But I'm gonna be too smart for him. Yes, sir. I can see it all now. I was a fool to get discouraged. For a minute. I'll be building you that house in town yet. And we'll be on our way to California in no time. Come on. Walk over to the field with me. I wouldn't want people to think I was a poor sport.

MRS. THORNTON: All right, Will. I'll be glad to.

[*Suddenly he stops. His hurt and anguish seize him again. He almost screams with pain.*]

WILL: Loula, Loula . . .

MRS. THORNTON: What is it, Will?

[*She runs to him.*]

WILL: Why does this come to a man? He's led on to believe, to expect . . . and then everything is knocked out of his hands. His hopes are dashed. There is failure again . . . I can't go through it anymore. I can't. It's better not to expect, not to hope . . . Oh, Loula . . . Loula . . . My heart is broken.

[*She takes him in her arms.*]

MRS. THORNTON: I know, Will . . . I know.

[*She is holding him, comforting him as she might a child.*]

Cry. Get it all out. It's better to let it all come out, then you'll be tired and able to sleep, and in the morning you'll be rested and can get on with the work to be done here . . .

WILL: Yes'm. But I won't ever hope again, Loula. I can't. There's too much hurt when it doesn't happen. Do you hear that, Loula?

MRS. THORNTON: Yes, I hear you. You think that now. But you won't stop hoping. You can't. And I wouldn't want you any other way. Not any other way in this world.

WILL: Wouldn't you, Loula?

MRS. THORNTON: No. Now come on . . . Let's go out to that field.

WILL: All right, Loula. All right.

[*She takes his arm. They go walking out of the yard left as the lights fade.*]

TIME STANDS STILL
BY DONALD MARGULIES

CHARACTERS

JAMES *and* SARAH *(both mid-40s) live together whenever both happen to be home, which happened rarely until* SARAH *was almost killed. She is a photojournalist working in dangerous war zones, and she is now recovering from wounds received in Iraq. He is a magazine reporter who is now feeling very guilty for abandoning her in Iraq before she suffered her injuries.*

SCENE

The modest Brooklyn apartment of James and Sarah. It is raining outside.

TIME

Late afternoon.

[JAMES *is watching a horror movie while taking notes on his laptop.* SARAH, *camera bag in hand, comes in from the rain.*]

JAMES: Hey!

SARAH: Hey.

[*He rushes to her aid.*]

JAMES: Why didn't your little intern help with this?

SARAH: I sent her home.

JAMES: You should've buzzed me. I would have come down.

SARAH: I could manage.

JAMES: How'd it go?

SARAH: Fine.

JAMES: You get some good stuff?

SARAH: Yeah.

JAMES: So . . . ?

SARAH: Let me catch my breath.

JAMES: Want something? Tea or uh . . .

SARAH: Something harder would be great.

JAMES: Got it.

[*He pours glasses of Scotch and hands one to her.*]

So tell me!

SARAH: It's not such a big deal.

JAMES: It *is* a big deal. Your first assignment in six months. That's a *very* big deal.

SARAH: How was *your* day?

JAMES: You're looking at it.

SARAH: What're you cooking?

JAMES: That chicken–black olive thing.

SARAH: Again?

JAMES: Thought I'd try not to make it rare this time.

SARAH: [*Regarding his laptop.*] What are you working on?

JAMES: My horror movie book.

SARAH: What about the pages for Richard? You promised he'd have it on Friday.

JAMES: I know; he will.

SARAH: You can't blow it off; you've got to do it.

JAMES: I am! I worked on it all day. Now I'm working on *this*.

[*A beat.*]

You okay? You seem wrecked.

SARAH: Long day.

JAMES: It was too much for you, wasn't it? I knew it would be too much. Didn't I say you weren't ready?

SARAH: It wasn't that. Physically I held up just fine.

[*Pause.*]

I had a flashback.

[*Pause.*]

JAMES: At the prison?

[*She nods.*]

What was it?

SARAH: Market bombing. Mosul. Couple of years ago.

JAMES: What happened today? What was the trigger?

[*Pause. She takes a deep breath.*]

SARAH: Today . . . I'm shooting these women. The inmates. With the babies they'd had in prison.

JAMES: Yeah . . .

SARAH: And *some* of these ladies are *seriously* bad. I mean, homicide; drug dealing, trying to kill their grandmother for her ATM card, that kind of thing . . . Anyway I'm shooting . . . sort of getting in the zone and this one woman . . . big . . . heavily tattooed with Hell's Angels kind of skulls with fire shooting out of the eye sockets, comes up to me, gets right in my face . . . and looks at me with such . . . contempt . . .

[*Brutish voice.*]

"What you want to take my picture for? Huh?" And . . . I was back in Mosul.

JAMES: Was I with you?

SARAH: You were off doing a story in the south; it was when I was there for the AP.

JAMES: What happened that day? I don't remember.

SARAH: That's because I never told you. I never told anybody.

JAMES: Tell me now.

[*She shakes her head. Gently.*]

Come on. Tell me.
[*Pause.*]

SARAH: I was . . . sitting in a café with the Reuters guys . . . And a car bomb went off, a block or two away, in this market. And I just *ran* to it, took off. Without even thinking.

[*A beat.*]

The carnage was . . . ridiculous. Exploded produce. Body parts. Eggplants. Women keening. They were digging in the rubble for their children. I started shooting. And suddenly this woman burst out from the smoke . . . covered in blood . . . her skin was raw and red and charred, and her hair was singed—she got so close I could smell it—and her clothes, her top was melted into her, and she was screaming at me.

[*Shouts.*]

"Go way, go way! No picture, no picture!" And she started pushing me, pushing my camera with her hand on the lens . . .

JAMES: What did you do?

SARAH: Nothing. I kept on shooting. Then, somehow, I ran the hell out of there. I stopped to catch my breath . . . and check out my cameras . . .

[*Pause.*]

There was blood on my lens.

[*Moved.*]

Her blood was smeared on my lens.

[*She breaks down.*]

I feel so ashamed . . .

JAMES: No. Why?

SARAH: It was wrong . . . What I did was so wrong.

JAMES: It wasn't wrong.

SARAH: It was indecent.

JAMES: You were doing your job.

SARAH: They didn't want me there! They did not want me taking pictures! They lost *children* in that mess! To them it was a sacred place. But there I was, like a, some kind of *ghoul* with a camera shooting away. No wonder they wanted to kill me; *I* would've wanted to kill me, too.

JAMES: [*Soothing.*] No . . .

SARAH: I live off the suffering of strangers. I built a *career* on the sorrows of people I don't know and will never see again.

JAMES: That's not true. You've helped them. In ways you can't see.

SARAH: Have I? Have I really? I'm such a fraud.

[*Long pause.*]

JAMES: Hey.

[*She looks at him. Pause.*]

We *don't* have to do this anymore, you know.

SARAH: What do you mean?

JAMES: We don't have to *do* this. We can stay home. We can *make* a home.

[*A beat.*]

Y'know? The past few months? Teaching myself how to cook, watching Netflix . . . writing while you napped, listening to you breathe . . . I've been so . . .

[*Chokes up.*]

happy. Y'know? Simple, boring, happy.

[*A beat.*]

For the first time in I don't know how long, I don't have giardia, or some nasty parasite I'm trying to get rid of . . . And my back doesn't ache from sleeping on the ground, or on lousy mattresses in shitty hotels. I realized: Wow, this is what it must feel like to be *comfortable.* I don't think I've ever known that feeling; maybe as a boy I did, I felt safe, but I didn't know what it was. Now I know! I just want to be comfortable! There! I said it! Does that make me a bad person?

SARAH: Of course not.

JAMES: I've been feeling like, We're going *back* there? *Why?* Unfinished business? Fuck unfinished business. I don't need to dodge bullets to feel alive anymore. Or step over mutilated corpses. Or watch children die. I want to watch children *grow*. And take vacations like other people. To . . . I don't know, *dude* ranches. Or Club Med. I don't want to be on a goddamn mission every time I get on a plane! I want to take our kids to Disney World and buy them all the crap they want.

SARAH: Our kids.

JAMES: [*Nods, then.*] Let's just do it. We keep putting it off, and putting it off. We're pushing our luck already. Let's just go ahead and do it. Now. Not six months from now.

[*Pause.*]

There'll always be something, some reason to put our lives on hold. The war *du jour*. Well, fuck it. It's our turn now.

[*A beat.*]

Let's stop running.

PAINTING CHURCHES

BY TINA HOWE

CHARACTERS
FANNY *(late 60s) and* GARDNER *(70s) are a long-married couple with a daughter, Mags (mid-30s) who is a visual artist living in New York City.* GARDNER *is a famous Pulitzer Prize–winning poet who is sliding into dementia;* FANNY *is an eccentric woman from a fine old family who is angry at the change in their circumstances.*

SCENE
The long-married couple's townhouse in the Beacon Hill area of Boston. They are in the midst of packing for a move to a beach house on Cape Cod. They are waiting for their daughter to show up, to help them pack and to paint their portrait.

TIME
Late morning.

[GARDNER *enters, singing. He's wearing mismatched tweeds and is holding a pack of papers, which keep drifting to the floor.*]

GARDNER: Oh, don't you look nice! Very attractive, very attractive!

FANNY: But I'm still in my bathrobe.

GARDNER: [*Looking around the room, leaking more papers.*] Well, where's Mags?

FANNY: Darling, you're dropping your papers all over the floor.

GARDNER: [*Spies the silver tray.*] I remember this! Aunt Alice gave it to us, didn't she?

[*He picks it up.*]

Good lord, it's heavy. What's it made of? Lead?!

FANNY: No, Aunt Alice did *not* give it to us. It was Mama's.

GARDNER: Oh, yes . . .

[*He starts to exit with it.*]

FANNY: Could I have it back, please?

GARDNER: [*Hands it to her, dropping more papers.*] Oh, sure thing . . . Where's Mags? I thought you said she was here.

FANNY: I didn't say Mags was here, I asked *you* to come here.

GARDNER: [*Papers spilling.*] Damned papers keep falling . . .

FANNY: I wanted to show you my new hat. I bought it in honor of Mags's visit. Isn't it marvelous?

GARDNER: [*Picking up the papers as more drop.*] Yes, yes, very nice . . .

FANNY: Gardner, you're not even looking at it!

GARDNER: Very becoming . . .

FANNY: You don't think it's too bright, do you? I don't want to look like a traffic light. Guess how much it cost.

GARDNER: [*A whole sheaf of papers slides to the floor; he dives for them.*] OH, SHIT!

FANNY: [*Gets to them first.*] It's alright, I've got them, I've got them.

[*She hands them to him.*]

GARDNER: You'd think they had wings on them . . .

FANNY: Here you go . . .

GARDNER: . . . damned things won't hold still!

FANNY: Gar? . . .

GARDNER: [*Has become engrossed in one of the pages.*] Mmmmm?

FANNY: HELLO?

GARDNER: [*Startled.*] What's that?

FANNY: [*In a whisper.*] My hat. Guess how much it cost.

GARDNER: Oh, yes. Let's see . . . ten dollars?

FANNY: Ten dollars . . . IS THAT ALL? . . .

GARDNER: Twenty?

FANNY: GARDNER, THIS HAPPENS TO BE A DESIGNER HAT!
DESIGNER HATS START AT FIFTY DOLLARS . . . SEVENTY-
FIVE!

GARDNER: [*Jumps.*] Was that the doorbell?

FANNY: No, it wasn't the doorbell. Though it's high time Mags were
here. She was probably in a train wreck!

GARDNER: [*Looking through his papers.*] I'm beginning to get fond
of Wallace Stevens again.

FANNY: This damned thing is going to kill me! Send me straight to
my grave!

GARDNER: [*Reading from a page.*]

The mules from angels ride come slowly down

The blazing passes, from beyond the sun.

Descensions of their tinkling bells arrive.

These muleteers are dainty of their way . . .

[*Pause.*]

Don't you love that! These muleteers are *dainty* of their way"!? . . .

FANNY: Gar, the hat. How much?

[GARDNER *sighs.*]

Darling? . . .

GARDNER: Oh, yes. Let's see . . . fifty dollars? Seventy-five?

FANNY: It's French.

GARDNER: Three hundred!

FANNY: [*Triumphant.*] No, eighty-five cents.

GARDNER: Eighty-five cents! . . . I thought you said . . .

FANNY: That's right . . . eighty . . . five . . . *cents!*

GARDNER: Well, you sure had me fooled!

FANNY: I found it at a thrift shop.

GARDNER: I thought it cost at least fifty dollars or seventy-five. You know, designer hats are very expensive!

FANNY: It was on the mark-down table.

[*She takes it off and shows him the label.*]

See that? Lily Dache! When I saw that label, I nearly keeled over right into the fur coats.

GARDNER: [*Handling it.*] Well, what do you know, that's the same label that's in my bathrobe.

FANNY: Darling, Lily Dache designed hats, not men's bathrobes!

GARDNER: Yup . . . Lily Dache . . . same name . . .

FANNY: If you look again, I'm sure you'll see . . .

GARDNER: . . . same script, same color, same size. I'll show you.

[*He exits.*]

FANNY: Poor lamb can't keep anything straight anymore.

[*Looks at herself in the tray again.*]

God, this is a good-looking hat!

GARDNER: [*Returns with a nondescript plaid bathrobe. He points to the label.*] See that? . . . What does it say?

FANNY: [*Refusing to look at it.*] Lily Dache was a *hat* designer! She designed ladies' *hats*!

GARDNER: What . . . does . . . it . . . say?

FANNY: Gardner, you're being ridiculous.

GARDNER: [*Forcing it on her.*] Read . . . the label!

FANNY: Lily Dache did *not* design this bathrobe, I don't care what the label says!

GARDNER: READ!

[FANNY *reads it.*]

ALL RIGHT, NOW WHAT DOES IT SAY? . . .

FANNY: [*Chagrined.*] Lily Dache.

GARDNER: I told you!

FANNY: Wait a minute, let me look at that again.

[*She does; then throws the robe at him in disgust.*]

Gar, Lily Dache never designed a bathrobe in her life! Someone obviously ripped the label off one of her hats and the sewed it into the robe.

GARDNER: [*Puts it on over his jacket.*] It's damned good-looking. I've always loved this robe. I think you gave it to me . . . Well, I've got to get back to work.

[*He abruptly exits.*]

FANNY: Where did you get that robe anyway? . . . I didn't give it to you, did I? . . .

[*Silence.* GARDNER *resumes typing.*]

FANNY: [*Holding the tray up and admiring herself.*] You know, I think I *did* give it to him. I remember how excited I was when I found it at the thrift shop . . . fifty cents and never worn! *I* couldn't have sewn that label in to impress him, could I? . . . I can't be that far gone! . . . The poor lamb wouldn't even notice it, let alone understand its cachet . . . Uuuuuuuh, this damned tray is even heavier than the coffee pot. They must have been amazons in the old days!

[*Writes on her pad.*]

"Empire tray, Parke-Bernet Galleries," and good riddance!

[*She wraps it and drops it into the carton with the coffee pot.*]

Where *is* that wretched Mags? It would be just like her to get into a train wreck! She was supposed to be here hours ago. Well, if she doesn't show up soon, I'm going to drop dead of exhaustion. God, wouldn't that be wonderful? . . . Then they could just cart me off into storage with all the old chandeliers and china . . .

GOOD PEOPLE
BY DAVID LINDSAY-ABAIRE

CHARACTERS
MARGARET WALSH *(50) and* DOCTOR MICHAEL DILLON *(50) are former high school classmates who have gone in very different directions.* MARGARET *wants to understand why.*

SCENE
Mike's very upscale home in an upscale Boston suburb.

TIME
Evening.

[MIKE *and his African American wife, Kate, have canceled their party for this night.* MARGARET *knows this, but she shows up anyway. Kate has just left the room, leaving* MARGARET *and* MIKE *alone.*]

MIKE: We have beer if you'd rather have beer.

MARGARET: [*Beat.*] Wine is fine.

MIKE: Red?

MARGARET: Sure.

[*He goes to the glassware cabinet and gets a wineglass, opens a bottle, pours her some wine.*]

I'm sorry, Mike, I misunderstood.

MIKE: How do you mean?

MARGARET: About the party. I didn't realize that—

MIKE: Right, I'm not sure how you could've done that.

MARGARET: I know.

MIKE: I thought I was pretty clear when we talked.

MARGARET: No, I know.

MIKE: I said Ally was sick, and so my wife wanted to cancel.

MARGARET: I thought you were lying, though.

MIKE: [*Beat.*] Ah.

MARGARET: I thought you were just making up an excuse to—

MIKE: Why would I lie?

MARGARET: I don't know. I just thought you didn't want me to come. It seemed suspicious. To cancel at the last minute like that.

MIKE: Ally got sick. Kate thought it'd be better if we called it off.

MARGARET: No, I know that *now*.

MIKE: You're paranoid.

[*He hands her the wine.* MARGARET *looks around.*]

So you found it okay.

MARGARET: No problem. That receptionist of yours gives good directions.

MIKE: I'll let her know.

MARGARET: I was early, though, so I walked around the block a few times.

MIKE: And you lived to tell the tale.

MARGARET: I should've figured out there was no party. Your driveway was empty. Most of your lights were off.

MIKE: Yeah, well.

MARGARET: The house is beautiful.

MIKE: Thanks.

MARGARET: I knew it would be.

[*Beat.*]

I pictured pillars, though.

MIKE: Pillars?

MARGARET: On the outside? Like columns?

MIKE: Like Tara?

MARGARET: Tara?

MIKE: *Gone With the Wind?*

MARGARET: I don't know, I guess. Yeah.

MIKE: That's funny.

MARGARET: It's still nice, though.

MIKE: But you would've preferred pillars.

MARGARET: I don't know.

[*They drink.*]

Should I go?

MIKE: No, you can't go now, Kate's getting cheese. You can't leave when she's getting cheese. She'll think I chased you off.

[*Beat.*]

Besides, she wanted to meet you.

MARGARET: [*Beat.*] She did?

MIKE: Yeah, she doesn't believe I grew up in Southie. You're my evidence.

MARGARET: Oh.

MIKE: You'll have to tell her what a hoodlum I was.

MARGARET: What do you mean?

MIKE: She only knows me as Mr. Doctor-Man.

MARGARET: Oh, I see.

MIKE: You gotta set her straight.

MARGARET: You want me to mention the Irish mob? How you ran with Whitey Bulger? How many bodies should I tell her you buried?

MIKE: All right. If you're gonna make fun of me—

MARGARET: Well, I don't know what you told her.

MIKE: I didn't *lie* to her.

MARGARET: Well, you said hoodlum.

MIKE: You know what I meant.

MARGARET: You were just a kid from the projects.

MIKE: Exactly.

MARGARET: So that means hoodlum?

MIKE: No. I didn't mean to say it like that. Forget it. How's the wine?

MARGARET: How the fuck should I know?

[*Pause; they drink.*]

What'd you tell her about me?

MIKE: I just said you might come to the party.

MARGARET: [*Beat.*] That's not very interesting. You must've said *something* else. Otherwise why would she want to meet me?

MIKE: Just that we ran in the same crowd when we were kids. And how you came by the office.

MARGARET: Looking for work.

MIKE: Yeah.

MARGARET: Okay.

[*Beat.*]

You didn't mention we used to go out?

MIKE: Oh God, no. I didn't mean—No.

MARGARET: How come?

MIKE: I don't know. That was such a blip.

MARGARET: Huh.

MIKE: A couple months.

MARGARET: No, I know.

MIKE: We were friends for so long before that. I just said we were friends.

MARGARET: [*A little chuckle.*] Okay. So she won't be weird about me at all?

MIKE: No.

MARGARET: Good.

MIKE: I mean, so long as you don't mention it.

MARGARET: [*Beat.*] Okay.

MIKE: I just said we were friends.

MARGARET: Right.

[*Pause as they drink.*]

So she *might* get weird? If she knew?

MIKE: No, I don't think so.

[*Beat.*]

I don't know. It's just . . . we're in a really good place right now, and I don't wanna . . .

MARGARET: Stir anything up?

MIKE: Exactly.

MARGARET: [*Beat. Smiles.*] What'd you do?

MIKE: Nothing.

MARGARET: "We're in a really good place right now."

MIKE: We *are.*

MARGARET: Which means at some point you *weren't.*

MIKE: Margaret—

MARGARET: What'd you do?

MIKE: Nothing.

MARGARET: It involves the Dominican receptionist, doesn't it?

MIKE: *Jesus. No.*

MARGARET: [*Laughs.*] I'm just bustin' balls.

MIKE: Can you just . . . not mention we dated?

MARGARET: All right.

MIKE: We were practically kids after all.

MARGARET: I'm not the one making a big deal out of it.

MIKE: I'm not making a big deal, I just wanna . . .

MARGARET: Keep it secret.

MIKE: Well, don't make it sound *dirty.*

MARGARET: *You* did that, not me.

THE MATCHMAKER
BY THORNTON WILDER

CHARACTERS
Wealthy merchant VANDERGELDER *(60) has hired matchmaker*
DOLLY LEVI *(somewhere over 50) to find him a wife. What he finds*
is something other than what he expected.

SCENE
The living room of Vandergelder's home in Yonkers, New York.

TIME
Early morning. The 1880s.

[*Enter* VANDERGELDER *at back. He has added a splendid*
plumed hat to his costume and is carrying a standard or small flag
bearing the initials of his lodge.]

MRS. LEVI: Oh, Mr. Vandergelder, how handsome you look! You
take my breath away. Oh, Mr. Vandergelder, I wish Irene Molloy
could see you now. But then! I don't know what's come over you
lately. You seem to be growing younger every day.

VANDERGELDER: Allowing for exaggeration, Mrs. Levi. If a man
eats careful there's no reason why he should look old.

MRS. LEVI: You never said a truer word.

VANDERGELDER: I'll never see fifty-five again.

MRS. LEVI: Fifty-five! Why, I can see at a glance that you're the sort that will be stamping about at a hundred—and eating five meals a day, like my uncle Harry. At fifty-five my uncle Harry was a mere boy. I'm a judge of hands, Mr. Vandergelder—show me your hand.

[*Looks at it.*]

Lord in heaven! What a life line!

VANDERGELDER: Where?

MRS. LEVI: From *here* to *here.* It runs right off your hand. I don't know where it goes. They'll have to hit you on the head with a mallet. They'll have to stifle you with a soft pillow. You'll bury us all! However, to return to our business—Mr. Vandergelder, I suppose you've changed your mind again. I suppose you've given up all idea of getting married.

VANDERGELDER: [*Complacently.*] Not at all, Mrs. Levi. I have news for you.

MRS. LEVI: News?

VANDERGELDER: Mrs. Levi, I've practically decided to ask Mrs. Molloy to be my wife.

MRS. LEVI: [*Taken aback.*] You have?

VANDERGELDER: Yes, I have.

MRS. LEVI: Oh, you have! Well, I guess that's just about the best news I ever heard. So there's nothing more for me to do but wish you every happiness under the sun and say good-bye.

[*She crosses as if to leave..*]

VANDERGELDER: [*Stopping her.*] Well—Mrs. Levi—Surely I thought—

MRS. LEVI: Well, I did have a little suggestion to make—but I won't. You're going to marry Irene Molloy, and that closes the matter.

VANDERGELDER: What suggestion was that, Mrs. Levi?

MRS. LEVI: Well—I *had* found *another* girl for you.

VANDERGELDER: Another?

MRS. LEVI: The most wonderful girl, the ideal wife.

VANDERGELDER: Another, eh? What's her name?

MRS. LEVI: Her name?

VANDERGELDER: Yes!

MRS. LEVI: [*Groping for it.*] Err . . . er . . . her *name*?—Ernestina—Simple. *Miss* Ernestina Simple. But now of course all that's too late. After all, you're engaged—you're practically engaged to marry Irene Molloy.

VANDERGELDER: Oh, I ain't engaged to Mrs. Molloy!

MRS. LEVI: Nonsense! You can't break poor Irene's heart now and change to another girl . . . When a man at your time of life calls four times on an attractive widow like that—and sends her a pot of geraniums—that's practically an engagement!

VANDERGELDER: That ain't an engagement!

MRS. LEVI: And yet—! If only you were free! I've found this treasure of a girl. Every moment I feel like a traitor to Irene Molloy—but let me tell you: I couldn't help it. I told this girl all about you, just as though you were a free man. Isn't that dreadful? The fact is: she has fallen in love with you already.

VANDERGELDER: Ernestina?

MRS. LEVI: Ernestina Simple.

VANDERGELDER: Ernestina Simple.

MRS. LEVI: Of course she's a very different idea from Mrs. Molloy, Ernestina is. Like her name—simple, domestic, practical.

VANDERGELDER: Can she cook?

MRS. LEVI: Cook, Mr. Vandergelder? I've had two meals from her hands and—as I live—I don't know what I've done that God should reward me with such meals. Her duck! Her steak!

VANDERGELDER: Eh! Eh! In this house we don't eat duck and steak every day, Mrs. Levi.

MRS. LEVI: But didn't I tell you?—that's the wonderful part about it. Her duck—what was it? Pigeon! I'm alive to tell you. I don't know how she does it. It's a secret that's comes down in her family. The greatest chefs would give their right hands to know it. And the steaks? Shoulder of beef—four cents a pound. Dogs wouldn't eat. But when Ernestina passes her hands over it—!

VANDERGELDER: Allowing for exaggeration, Mrs. Levi.

MRS. LEVI: No exaggeration. I'm the best cook in the world myself, and I *know* what's good.

VANDERGELDER: Hm. How old is she, Mrs. Levi?

MRS. LEVI: Nineteen, well—say twenty.

VANDERGELDER: Twenty, Mrs. Levi? Girls of twenty are apt to favor young fellows of their own age.

MRS. LEVI: But you don't listen to me. And you don't know the girl. Mr. Vandergelder, she has a positive horror of flighty, brainless young men. A fine head of gray hair, she says, is worth twenty shined up with goose grease. No, sir. I like a man that's *settled*"— in so many words she said it.

VANDERGELDER: That's . . . that's not usual, Mrs. Levi.

MRS. LEVI: Usual? I'm not wearing myself to the bone hunting up *usual* girls to interest you, Mr. Vandergelder. Usual, indeed. Listen to me. Do you know the sort of pictures she has on her wall? Is it any of these young Romeos and Lochinvars? No!—it's Moses on the mountain—that's what she's got. If you want to make her happy, you give her a picture of Methuselah surrounded by his grandchildren. That's my advice to you.

[*Following passage—based on Moliere—has generally been cut in performance.*]

VANDERGELDER: I hope . . . hm . . . that she has some means, Mrs. Levi. I have a large household to run.

MRS. LEVI: Ernestina? She'll bring you five thousand dollars a year.

VANDERGELDER: Eh! Eh!

MRS. LEVI: Listen to me, Mr. Vandergelder, You're a man of sense, I hope. A man that can reckon. In the first place, she's an orphan. She's been brought up with a great saving of food. What does she eat herself? Apples and lettuce. It's what she's been used to eat and what she likes best. She saves you two thousand a year right there. Secondly, she makes her own clothes—out of old tablecloths and window curtains. And she's the best-dressed woman in Brooklyn this minute. She saves you a thousand dollars right there. Thirdly, her health is of iron—

VANDERGELDER: But, Mrs. Levi, that's not money in the pocket.

MRS. LEVI: We're talking about marriage, aren't we, Mr. Vandergelder? The money she saves while she's in Brooklyn is none of your affair—but if she were your wife that would be *money*. Yes, sir, that's money.

VANDERGELDER: What's her family?

MRS. LEVI: Her father?—God be good to him! He was the best— what am I trying to say?—the best undertaker in Brooklyn, respected, esteemed. He knew all the best people—knew them well, even before they died. So—well, that's the way it is.

[*Lowering her voice, intimately.*]

Now let me tell you a little more of her appearance. Can you hear me: as I say, a beautiful girl, beautiful, I've seen her go down the street—you know what I mean?—the young men get dizzy. They have to lean against lampposts. And she? Modest, eyes on the ground—I'm not going to tell you anymore . . . Couldn't you come to New York today?

VANDERGELDER: I was thinking of coming to New York this afternoon . . .

MRS. LEVI: You were? Well, now, I wonder if something could be arranged—oh, she's so eager to see you! Let me see . . .

VANDERGELDER: Could I . . . Mrs. Levi, could I give you a little dinner, maybe?

MRS. LEVI: Really, come to think of it, I don't see where I could get the time. I'm so busy over that wretched lawsuit of mine. Yes. If I win it, I don't mind telling you, I'll be what's called a very rich woman. I'll own half of Long Island, that's a fact. But just now I'm at my wit's end for a little help, just enough money to finish it off. My wit's end!

[*She looks in her handbag. In order not to bear this,* VANDERGELDER *has a series of coughs, sneezes, and minor convulsions.*]

MRS. LEVI: But perhaps I could arrange a little dinner; I'll see. Yes, for that lawsuit all I need is fifty dollars, and Staten Island's as good as mine. I've been trotting all over New York for you, trying to find you a suitable wife.

VANDERGELDER: Fifty dollars!

MRS. LEVI: Two whole months I've been . . .

VANDERGELDER: Fifty dollars, Mrs. Levi . . . is no joke.

[*Producing purse.*]

I don't know where money's gone to these days. It's in hiding . . . There's twenty . . . well, there's twenty-five. I can't spare no more, not now I can't.

MRS. LEVI: Well, this will help—will help somewhat. Now let me tell you what we'll do. I'll bring Ernestina to that restaurant on the Battery. You know it: the Harmonia Gardens. It's good, but it's not flashy. Now, Mr. Vandergelder, I think it'd be nice if just this once you'd order a real nice dinner. I guess you can afford it.

VANDERGELDER: Well, just this once.

MRS. LEVI: A chicken wouldn't hurt.

VANDERGELDER: Chicken!—Well, just this once.

MRS. LEVI: And a little wine.

COUNTING THE WAYS
BY EDWARD ALBEE

CHARACTERS
HE *and* SHE *have been married a long time and things have been going on in the same vein for quite a while. But all of a sudden something has changed, something is different. And* HE *can't understand why.*

SCENE
An empty stage.

TIME
Yes, there is time. There will always be time. Except when there won't be.

[*Stage empty. They enter,* SHE *first,* HE *urgently following after.*]

SHE: I don't want to discuss it!

HE: [*Persisting.*] When did it happen!?

SHE: I do *not* wish to *discuss* it!

HE: Well, I *do.*

SHE: [*Smiles a small, superior smile.*] Then we are at an impasse.

HE: No, we are not; we will discuss it.

SHE: If I will not, and only you will, that is not a discussion.

HE: Silence is a reply.

SHE: Of sorts. For some, I suppose. Martyrs in the desert? Old people at the post office?

HE: When did it happen?

SHE: What? I have no idea what.

HE: Two beds.

SHE: So.

HE: [*Voice rising.*] There are two beds!

SHE: [*Straining to remain calm.*] Yes; there are two beds.

HE: [*Suddenly; loud, hysterical.*] WHY!!??

SHE: Well; let us sit down and discuss it.

   [SHE *sits.*]

   With calm and reason.

HE: [*Bolts down into the other chair; urgent if softer.*] Okay! Right! Okay!

SHE: Greater calm.

HE: [*Softer, but still urgent.*] Okay. Right. Okay.

SHE: And reason.

HE: Reason? Sure! All of a sudden there are two beds. Once upon a time there was one.

SHE: I . . . I *noticed* that.

HE: I wake up this morning . . . in our king-size bed . . .

SHE: You've moved into the historical present, I hope you realize.

HE: [*Tries to ignore her; voice tenser.*] I wake up this morning in our king-size bed . . .

SHE: [*To the audience.*] It's an odd tense, isn't it—sort of common, if you know what I mean. It's useful, I know, but . . . *still.*

HE: I won't be put *off.*

SHE: [*Back to him, reassuring, not patronizing.*] No, no; of course not!

HE: I wake up this morning in our king-size bed, the one I've waked in every day for all our marriage . . .

SHE: I know.

HE: . . . and so have you—save trips and hospitals—the bed I can reach across and touch you in the dark . . . in the night . . .

SHE: I know the *bed.*

HE: I wake up there; I find you gone.

SHE: To the kitchen; for your tea, for my coffee.

HE: It's the same every day.

   [*Tiny pause.*]

   Is it *not?*

SHE: Yes; yes, it is.

HE: This morning I wake in the king-size bed; I find you gone; I find you in the kitchen; I find nothing amiss.

SHE: No; nothing. I understand you.

HE: It's a day like every other day.

SHE: And I sympathize with you. I understand you, and I sympathize with you.

HE: We are each other's rod?

SHE: [*After a pause.*] So to speak.

HE: Nothing is amiss—except perhaps the coffee.

SHE: Now, now.

   [*Afterthought.*]

   You should taste the *tea.*

HE: It's a day like every other day—*except!*

SHE: Yes, I know.

HE: *Except!*

SHE: I said: I know.

HE: This afternoon you come to me and say you want flowers for a vase *between* our *beds.*

SHE: Yes.

HE: *Between . . .* our *beds.*

SHE: Yes; yes!

HE: When did it happen?

SHE: Hm?

HE: When did it happen? When did our lovely bed . . . split and become two? When did a table appear where there had been no space, in the center of our lovely bed?

SHE: [*Very reasonable.*] Well, I suspect it's been coming.

HE: Pardon?

SHE: [*Closes her eyes momentarily.*] I suspect it's been coming.

HE: And those *beds!* They're not wide, those beds; they're single; they're for a solitary, or for a corpse!

SHE: These things sneak up on you.

HE: Did you have someone in? Hm?

[SHE *shakes her head.*]

Did the bed people come and take our lovely bed away and leave these . . . these pallets? Hm?

SHE: No one came: these things happen. We've been lucky.

HE: I want an *answer* for this!

[SHE *sighs, smiles, shrugs.*]

I want an ANSWER for this!

SHE: Well, it happens sooner or later; look around you; look at our friends. Sooner or later it happens. Maybe we'll be lucky and it won't go any further.

HE: [*After a second.*] Further? *Further!?*

SHE: [*Quietly; shrugs.*] Of course: separate rooms.

HE: [*Pause; quietly.*] Separate . . . oh, *God.*

[*Pause.*]

THE HOUSE OF BLUE LEAVES

BY JOHN GUARE

CHARACTERS
ARTIE *(45) is an aging aspiring songwriter, who longs to be acclaimed. He is married to* BANANAS, *but* BANANAS *is, well, bananas.* BUNNY *(40) is Artie's girlfriend, and she is very excited by the Pope's impending visit to New York City.*

SCENE
Artie's apartment in Queens, New York.

TIME
Late night, 1963.

ARTIE: [*Thoughtfully, sings.*]

  Bridges are for burning

  Tables are for turning—

  [*He turns on all the lights. He pulls* BUNNY *by the pudgy arm over to the kitchen.*]

  I'll go see the Pope—

BUNNY: [*Hugging him.*] Oh, I love you!

ARTIE: I'll come if—

BUNNY: You said you'll come. That is tantamount to a promise.

ARTIE: I will if—

BUNNY: Tantamount. Tantamount. You hear that? I didn't work in a law office for nix. I could sue you for breach.

ARTIE: [*Seductively.*] Bunny?

BUNNY: [*Near tears.*] I know what you're going to say—

ARTIE: [*Opening a ketchup bottle under her nose.*] Cook for me?

BUNNY: [*In a passionate heat.*] I knew it. I knew it.

ARTIE: Just breakfast.

BUNNY: You bend my arm and twist my heart but I got to be strong.

ARTIE: I'm not asking any ten-course dinner.

[BUNNY *runs over to the piano where his clothes are draped to get away from his plea.*]

BUNNY: Just put your clothes on over the ski pj's I bought you. It's thirty-eight degrees and I don't want you getting your pneumonia back—

ARTIE: [*Holding up two eggs.*] Eggs, baby. Eggs right here.

BUNNY: [*Holds out his jingling trousers.*] Rinse your mouth out to freshen up and come on let's go?

ARTIE: [*Seductively.*] You boil the eggs and pour lemon sauce over—

BUNNY: [*Shaking the trousers at him.*] Hollandaise. I know Hollandaise.

[*Plopping down with the weight of the temptation, glum.*]

It's really cold out, so dress warm—Look, I stuffed the *New York Post* in my booties—plastic just ain't as warm as it used to be.

ARTIE: And you pour the Hollandaise over the eggs on English muffins—and then you put the grilled ham on top—I'm making a scrapbook of all the foods you tell me you know how to cook and then I go through the magazines and cut out pictures of what it must look like.

[*He gets the scrapbook.*]

Look—veal parmesan—eggplant meringue.

BUNNY: I cooked that for me last night. It was so good I almost died.

ARTIE: [*Sings, as* BUNNY *takes the book and looks through it with great despair.*]

If you cooked my words

Like they was veal

I'd say I love you

For every meal.

Take my words,

Garlic and oil them,

Butter and broil them,

Sauté and boil them—

Bunny, let me eat you!

[*Speaks.*]

Cook for me?

BUNNY: Not till after we're married.

ARTIE: You couldn't give me a little sample right now?

BUNNY: I'm not that kind of girl. I'll sleep with you anytime you want. Anywhere. In two months I've known you, did I refuse you once? Not once! You want me to climb in the bag with you now? Unzip it—go on—unzip it—Give your fingers a smack and I'm flat on my back. I'll sew those words into a sampler for you in our new home in California. We'll hang it right by the front door. Because, Artie, I'm a rotten lay. I know it and you know it and everybody knows it—

ARTIE: What do you mean? Everybody knows it—

BUNNY: I'm not good in bed. It's no insult. I took that sex test in the *Reader's Digest* two weeks ago and I scored twelve. Twelve, Artie! I ran out of that dentist office with tears gushing out of my face. But I face up to the truth about myself. So if I cooked for you now and said I won't sleep with you till we're married, you'd look forward to sleeping with me so much that by the time we did get to that motel near Hollywood, I'd be such a disappointment, you'd never forgive me. My cooking is the only thing I got to lure you on with and hold you with. Artie, we got to keep some magic for the honeymoon. It's my first honeymoon and I want it to be so good, I'm aiming for two million calories. I want to cook for you so bad I walk by the A&P, I get all hot jabs of chili powder inside my thighs . . . but I can't till we get those tickets to California safe in my purse, till Billy knows we're coming, till I got that ring right on my cooking finger . . . Don't tempt me . . . I love you . . .

ARTIE: [*Beaten.*] Two eggs over easy.

BUNNY: [*Shakes her head no.*] And I'm sorry last night went sour . . .

ARTIE: [*Sits down, depressed.*] They make me buy my own beers . . .

BANANAS: [*Calling from the bedroom.*] Is it light? Is it daytime already?

[ARTIE *and* BUNNY *look at each other.*]

BUNNY: I'll pour your cornflakes.

ARTIE: [*Nervous.*] You better leave.

BUNNY: [*Standing her ground.*] A nice bowlful?

ARTIE: I don't want her to know yet.

BUNNY: It'll be like a coming attraction.

ARTIE: [*Pushing her into the kitchen.*] You're a tease, Bunny, and that's the worst thing to be.

[*He puts on his green shirt and pants over his pajamas.*]

THE TALE OF THE ALLERGIST'S WIFE

BY CHARLES BUSCH

CHARACTERS

MARJORIE *and* IRA *(both 50s) are a well-off married couple living in Manhattan. IRA is a successful allergist, now retired, good-looking and highly energetic. MARJORIE is attractive and stylish, and in the "throes of an epic depression. It's not quite depression but raging frustration. She's a volcano that explodes, simmers down, and then explodes again."*

SCENE

Upper West Side condo apartment, comfortably and tastefully furnished.

TIME

Late morning.

[MARJORIE *is still wearing her bathrobe—and has a bandage on one wrist.* IRA, *who has recently come in, is wearing a jogging suit and headband.*]

IRA: When I left this morning, you were sleeping on the sofa. Did you spend the whole night out here?

MARJORIE: Apparently so.

IRA: Was it my snoring? I don't know what to do.

MARJORIE: It's not the snoring.

IRA: Then what is it, darling? Please, tell me.

MARJORIE: [*A long sigh.*] *Perdu.*

IRA: What?

MARJORIE: *Perdu.* Utter damnation. The loss of my soul.

IRA: I'm opening these drapes.

[*He pushes apart the curtains.*]

Marjorie, you've got to rouse yourself from this *perdu.* You've spent how many weeks lying out here in the dark? I'm really worried. Perhaps you should see someone.

MARJORIE: A therapist? My therapist died. I cannot replace that remarkable woman as easily as I would a dead schnauzer.

IRA: Marjorie, I did not mean to disparage your relationship with Reba Fabrikant. But you cannot allow her passing to be a catalyst for a complete breakdown. Am I the problem? I know I'm far from perfect. It took me over thirty years to get the point that you hated my jokes. Have you heard a single joke from me in months, a play on words, a pun?

MARJORIE: It was wrong of me to censor you. I should be ashamed of myself.

IRA: No, you were right. People who constantly make puns aren't really listening. I'm glad you criticized me. I am grateful.

MARJORIE: Please don't say that. Have you heard from the Disney Store?

IRA: Yes. Good news. They're not going to press charges. They're being very understanding.

MARJORIE: What do they understand?

IRA: Well, that you had just left a memorial service for your beloved therapist and you had a—

MARJORIE: The memorial service was nearly a month before.

IRA: Doesn't matter. You were out of control.

MARJORIE: It was an accident. People drop things.

IRA: Within three minutes, you dropped six porcelain figurines. They tell me the Goofy alone was two hundred and fifty dollars.

MARJORIE: And you had to pay for everything?

IRA: Forget the expense. What is money but a conduit to help people? It's you I worry about.

MARJORIE: It was an accident.

IRA: I know but they thought you were making some kind of political statement about the Disney Corporation. You know what? I think you should get dressed and go outside.

[*Eyes the calendar taped to the refrigerator.*]

Let's see what you had going for today. Tuesday the seventh. One-thirty, lecture on the literary legacy of Hermann Hesse at Goethe House. "Hiroshima/ Vagina," multimedia landscapes, Landsberg Gallery, SoHo. Five o'clock, Regina Resnik opera symposium, Florence Gould Auditorium. You've got quite a day mapped out for yourself.

MARJORIE: I should be barred from all of those places. I'm of limited intellect. Never have had one original thought.

IRA: That is not true. If I were half as intellectually curious as you.

MARJORIE: Curious, yes. Profound, no.

IRA: What do you call "profound"?

MARJORIE: The ability to think in the abstract. Oh, Ira, can't we just face it? We're Russian peasants with the *shtetl*. We have no right to be attending art installations at the Whitney. We should be tilling the soil, pulling a plow.

[IRA*'s beeper goes off. He takes out his phone and dials the number.*]

IRA: Jeffrey Krampf, one of my grad students. Brilliant, tortured mind. I think he's on crack. What can I do? Let him flounder? Now, the line's busy. You're so tough on us. You know, that last production of *Waiting for Godot* affected me deeply. I had the sense that I finally understood what that play was about.

MARJORIE: You understood the story. You think it's about two guys who get stranded by the Tappan Zee Bridge. They're not waiting for Triple A. It's about—I can't even explain what it's about. That is my conundrum. I don't understand the play any better than you. I'm a fraud. A cultural poseur. To quote Kafka, "I am a cage in search of a bird."

IRA: You're hungry.

MARJORIE: Yes, I'm hungry.

[*An agonized cry.*]

Hungry for meaning!

IRA: You need food, real food. You made that wonderful meatloaf and didn't eat a bite. You're gonna lose potassium. I'm cutting you off a square of this Entenmanns. Just to nibble. You'll end up in the hospital with an IV at this rate.

[IRA *hands her the piece of cake.*]

MARJORIE: Thank you, Ira.

[*Eating a bite and yielding a bit.*]

It is good.

THE HOUSE OF RAMON IGLESIA

BY JOSÉ RIVERA

CHARACTERS

RAMON IGLESIA *(50s) has the dream of quitting his janitorial job and moving his wife,* DOLORES *(50), and their three sons from their Long Island home back to Puerto Rico (where* RAMON *and* DOLORES *are from). But life is not being very cooperative with* RAMON*'s dream.*

SCENE

The Iglesia family's Long Island home.

TIME

Evening. (The play was produced in 1983.)

[DOLORES *continues to write.* RAMON *sits.*]

RAMON: [*Suspiciously.*] What are you writing?

DOLORES: Nothing, Ramon. It's nothing.

RAMON: Dolores, what is it?

DOLORES: I'm writing to Doña Perez. I'm writing about . . . how much I'm sad about Julio. How much I miss him, Ramon.

RAMON: He had to do what he had to do. There was nothing for Julio to do in Holbrook.

DOLORES: He could die where he's going. What if he dies?

RAMON: He's not going to die. Julio is a beast!

DOLORES: If they hurt my little boy, I don't know what I'll do . . .

RAMON: [*Crossing to* DOLORES.] Come on, old lady, stop.

DOLORES: [*Crossing to sofa, sits.*] He never *relaxed,* Ramon. He worked after school every day—

RAMON: [*Reading her letters.*] He loves responsibility. Loves to give orders!

DOLORES: [*Packing clothes in a box.*] Was he angry with us, Ramon?

RAMON: *Mamacita,* please . . .

[RAMON *crumples her letter and puts it in his pocket.*]

I don't want you talking about this and writing it in your letters! You have no proof, Dolores!

DOLORES: Javier is my proof! When he came home from school he was a stranger. The same will happen to Julio: they'll change him.

RAMON: Shhhhhh, Javier will hear.

DOLORES: Javier doesn't kiss you good night anymore. Up to the day he left he kissed you good night. That made me feel so good.

RAMON: I don't know what's wrong with him but he's still my Javier! Maybe he'll come to Puerto Rico one day.

DOLORES: No, he won't. And we won't beg him! Do you hear? I'll never beg for my son's affection and neither will you!

DOLORES: I heard what he said, Ramon—.

RAMON: You always understand when you want to understand, don't you?

DOLORES: You can't let him buy another house! He has to take this one! This house!

RAMON: This house is Ramon Iglesia's house.

DOLORES: Ramon Iglesia's house is in Puerto Rico.

RAMON: [*Crossing to* DOLORES.] Do you really think I can start a little business down there? Can you really see us going back there? Back to the little farms and the hills and the people who never left? What I'm going to do down there?

[DOLORES *crosses away from* RAMON.]

I thought about this all week, about my house, about the way it's grown with things, for nineteen years, all the bits and pieces of Ramon Iglesia. Even the accidents—.

DOLORES: Not accidents, Ramon: mistakes.

RAMON: Mistakes then. What. The night I lost the diner and the boys and I filled the station wagon with all the food and things we could save from it. Brought it here. Boxes of pots and plates and bags of rice. The house was full and fat and beautiful.

DOLORES: I swear on the spirit of my little Felicia, if you keep me here another year, it'll be our last year together. Every year you promise me we'll go back and every year you break your promise. No more, Ramon! I let you do what you want to do for nineteen years, now I do what I want. If you don't, Ramon, I'll leave you. I'll go home by myself.

RAMON: *We don't have any money!*

DOLORES: There's somebody in this house with enough money to help you.

RAMON: I'm not going to go to him, I can't go to him.

DOLORES: [*Pointing offstage.*] He's right there. He knows what we need. When he returned from school what did we hear but some big, big talk about helping the poor? Giving to the poor! Well, Ramon, *we* are the poor. You and me.

RAMON: I can't take from him, Dolores, will you listen to what I say!

DOLORES: No! Because it's only fear talking to me. You're so afraid of him, I turn red with shame thinking about it!

RAMON: I'm not afraid of Javier—.

DOLORES: You're afraid of him and he's ashamed of you!

RAMON: Javier is not ashamed of his father! I wouldn't let him live in the house—!

DOLORES: You let him live in the house! You let him eat your food and spit it back in your face! You let him keep you in this country because you're afraid of him!

RAMON: Dolores, don't you use that word with me again!

DOLORES: Coward! Coward!

A DELICATE BALANCE

BY EDWARD ALBEE

CHARACTERS

AGNES *(late 50s) is a handsome and elegant woman;* TOBIAS *(early 60s) is her husband.*

SCENE

The living room of a large and well-appointed suburban home.

TIME

Seven-thirty in the morning.

[TOBIAS *alone, in a chair, wearing pajamas and a robe, slippers. Awake.* AGNES *enters, wearing a dressing gown which could pass for a hostess gown. Her movements are not assertive, and her tone is gentle.*]

AGNES: [*Seeing him.*] Ah, there you are.

TOBIAS: [*Not looking at her, but at his watch; there is very little emotion in his voice.*] Seven-thirty a.m., and all's well . . . I guess.

AGNES: So odd.

TOBIAS: Hm?

AGNES: There was a stranger in my room last night.

TOBIAS: Who?

AGNES: You.

TOBIAS: Ah.

AGNES: It was nice to have you there.

TOBIAS: [*Slight smile.*] Hm.

AGNES: *Le temps perdu.* I've never understood that; *perdu* means lost, not merely . . . past, but it was nice to have you there, though I remember, when it was a constancy, how easily I would fall asleep, pace my breathing to your breathing, and if we were touching! Ah, what a splendid cocoon that was. But last night—what a shame, what sadness—you were a stranger, and I stayed awake.

TOBIAS: *I'm* sorry.

AGNES: Were you asleep at all?

TOBIAS: No.

AGNES: I would go half, then wake—your unfamiliar presence, sir. I *could* get used to it again.

TOBIAS: Yes?

AGNES: I think.

TOBIAS: You didn't have your talk with Julia—your all-night lulling.

AGNES: No; she wouldn't let me stay. "Look to your own house" is what she said. You stay down long?

TOBIAS: When?

AGNES: After . . . before you came to bed.

TOBIAS: Some.

[*Laughs softly, ruefully.*]

I almost went into *my* room . . . by habit . . . by mistake, rather, but then I realized that your room is my room because my room is Julia's because Julia's room is . . .

AGNES: . . . yes.

[*Goes to him, strokes his temple.*]

And I was awake when you left my room again.

TOBIAS: You could have said.

AGNES: I felt shy.

TOBIAS: Hm!

AGNES: Did you go to Claire?

TOBIAS: I never go to Claire.

AGNES: Did you go to Claire to talk?

TOBIAS: I never go to Claire.

AGNES: We must always envy someone we should not, be jealous of those who have so much less. You and Claire make so much more sense together, talk so well.

TOBIAS: I never go to Claire at night, or talk with her alone—save publicly.

AGNES: [*Small smile.*] In public rooms . . . like this.

TOBIAS: Yes.

AGNES: Have *never.*

TOBIAS: Please?

AGNES: Do we dislike happiness? We manufacture such a portion of our own despair . . . such busy folk.

TOBIAS: We are a highly moral land: we assume we have done great wrong. We find the things.

AGNES: I shall start missing you again—when you move from my room . . . if you do. I had stopped, I believe.

TOBIAS: [*Little chuckle.*] Oh, you're an honest woman.

AGNES: Well, we need *one* . . . in every house.

TOBIAS: It's very strange . . . to be downstairs, in a room where everyone has been, and is gone . . . very late, after the heat has gone—the furnace *and* the bodies: the hour or two before the sun comes up, the furnace starts again. And tonight especially: the cigarettes still in the ashtrays—odd, metallic smell. The odors of a room don't mix, late, when there's no one there, and I think the silence helps it . . . and the lack of bodies. Each . . . thing stands out in its place.

AGNES: What did you decide?

TOBIAS: And when you *do* come down . . . if you do, at three, or four, and you've left a light or two—in case someone should come in late, I suppose, but who is there left? The inn is full—it's rather . . . Godlike, if I may presume: to look at it all, reconstruct, with such . . . de*tach*ment, see your*self* you, Julia . . . Look at it all . . . play it out again, *watch*.

AGNES: Judge?

TOBIAS: No; that's being in it. Watch. And if you have a drink or two . . .

AGNES: Did you?

TOBIAS: And if you have a drink or two, very late, in the quiet, tired, the mind . . . lets loose.

AGNES: Yes?

TOBIAS: And you watch it as it reasons, all with a kind of . . . grateful delight, at the same time sadly, 'cause you know that when the daylight comes the pressures will be on, and all the insight won't be worth a damn.

AGNES: What did you decide?

TOBIAS: You can sit and watch. You can have . . . so clear a picture, see everybody moving through his own jungle . . . an insight into all the reasons, all the needs.

AGNES: Good. And what did you decide?

TOBIAS: [*No complaint.*] Why is the room so dirty? Can't we have better servants, some help who . . . help?

AGNES: They keep far better hours than we, that's all. They are a comment on our habits, a reminder that we are out of step—that is why we pay them . . . so very, very much. Neither a servant nor a master be. Remember?

TOBIAS: I remember when . . .

AGNES: [*Picking it right up.*] . . . you were very young and lived at home, and the servants were awake whenever you were: six a.m. for your breakfast when you wanted it, or five in the morning when you came home drunk and seventeen, washing the vomit from the car, and you, telling no one; stealing just enough each month, by arrangement with the stores, to keep them in a decent wage; generations of them: the laundress, blind and always dying, and the cook, who did a better dinner drunk than sober. Those servants? Those days? When you were young, and lived at home?

TOBIAS: Hmmm.

AGNES: [*Sweet, sad.*] Well, my darling, you are not young now, and you do not live at home.

TOBIAS: Where do I live?

AGNES: The dark sadness. Yes?

TOBIAS: What are we going to do?

AGNES: What did you decide?

TOBIAS: [*Pause; they smile.*] Nothing.

AGNES: Well, you must. Your house is not in order, sir. It's full to bursting.

TOBIAS: Yes. You've got to help me here.

AGNES: No. I don't *think* so.

TOBIAS: No?

AGNES: No. I thought a little last night, too: while you were seeing everything so clearly here. I lay in the dark, and I . . . revisited— our life, the years and years. There are many things a woman does: she bears the children—if there *is* that blessing. Blessing? Yes, I suppose, even with the sadness. She runs the house, for what that's worth: makes sure there's food, and not just anything, and decent linen; looks well; assumes whatever duties are demanded—if she is in love, or loves; and plans.

TOBIAS: [*Mumbled.*] I know, I know . . .

AGNES: And plans. Right to the end of it; expects to be alone one day, abandoned by the heart attack or the cancer, *prepares* for that. And prepares earlier, for the children to become *adult* strangers instead of growing ones, for that loss, and for the body chemistry, the end of what the Bible tells us is our usefulness. The reins we hold! It's a team of twenty horses, and we sit there, and we watch the road and check the leather . . . if our . . . man is so disposed. But there are things we do not do.

TOBIAS: Yes?

AGNES: Yes.

[*Harder.*]

We don't decide the route.

TOBIAS: You're copping out . . . as they say.

AGNES: No, indeed.

TOBIAS: [*Quiet anger.*] *Yes,* you are!

AGNES: [*Quiet warning.*] Don't you yell at me.

TOBIAS: You're copping *out*!

AGNES: [*Quiet, calm, and almost smug.*] We follow. We let our . . . men decide the moral issues.

TOBIAS: [*Quite angry.*] Never! You've never done that in your life!

AGNES: Always, my darling. Whatever you decide . . . I'll make it work; I'll run it for you so you'll never know there's been a change in anything.

TOBIAS: [*Almost laughing, shaking his head.*] No. No.

AGNES: So, let me know.

TOBIAS: I *know* I'm tired. I know I've hardly slept at all: I know I've sat down here, and thought . . .

AGNES: And made your decisions.

TOBIAS: But I have not *judged.* I told you that.

AGNES: Well, when you have . . . you let me know.

TOBIAS: NO!

AGNES: You'll wake the house.

TOBIAS: *I'll wake* the house!

AGNES: This is not the time for you to lose control.

TOBIAS: I'LL LOSE CONTROL! I have *sat* here . . . in the cold, in the empty cold, I have sat here alone, and . . . I've looked at *every*thing, *all* of it. I thought of it, and Julia, and Claire . . .

AGNES: And Edna? And Harry?

TOBIAS: [*Tiny pause.*] Well, of course! What do you think!

AGNES: [*Tiny smile.*] I don't know. I'm listening.

PART II

SCENES FOR TWO WOMEN

THE OLD SETTLER

BY JOHN HENRY REDWOOD

CHARACTERS

ELIZABETH *(55) and her sister,* QUILLY *(53), are trying to make ends meet in 1943 Harlem. Then* ELIZABETH *decides to take in a boarder, the much younger Husband.*

SCENE

The living room of the apartment of Elizabeth Borny in Harlem, New York City.

TIME

Friday, early evening. Early spring, 1943.

[*The apartment door opens and* ELIZABETH (BESS) BORNY, *a black woman of fifty-five, enters leaving the door open. She is carrying a black pocketbook, black gloves, and a paper plate of food covered with wax paper. Elizabeth crosses into the kitchen and puts the plate on top of the stove. She then crosses and turns off the radio. After a beat, another black woman,* QUILLY MCGRATH, *fifty-three, enters laboriously, closing the door. She is carrying a white pocketbook and white gloves.* QUILLY *stops in the doorway catching her breath.*]

QUILLY: Oh, Lord have mercy! Whew! Them stairs. Shoot!

ELIZABETH: You forgot to turn the lights off again, Quilly.

[QUILLY *crosses to a chair and sits.*]

QUILLY: I left it on so these robbers and rapists would think somebody's home. That's the way I did it in Brooklyn.

ELIZABETH: You ain't living in Brooklyn no more. I've got to pay the electric here.

QUILLY: Shoot!

[*She picks up a hand fan from under an end table and begins to fan herself.*]

Goodness, it's hot already. What we got to eat, Bess?

ELIZABETH: You're supposed to be cooking this week. What you asking me for?

[*She enters from the kitchen.*]

QUILLY: If you cook tonight, I'll take two of your nights next week.

ELIZABETH: No you won't. You'll scheme and connive to get out of it just like you're doing now. Cooking all that food on Saturday and then we eat the same old leftovers all week long.

QUILLY: Shoot, Bess, I'm tired. That's the God's honest truth.

ELIZABETH: I don't understand it. You're two years younger than I am and you act like you're five years older.

[*She exits the bedroom taking off her hat.*]

QUILLY: [*Calling offstage.*] Age ain't got nothing to do with it, shoot.

ELIZABETH: [*From offstage.*] You should be tired. Running around like a chicken with his head cut off trying to get to that funeral.

QUILLY: And you still made us late.

ELIZABETH: I'm in no rush to get to no funeral; mine or somebody else's.

QUILLY: I wanted to get a good seat.

ELIZABETH: There's no such thing as a good seat at a funeral, Quilly.

QUILLY: I wanted to get where I could see.

ELIZABETH: I'm surprised you didn't get one of them folding chairs and sit right up front next to the casket.

QUILLY: [*Ignoring* ELIZABETH.] Did you see that dress they put on her? That was one ugly dress.

[ELIZABETH *re-enters from the bedroom buttoning her housedress.*]

ELIZABETH: Her sister said that was her favorite dress. Said, her husband wanted to put her away in something she liked and wore when she was living . . .

QUILLY: It was ugly then too, shoot.

ELIZABETH: . . . so her sister picked out that dress.

QUILLY: Quiet as it's kept, that dress probably killed her. Then they put her in all that bright red lipstick! Now they know she was too dark for all that bright red lipstick. Shoot. She looked better when she was living.

ELIZABETH: You're supposed to, Quilly.

QUILLY: That sure is some way to spend eternity, in an ugly dress and bright red lipstick.

ELIZABETH: Quilly, will you please be quiet about that woman!

QUILLY: All I'm saying is, we're sisters, and I hope whichever one of us goes first, the other one does better by her than that poor woman was done by her husband and her sister. That's all I'm saying, shoot.

[*Pause.*]

You think he's ever going to get married again?

ELIZABETH: The woman's not in the ground good, Quilly. He's got to let a decent amount of time pass.

QUILLY: What for? She ain't going to get no deader.

[*She stands and begins pulling on her girdle.*]

I sure hope they didn't put no girdle on her. She'll be pulling on that thing forever, shoot.

(*Pause.*)

You getting ready to cook.

ELIZABETH: I told you I wasn't cooking. I'm going to eat that dinner I brought back from the church.

[*She exits to the kitchen and begins to eat.*]

QUILLY: See now, that ain't right. You went down there and got you a dinner and didn't get me one.

ELIZABETH: They ran out of food. I told you, I said, "Quilly, come on now, let's get us a dinner." But no, you wanted to sit there until the last minute waiting for them to close that coffin.

QUILLY: It wasn't no such thing. I didn't want all them snotty-nose kids, running around down there with their greasy hands, to touch my dress. I ain't got no money to be buying another white dress, shoot.

ELIZABETH: You didn't have to wear that dress today, Quilly. You wasn't doing nothing but showing off.

QUILLY: The Ladies of the Golden Scepter were . . .

ELIZABETH: Don't nobody in that church know nothing about no Ladies of the Golden Scepter . . . except you and Sister Wallace. You ain't been to a mattering since you moved back here from Brooklyn a month ago. Over fifty and you and her running around the church in some old ugly uniform looking like the Gold Dust Twins.

QUILLY: Oh, you just jealous.

ELIZABETH: All right, I'm jealous. But I tell you this, you opened your mouth about frying chicken for Sister Wallace and her children to take on the train when they go back down to Georgia for Mother's Day. Now, don't you fix it in your head to try and connive me into frying that chicken because that's my week to cook. She's your lodge sister.

QUILLY: I ain't going to ask you nothing.

ELIZABETH: I'm just saying. I know you, Quilly.

QUILLY: I ain't studying you.

[*Pause.*]

I sure wish I had somebody to go to Singleton's restaurant and get me something to eat. I can't climb them stairs no more today . . . not with this girdle on, shoot.

ELIZABETH: Then take it off and stop complaining.

[*Pause.*]

Ain't no use you looking, Quilly. You ain't getting none of my pig feet. Now you go on and eat them leftovers you cooked for the whole week.

[*The doorbell rings.*]

Look and see who it is.

QUILLY: Shoot.

[*She crosses to the window and looks out. Calling.*]

Who is it?

[*Pause.*]

Oh, it's you . . . When you ring the bell, come out and stand on the sidewalk so we can see who . . .

ELIZABETH: Who are you talking to like that?

QUILLY: Your "roomer."

ELIZABETH: Husband?

QUILLY: Yeah, "Husband."

ELIZABETH: Did you throw the key down to him?

QUILLY: I had to find out who it was first. How many times have we told him to come out and stand where we can see him after he rings the bell. He rings the bell then stands in the hallway. Now how are we supposed to know who we're throwing the key to if he stands in the hallway where nobody can see him? Shoot! What happened to the keys you gave him?

ELIZABETH: I don't know. Just throw him the key, Quilly.

QUILLY: [*Looking for the key.*] I don't know why you want to take in some strange man anyway . . .

[*She finds the key tied to a handkerchief.*]

You don't know nothing about him . . .

[*She crosses to the window and throws the key out. She shouts out the window.*]

Here!

[*To* Elizabeth.]

You don't know who you're letting into our house . . . He could be a rapist or something.

ELIZABETH: Well, unless something is wrong with him, you and me don't have nothing to worry about.

QUILLY: I don't know what you're talking about. You better talk for yourself, shoot.

[Elizabeth *stands in the doorway and talks as she eats.*]

ELIZABETH: He wrote to me a couple of times after we agreed about him renting the room . . . and I wrote him back. He's a very nice, polite, young man. Now, I want you to try and be nice to him. We need the money.

QUILLY: Where's he going to get money from? He ain't got no job.

ELIZABETH: How's he going to get a job when he's only been up here for three days, Quilly?

QUILLY: Well, if he'd stop running all over Harlem looking for that woman every single day, he might be able to find him a job. And why ain't he in the army like a lot of young men his age? There's a war going on. You ever ask yourself that . . . or him?

ELIZABETH: No, I never asked myself that . . . or him. And if he wants me . . . or you to know, he'll tell us. And as far as his money goes, as long as he gets it honest, it's none of our business where he gets it from.

QUILLY: Well, if it's none of our business where he gets it from, then we don't know where he gets it from, so we don't know if he gets it honest or not.

ELIZABETH: The man ain't going to be up here forever, Quilly. Just as soon as he finds his girlfriend, he's going back down home.

QUILLY: Yeah, that's what they all say until they get up here and I starts getting good to them. What's taking him so long to come upstairs?

ELIZABETH: Deacon Slater said that Husband came into some money from selling some of the land left to him after his mama passed on. Now, he's paid a month's rent in advance and Deacon Slater has spoken for him and that's enough for me.

QUILLY: Well, Deacon Slater don't have to live with him. That's all I've got to say, shoot. And you can't trust no gator-tail eating geechees no way. And both of them from the same hometown too. And one geechee is up here looking for another geechee who ran away from him . . . What's the name of that place he comes from?

ELIZABETH: [*Whispering.*] You just remember that his rent is helping us keep this apartment.

QUILLY: I don't want to have nothing to do with him. All I want him to do is stay out of my way.

MARVIN'S ROOM
BY SCOTT MCPHERSON

CHARACTERS

BESSIE *(40) is a woman who has been the caretaker for her dying father, Marvin, for the past twenty years; she also looks after her aunt* RUTH *(70), who has several collapsed vertebrae, for which she wears an electrode pack on her waist to control her constant pain. But* BESSIE's *health is also in crisis—she has recently been told that she has leukemia.*

SCENE
Bessie's home in Florida.

TIME
5:25 p.m.

> [BESSIE's *home.* RUTH, *a woman of seventy with a slight hunchback, sleeps in a chair.* BESSIE *enters with groceries. Her arms are bruised from the doctor's attempts to draw blood.*]

BESSIE: Aunt Ruth? Ruth?

RUTH: Hmmm.

BESSIE: Ruth, you're not supposed to sleep sitting in a chair, honey. It puts too much pressure on your lower spine.

RUTH: You're home.

BESSIE: Do you want to go lie down?

RUTH: Don't you look pretty.

BESSIE: Do you want to lie down?

RUTH: No, no. Don't you bother about me now. I'm just fine.

BESSIE: You're sleeping in the chair.

RUTH: I am?

BESSIE: You were, when I came in. That's not good for you.

RUTH: Oh, stupid me. You tell me right away when I'm sleeping because I don't always know.

BESSIE: I just got home. I couldn't tell you sooner.

RUTH: Look, this control box pulled my sweater. I'm going to have a hole there. It's my own fault.

BESSIE: How's Dad?

RUTH: What did the doctor say?

BESSIE: Oh, he made a big to-do so I wouldn't feel like he was overcharging me.

RUTH: He's a very nice man, isn't he? He has very handsome hands.

BESSIE: It wasn't Dr. Serat.

RUTH: Bessie, oh, what happened to your arms?

BESSIE: They took a little blood.

RUTH: It looks tender. Should you see a doctor?

BESSIE: I just came from the doctor.

RUTH: Did you show him your arms?

BESSIE: Yes, he just had some trouble finding my veins.

RUTH: That sounds serious.

BESSIE: I have a vitamin deficiency, Ruth, that's all.

RUTH: It's because you don't make stinky often enough.

BESSIE: I do so.

RUTH: Stinky is poison. You have to get rid of it. That's why when you're constipated you have a headache.

BESSIE: [*Picking up Marvin's pills.*] Did you give Dad his five o'clock?

RUTH: What did I do? What time is it now?

BESSIE: Five twenty-five.

RUTH: No, but I was going to.

BESSIE: Honey, I asked you to do one thing.

RUTH: I'm so stupid. I'm useless, you know.

BESSIE: You are not.

RUTH: It's my cure, I think. It's because I have these wires in my brain.

BESSIE: It's not your cure. You blame your cure for everything.

RUTH: I can feel them. They tingle when I bathe.

BESSIE: You used to blame your pain, now you blame your cure.

RUTH: It's gotten so I'm afraid to get in the tub.

BESSIE: You've always been afraid to get in the tub.

RUTH: Oh, no, no, no. I've never been afraid to get in the tub.

BESSIE: You make me come in and towel down the floor.

RUTH: That's because I'm afraid to get *out* of the tub. The floor gets so wet. Do you remember Mrs. Steingetz fell and the poor thing cracked her head wide open? No one found her until her family came down for Thanksgiving, and even then not until the end of their visit.

BESSIE: I remember.

RUTH: She'd still be there if they hadn't run out of towels in the guest bath.

BESSIE: I know.

RUTH: I don't want to be lying on the tiles till the holiday season.

BESSIE: You won't.

RUTH: I mean, my goodness, it's only just June.

BESSIE: I hope you remembered to give Dad his four o'clock.

RUTH: Oh, stupid me.

BESSIE: Ruth, he is supposed to get his pills at the same time every day.

RUTH: I know, but—

BESSIE: You never forget to watch your program, do you? You never forget what time your show comes on.

RUTH: You usually give Marvin his pills.

BESSIE: Today I asked you to.

[BESSIE *goes into Marvin's room to give him his pills while* RUTH *crosses to the kitchen to get her vitamins.*]

BESSIE: [*To Marvin, who is lying inert in the bed.*] I have been running all over today. Would you quit hogging the bed so I can sit down! Here. Take these now. We're a little off schedule today . . . Have you been pulling at your sheets? You've got them all twisted. That can't be very comfortable . . . What does that face mean? Mr.

Innocent! . . . How about some tomato soup? And some juice? . . . Water? . . . Juice? . . . Which? . . . Juice.

[*She re-enters.*]

He's confused. He doesn't know why he's getting his four o'clock at five-thirty.

RUTH: [*With her pills.*] Do you want to take one of mine for your deficiency?

BESSIE: I'll get some real vitamins later.

RUTH: These are real. They're just easier to swallow because I don't like to swallow things. Do you want Pebbles or Bam-Bam?

BESSIE: Ruth.

RUTH: Dino came out.

BESSIE: Dino's fine.

RUTH: Chew it up good. We have to take care of you, too.

[*Slight pause.*] That cat came around today.

BESSIE: Honey, it's just a little kitty. It won't bother you.

RUTH: It came right up to the house and stared in at me. It sat there like it was a stone.

BESSIE: Uh-huh.

RUTH: What do you think it wants?

BESSIE: I don't think it wants anything.

RUTH: I know you have things you have to do and it's hard getting someone to come in, but I wish you wouldn't leave me at home alone.

BESSIE: Honey, you do fine.

RUTH: But I'm so useless. What if Marvin were to choke on something again? What if he gets hold of the Yahtzee dice or tries to kill himself with the Parcheesi men?

BESSIE: Dr. Serat explained this to you. He puts things in his mouth because it gives him pleasure. He likes the way it feels. You know how much he likes it when you bounce the light off your compact mirror? This is another thing he likes. He's not trying to choke himself.

RUTH: What if he dies while you're out of the house?

BESSIE: Then you'll call me and I'll come home.

[*Pause.*]

You've got your cure now. There's no reason you can't help out around here. I don't ask you too much.

RUTH: Do you want me to make the tomato soup?

BESSIE: No. You'd make a mess of it.

[*She starts to make the soup.*]

RUTH: I'll go bounce the light around Marvin's room.

BESSIE: That's a good idea. Why don't you do that. And later we'll watch some TV. All right?

RUTH: All right.

[*She goes into Marvin's room.*]

BESSIE: [*Pouring a can of soup into a metal pan.*] Do you remember all the foods Dad used to like—flapjacks and bacon and eggs—

[RUTH *moves her mirror above Marvin's bed.*]

—and grits and biscuits and roast beef and green beans and mashed potatoes and apple pie and ice cream he churned himself.

SHTICK
BY HENRY MEYERSON

CHARACTERS

HELEN *(60) is the very practical and capable wife of Murray, an aging comedian;* GLADYS *(55) is* HELEN*'s younger sister, more freewheeling, stylishly attired, and carefree than* HELEN.

SCENE
A hospital waiting area.

TIME
The present.

[HELEN *is pacing.* GLADYS *enters.*]

HELEN: Thanks for coming, Gladys. Hospitals are not really people-friendly places.

GLADYS: Not a problem. We're sisters, right? Where else should I be. So tell me what happened.

HELEN: He was in the middle of one of his jigs . . .

GLADYS: He was dancing?

HELEN: I meant gigs. I always get that wrong. Gigs.

GLADYS: Where?

HELEN: What difference does it make?

GLADYS: No difference. Go ahead.

HELEN: I will if you promise not to ask a bunch of your silly questions.

GLADYS: Go ahead.

HELEN: He was in the middle of one of his . . . performances . . . in New Jersey, okay?

GLADYS: Figures. Okay.

HELEN: Why does it figure?

GLADYS: He loved New Jersey.

HELEN: How do you know?

GLADYS: It's not important. Go ahead.

HELEN: So Jack said . . .

GLADYS: His agent?

HELEN: Yes, his agent. How do you know his agent?

GLADYS: Never mind. Go ahead.

HELEN: Jack said . . . he said . . .

   [*She begins to cry.*]

GLADYS: That's okay, Helen.

HELEN: I'm not asking permission, Gladys.

GLADYS: So Jack said . . .

HELEN: Jack said Murray just collapsed. Just fell over. The microphone fell on top of him. He fell and didn't move.

GLADYS: Then?

HELEN: Then? He just laid there, Gladys. The audience thought it was part of the act. He laid there with the Goddamn microphone on top of him, and the audiences laughed their asses off. Finally, Jack got some guys to carry him off and he wound up here.

GLADYS: How awful.

HELEN: I got the call last night. They rushed him here.

GLADYS: This is a great place, Helen. He'll get great care.

HELEN: How do you know?

GLADYS: I dated some doctors from here.

HELEN: You dated doctors from everywhere.

GLADYS: Let's not discuss my sex life now.

HELEN: You're right. I'm sorry.

GLADYS: You've always been critical of my dating.

HELEN: Only because you haven't been.

GLADYS: Haven't been dating?

HELEN: Haven't been critical.

GLADYS: I'm here for you, Helen. Get off me.

HELEN: "Get off me" is a line that Murray would never pass up, but I'll let it go.

GLADYS: Given the situation, the news about Murray, I have to tell you something, Helen. I just hope this doesn't cause tension between us.

HELEN: No more than I'm feeling by this conversation at this moment.

GLADYS: Good. Because not only are we sisters but good friends, and you have to believe I treasure our relationship.

HELEN: This is starting to worry me, Gladys. Tell me now. What the hell are you getting at?

GLADYS: [*Almost unintelligible.*] I had an affair with Murray.

HELEN: What? I didn't . . .

GLADYS: [*As before.*] I had an affair with Murray.

HELEN: If you don't slow down, I'm going to hit you.

GLADYS: [*Normal.*] I had an affair with Murray.

HELEN: What?

GLADYS: I had an affair . . .

HELEN: STOP! I heard you, I just don't understand you.

GLADYS: It started three years ago. I thought it would be important for you to know, in case you know . . . Murray . . . well . . .

HELEN: I still don't . . .

GLADYS: We bumped into each other at the Jersey Shore . . . He was appearing at . . .

HELEN: . . . yeah I know what he does, Gladys.

GLADYS: We talked, had a few drinks . . .

HELEN: . . . I said I know what he does, Gladys. What I want to know is why.

GLADYS: Maybe it was the alcohol.

HELEN: For three years? What the hell were you two drinking?

GLADYS: No, I meant . . .

HELEN: What the hell were you two thinking?

GLADYS: I'm not sure what . . .

HELEN: HOW COULD YOU DO THIS TO ME?

GLADYS: Stop yelling at me. This is very difficult for me too.

HELEN: Not like for me, Gladys. And why would you tell me? Did I really need to know this? Did I really need to know this now?

GLADYS: I've always believed that before a person dies, everything should be laid out on the table.

HELEN: Just like you were laid out in bed.

GLADYS: That's uncalled for, Helen.

HELEN: You figured when you told me I was going to kill you, and you wanted to make sure you died with a confession on your lips.

GLADYS: I was talking about Murray, not me. You're misinterpreting what I said.

THINNER THAN WATER

BY MELISSA ROSS

CHARACTERS

RENEE *(40)* is a working-class mother whose dad is dying; and
GWEN *(50) has been shacked up with* RENEE*'s dad for several years.*

SCENE

Hospital parking lot.

TIME

The present.

[RENEE *sits alone crying.* GWEN *enters. She calmly lights a
cigarette and hands it to* RENEE. *She lights one for herself. She
sits next to her. They smoke silently. They do not look at each other
throughout the scene.*]

RENEE: I thought you wanted cigarettes to be illegal.

GWEN: I do. I also think guns should be illegal. Doesn't mean I
don't wanna shoot people sometimes.

RENEE: Fair enough.

[Silence. They smoke.]

Hey, Gwen?

GWEN: Uh-huh?

RENEE: Who would you shoot? If you got a free pass. No repercussions.

GWEN: Anybody at all?

RENEE: Uh-huh.

GWEN: Do I only get one?

RENEE: Is there a list?

GWEN: Depends on the day.

RENEE: Okay. Today then. Who would you shoot if you got the chance today?

GWEN: Today . . .

RENEE: Uh-huh.

GWEN: That doctor.

RENEE: Which one.

GWEN: That one with the name we couldn't remember.

RENEE: Was that Asshole Doctor Number One? Or Asshole Doctor Number Two?

GWEN: The one with the lisp and the shifty eyes.

RENEE: One. That was One.

GWEN: All right then. I would shoot Asshole Doctor Number One.

RENEE: Okay. You get One—I'll get Two. We'll take 'em both out, Gwen. You and me.

GWEN: Deal. And maybe that nurse?

RENEE: Which one?

GWEN: The one who kept clicking her tongue.

RENEE: The tsk-tsker?

GWEN: Yeah her. She was so condescending.

RENEE: She sure was. Okay. We can get rid of her too.

[*Pause.*]

And the cell phone guy!

GWEN: The one breaking up with his girlfriend?

RENEE: Yeah, him. And the girlfriend?

GWEN: [*Pause.*] And the smelly food woman.

RENEE: Oh God yes. Her too. Gone.

GWEN: People shouldn't be allowed to eat tuna in public.

RENEE: I'll smoke to that.

[*They smoke.*]

And family?

GWEN: What about 'em?

RENEE: Can I shoot my family?

GWEN: Today?

RENEE: Yeah.

GWEN: Today you can shoot anybody you want.

RENEE: Okay then. I wanna shoot my family. All of 'em.

[*Pause.*]

Except my kids. I'll spare my kids.

GWEN: You got it.

[*They smoke.*]

Doesn't it feel great?

RENEE: Shooting people?

GWEN: Smoking.

RENEE: Ugh. It's disgusting. It's so disgusting. I feel disgusting.

[*She takes a long drag.*]

I only smoke when I already hate myself and wanna die anyway so I figure why the hell not. Like today? Today I wanna shoot everybody in the world and then I wanna shoot myself.

GWEN: You'd regret it tomorrow.

RENEE: Yeah, but I'd be dead, so it wouldn't matter.

[*Pause.*]

You didn't have to come out here.

GWEN: I know. You say that a lot. Tell people what they don't have to do.

RENEE: I don't like to be fussed over.

GWEN: I don't believe that. I think you're someone who could use some fussing. Maybe you should just try saying thank you.

DINNER WITH FRIENDS

BY DONALD MARGULIES

CHARACTERS

KAREN *and* BETH *(both 40s) are best friends. A while ago,* BETH *was left by her now ex-husband, Tom, who* KAREN *and her husband, Gabe, had set* BETH *up with.*

SCENE

Karen and Gabe's garden patio.

TIME

Present day. Spring.

[KAREN *and* BETH *set the patio table and proceed to have lunch.*]

BETH: [*Entering, mid-conversation.*] When you promise your little girl you're gonna call at eight o'clock and eight o'clock comes and goes . . .

KAREN: Oh no . . .

BETH: [*Continuous.*] *And* nine, *and* ten . . .

KAREN: That's terrible.

BETH: She's devastated—sobbing!—and *I'm* the one who has to do damage control!

KAREN: The poor kid . . .

BETH: [*Continuous.*] *He's* out there somewhere cavorting with his *girl*friend, and Laurie's leaving all these heartbreaking messages on his voice mail: "Daddy, where are you, Daddy?"

KAREN: Oh, God . . .

BETH: [*Continuous.*] He just doesn't get it!

KAREN: Did he finally call?

BETH: Yeah! At one o'clock in the morning!

KAREN: No!

BETH: "Tell Laurie I'm really sorry."

KAREN: What a schmuck.

BETH: "If you want to tell your daughter you're sorry, call her when she's *awake* and tell her yourself!"

KAREN: Unbelievable. Was he always like this or is this what happens to people when they break up? Do they get stupid, or what?

BETH: I know!

KAREN: I'm telling you, this whole thing with you and Tom . . . It's like men get by for years without really talking to you and then, one day, when they finally do, it's to tell you they're leaving.

BETH: You and *Gabe* talk . . .

KAREN: [*Equivocally.*] Yeah . . .

[*A beat.*]

You sure you don't mind eating outside?

BETH: Not at all; the sun feels great.

KAREN: I feel like I haven't seen you in ages!

BETH: I know.

KAREN: You look wonderful! You really do!

BETH: Thank you.

KAREN: We were worried about you.

BETH: Really?

KAREN: You disappeared on us.

BETH: I didn't mean to.

KAREN: I'd leave messages and you wouldn't call back right away . . .

BETH: [*Over ". . . right away . . ."*] I know, I'm sorry, I needed some time to myself. *You* know.

KAREN: [*Nods, then.*] You're not mad at me or anything, are you?

BETH: [*Over ". . . are you?"*] Mad at you? Why should I be mad at you?

KAREN: I don't know . . . when this thing first happened, we talked all the time.

BETH: I know.

KAREN: You dropped *by* all the time, then after a while . . .

BETH: I thought you were getting sick of me.

KAREN: No . . .

BETH: *I* was getting sick of me.

KAREN: Are you sure I didn't offend you in some way?

BETH: [*Over ". . . in some way?"*] Karen, why would you have offended me?

KAREN: You don't think, on some level, you blame me for this whole thing?

BETH: [*Over ". . . whole thing?"*] Oh, God, that is ridiculous.

KAREN: It was my idea to introduce you.

BETH: So what?! We were grown-ups, we knew what we were doing.

KAREN: Yeah, but I set this whole thing in motion. All the rancor and rage, the pain the kids are going through . . .

BETH: It was out of your control. That we came together was as much out of your control as our falling apart. You can't control everything, Karen, even though you'd like to think you can.

[*Silence.*]

KAREN: So, I guess you immersed yourself in your work all this time, which was probably the healthiest thing you could've done . . .

BETH: Well, actually, no. I haven't been in my studio in weeks.

KAREN: How come?

BETH: The pressure to paint has totally lifted.

KAREN: Oh, that'll pass . . .

BETH: Oh, I'm not worried about it; I don't want to paint anymore.

KAREN: Why?

BETH: Right after Tom left . . . This *unburdening* took place. I looked at what I'd been doing with my life and it seemed so insignificant to me.

KAREN: [*Reassuring.*] No . . .

BETH: Yes. I realized Tom was right: I *was* using painting as an excuse not to get on with my life.

KAREN: How can you say that? After all these years? All that hard work?

BETH: Let's face it, I was never very good.

KAREN: That's not true, you're *very* good.

BETH: Karen, you don't have to say that anymore.

KAREN: I *like* your stuff.

BETH: It's okay; I'm over it; it's not important anymore.

KAREN: Wow. So what have you been doing with yourself all winter

BETH: Well, therapy twice a week . . .

KAREN: Good . . .

BETH: And . . . I'm seeing someone.

KAREN: [*A bit taken aback.*] Why, you little devil. Isn't that great!

BETH: It is. He's a wonderful man.

KAREN: What's his name?

BETH: David.

KAREN: Uh-huh. How'd you meet him?

BETH: Actually, I met him years ago, like ten years ago or something

KAREN: Oh yeah?

BETH: He and Tom used to work together.

KAREN: Uh-oh: another lawyer.

BETH: Yeah, right.

KAREN: Oh, well, can't have everything.

BETH: *Any*way, he just happened to call, for Tom . . .

KAREN: Uh-huh.

BETH: [*Continuous.*] . . . and I filled him in on what was going on . .

KAREN: Uh-huh.

BETH: [*Continuous.*] . . . and he was very compassionate and it turned out *his* marriage was falling apart, too . . .

KAREN: Uh-huh.

BETH: [*Continuous.*] So we met for a drink and, *you* know, it turned out we had a lot in common. And I've been seeing him ever since.

KAREN: Well, it certainly seems to agree with you.

BETH: Oh, it's been . . .

KAREN: I think it's great you're getting your feet wet. The hell with Tom.

BETH: Well, actually, it's a bit more serious than wet feet.

[KAREN *looks at her intently;* BETH *giggles.*]

I'm sorry. Isn't it silly. This is like high school: I'm blushing. It's been so exciting, stealing away when we can . . .

KAREN: How long has this been going on?

BETH: A few months.

KAREN: Uh-huh.

BETH: We're having such a good time.

KAREN: A few *months*?

BETH: [*Continuous.*] He's teaching me how to rollerblade!

KAREN: Oh, God.

BETH: I'm getting pretty good at it, too. We play hooky some afternoons and he takes me out to, *you* know, along the canal?

KAREN: Do you wear knee-pads and a helmet and everything?

BETH: Yes.

KAREN: 'Cause you could really hurt yourself on those things.

BETH: It's fun. You should try. We'll give you and Gabe a lesson.

KAREN: Yeah, I could just see Gabe . . .

BETH: He's so full of life: David; he's so open and optimistic. He's a playmate, *that's* what he is, a wonderful playmate.

KAREN: Boy, that was fast.

BETH: What?

KAREN: Tom is barely out the door . . .

BETH: Oh, Karen . . .

KAREN: You didn't want to be alone for a while? You haven't been alone in a dozen years.

BETH: I've always been alone, don't you see? I spent my *marriage* alone.

KAREN: But to get *involved* with someone, right away?

BETH: [*Over ". . . right away?"*] I'm in love with him.

KAREN: [*A beat.*] How could you be in love with him?

BETH: I am.

KAREN: [*Continuous.*] You've only just started seeing him.

BETH: I knew him years ago, I said.

KAREN: Through Tom.

BETH: Right. We went out socially a few times, the two couples.

KAREN: But that's different.

BETH: I mean, it's not like he's a stranger. The preliminaries were out of the way. There's a history there. There was already a kind of shorthand.

KAREN: I can understand its being exciting, I can understand that. But love?

BETH: Why is that so hard to believe? I fell in love with Tom that first weekend in the Vineyard.

KAREN: Okay, and look where *that* got you. Sorry.

[*A beat.*]

I just think you have to be careful.

BETH: Karen . . .

KAREN: [*Continuous.*] You're very vulnerable right now.

BETH: Oh, please . . .

KAREN: I don't want you to get hurt.

BETH: I'm gonna marry him.

[*A tense pause.*]

David is not Tom. He's not. They're very different men. There's no hidden agenda with him. What you see is what you get. You know? He *talks* to me. He tells me what he's thinking. He lets me in.

[*A beat.*]

So much of my marriage to Tom was this dark little tango, this adagio dance. I don't want that anymore. I want another shot at it. With David. And David wants me.

KAREN [*Nods, then.*] I wish you well.

BETH: Thanks.

[*Pause.*]

He's great with the kids. You should see him with them. They're crazy about him. Particularly Sammy. He's all over him. Things were so gloomy, after Tom left, you have no idea . . .

KAREN: I know.

BETH: I never thought my kids would laugh again, I mean it, it was that grim.

KAREN: I'm sure.

BETH: I know what I'm doing, Karen. This is the man I was meant to be with. I really believe that. I had to survive Tom so I could end up with David. It was my fate.

KAREN: That may be, but, still, I wish you'd give it more time.

BETH: And let this moment pass? No way. I don't want to let this moment—look, why do I even bother?

KAREN: What?

BETH: You think I'm crazy.

KAREN: I never said that . . .

BETH: [*Continuously.*] This is my opportunity for a real marriage, a real partnership. But you don't want me to have that, do you.

KAREN: [*Over ". . . do you."*] What an outrageous thing to say! Of course I do!

BETH: [*Over ". . . of course I do!"*] I'm finally feeling whole, finally feeling like I'm on the right track, for the first time in my life, and what do you do? You undermine me!

KAREN: I am not undermining you, I'm only thinking of what's best for you.

BETH: Oh, I see.

KAREN: Try being alone for a while. That's what *I* would do . . .

BETH: [*Over "That's what I would do . . ."*] What's so great about being alone? Huh? What's so great about it?

KAREN: [*Continuous.*] I would *indulge* myself; get to know myself better . . .

BETH: That's easy for you to say: You have Gabe, you have this life . . .

KAREN: Beth . . .

BETH: You know what I think? I think you *love it* when I'm a mess.

KAREN: What?!

BETH: You do. You love it when I'm all over the place, flailing about. I finally find someone who's like a, like an *anchor* and you don't want to hear about it!

KAREN: That is not true.

BETH: As long as I'm artsy and incompetent, everything is fine. The minute I show any signs of being on an equal footing with you, forget it; you can't deal with it, you have to knock me over!

KAREN: How can you say that?

BETH: Come on, you *need* me to be a mess; you're *invested* in it. Every Karen needs a Beth.

KAREN: That really isn't fair.

BETH: We all play the parts we're handed. I was the Mess, the Ditz, the Comic Relief. You got to be Miss Perfect: everything just right. Just the right wine, just the right spice, just the right husband. How was I supposed to compete with that?

KAREN: Nobody was asking you to compete with anything.

BETH: You're right, there was no contest; I couldn't possibly reciprocate . . . The hostess gifts you would give me! I could never tell if you were being remedial or just plain hostile.

KAREN: I had no idea you felt this way . . .

BETH: We can't all be like you, Karen. God knows I've tried. No matter how much *I* stir, my soup still sticks to the pot.

[*Pause. In a conciliatory gesture,* BETH *takes* KAREN'*s hand.*]

KAREN: We loved nothing more than having you in our home and cooking you meals.

BETH: We loved it, too.

KAREN: You're my family.

BETH: I know.

KAREN: I spent my first twenty years doing whatever the hell I could do to get *away* from my family and my second twenty years doing everything I could do to cobble together a family of my own. I thought if I could *choose* my family this time, if I could make my *friends* my family . .

BETH: Congratulations. The family you've chosen is just as fucked up and fallible as the one you were born into.

[*They resume eating in silence.*]

How are the boys?

[KAREN, *distracted, nods.*]

And you and Gabe?

KAREN: We're good. We're fine.

[BETH *nods. Silence.*]

'NIGHT, MOTHER

BY MARSHA NORMAN

CHARACTERS

JESSIE *(40) has told her mother that she can't take the disappointment of her life anymore and intends to kill herself.* MAMA *(late 60s) is doing whatever she can to talk her daughter out of it.*

SCENE

The living room/kitchen of a small country home on an isolated lane.

TIME

Evening.

[JESSIE *sits down with a gun and starts cleaning it, pushing the cylinder out, checking to see that the chambers and barrel are empty, then putting some oil on a small patch of cloth and pushing it through the barrel with the pushrod that was in the box.* MAMA *goes to the kitchen and washes her hands, as instructed, trying not to show her concern about the gun.*]

MAMA: I shoulda got you to bring down that milk can. Agnes Fletcher sold hers to somebody at a flea market for forty dollars apiece.

JESSIE: I'll go back and get it in a minute. There's a wagon wheel up there, too. There's even a churn. I'll get it all if you want.

MAMA: [*Coming over now, taking over now.*] What are you doing?

JESSIE: The barrel has to be clean, Mama. Old powder, dust gets in it . . .

MAMA: What for?

JESSIE: I told you.

MAMA: [*Reaching for the gun.*] And I told you, we don't get criminals out here.

JESSIE: [*Quickly pulling it to her.*] And I told you . . .

[*Then trying to be calm.*]

The gun is for me.

MAMA: Well, you can have it if you want. When I die, you'll get it all, anyway.

JESSIE: I'm going to kill myself, Mama.

MAMA: [*Returning to the sofa.*] Very funny. Very funny.

JESSIE: I am.

MAMA: You are not! Don't even say such a thing, Jessie.

JESSIE: How would you know if I didn't say it? You want it to be a surprise? You're lying there in your bed or maybe you're just brushing your teeth and you hear this . . . noise down the hall?

MAMA: Kill yourself.

JESSIE: Shoot myself. In a couple of hours.

MAMA: It must be time for your medicine.

JESSIE: Took it already.

MAMA: What's the matter with you?

JESSIE: Not a thing. Feel fine.

MAMA: You feel fine. You're just going to kill yourself.

JESSIE: Waited until I felt good enough, in fact.

MAMA: Don't make jokes, Jessie. I'm too old for jokes.

JESSIE: It's not a joke, Mama.

[MAMA *watches for a moment in silence.*]

MAMA: That gun's no good, you know. He broke it right before he died. He dropped it in the mud one day.

JESSIE: Seems okay.

[*She spins the chamber, cocks the pistol, and pulls the trigger, The gun is not yet loaded, so all we hear is the click, but it will definitely work. It's also obvious that* JESSIE *knows her way around a gun.* MAMA *cannot speak.*]

I had Cecil's all ready in there, just in case I couldn't find this one, but I'd rather use Daddy's.

MAMA: Those bullets are at least fifteen years old.

JESSIE: [*Pulling out another box.*] These are from last week.

MAMA: Where did you get those?

JESSIE: Feed store Dawson told me about.

MAMA: Dawson!

JESSIE: I told him I was worried about prowlers. He said he thought it was a good idea. He told me what kind to ask for.

MAMA: If he had any idea . . .

JESSIE: He took it as a compliment. He thought I might be taking an interest in things. He got through telling me all about the bullets and then he said we ought to talk like this more often.

MAMA: And where was I while this was going on?

JESSIE: On the phone with Agnes. About the milk can, I guess. Anyway, I asked Dawson if he thought they'd send me some bullets and he said he'd just call for me, because he knew they'd send them if he told them to. And he was absolutely right. Here they are.

MAMA: How could he do that?

JESSIE: Just trying to help, Mama.

MAMA: And then I told you where the gun was.

JESSIE: [*Smiling, enjoying this joke.*] See? Everybody's doing what they can.

MAMA: You told me it was for your protection!

JESSIE: It *is*! I'm still doing my nails, though. Want to try that new Chinaberry color?

MAMA: Well, I'm calling Dawson right now. We'll just see what he has to say about this little stunt.

JESSIE: Dawson doesn't have any more to do with this.

MAMA: He's your brother.

JESSIE: And that's all.

MAMA: [*Stands up, moves toward the phone.*] Dawson will put a stop to this. Yes he will. He'll take the gun away.

JESSIE: If you call him, I'll just have to do it before he gets here. Soon as you hang up the phone, I'll just walk in the bedroom and lock the door. Dawson will get here just in time to clean you up. Go ahead, call him. Then call the police. Then call the funeral home. Then call Loretta and see if *she'll* do your nails.

MAMA: You will not! This is crazy talk, Jessie!

[MAMA *goes directly to the telephone and starts to dial, but* JESSIE *is fast, coming up behind her and taking the receiver out of her hand, putting it back down.*]

JESSIE: [*Firm and quiet.*] I said no. This is private. Dawson is not invited.

MAMA: Just me.

JESSIE: I don't want anybody else over here. Just you and me. If Dawson comes over, it'll make me feel stupid for not doing it ten years ago.

MAMA: I think we better call the doctor. Or how about the ambulance. You like that one driver, I know. What's his name, Timmy? Get you somebody to talk to.

JESSIE: [*Going back to her chair.*] I'm through talking, Mama. You're it. No more.

MAMA: We're just going to sit around like every other night in the world and then you're going to kill yourself?

[JESSIE *doesn't answer.*]

You'll miss.

[*Again there is no response.*]

You'll just wind up a vegetable. How would you like that? Shoot your ear off. You know what the doctor said about getting excited. You'll cock the pistol and have a fit.

JESSIE: I think I can kill myself, Mama.

MAMA: You're not going to kill yourself, Jessie. You're not even upset!

[JESSIE *smiles, or laughs quietly, and* MAMA *tries a different approach.*]

People don't really kill themselves, Jessie. No, ma'm, doesn't make sense, unless you're retarded or deranged, and you're as normal as they come, Jessie, for the most part, We're all *afraid* to die.

JESSIE: I'm not, Mama. I'm cold all the time, anyway.

MAMA: That's ridiculous.

JESSIE: It's exactly what I want. It's dark and quiet.

MAMA: So is the backyard, Jessie! Close your eyes. Stuff cotton in your ears. Take a nap! It's quiet in your room. I'll leave the TV off all night.

JESSIE: So quiet I don't know it's quiet. So nobody can get me.

MAMA: You don't know what dead is like. It might not be quiet at all. What if it's like an alarm clock and you can't wake up so you can't shut it off. Ever.

JESSIE: Dead is everybody and everything I ever knew, gone. Dead is dead quiet.

MAMA: It's a sin. You'll go to hell.

JESSIE: Uh-huh.

MAMA: You will!

JESSIE: Jesus was a suicide if you ask me.

MAMA: You'll go to hell just for saying that. Jessie!

JESSIE: [*With genuine surprise.*] I didn't know I thought that.

MAMA: Jessie!

[JESSIE *doesn't answer. She puts the now-loaded gun back in the box and crosses to the kitchen. But* MAMA *is afraid she's headed for the bedroom.*]

MAMA: [*In a panic.*] You can't use my towels! They're my towels! I've had them for a long time. I like my towels.

JESSIE: I asked you if you wanted that swimming towel and you said you didn't.

MAMA: And you can't use your father's gun, either. It's mine now, too. And you can't do it in my house.

JESSIE: Oh, come on.

MAMA: No, You can't do it. I won't let you. The house is in my name.

JESSIE: I have to go in the bedroom and lock the door behind me so they won't arrest you for killing me. They'll probably test your hands for gunpowder, anyway, but you'll pass.

MAMA: Not in my house!

JESSIE: If I'd known you were going to act like this, I wouldn't have told you.

MAMA: How am I supposed to act? Tell you to go ahead? Okay by me, sugar? Might try it myself. What took you so long?

JESSIE: There's just no point in fighting me over it, that's all. Want some coffee?

MAMA: Your birthday's coming up, Jessie. Don't you want to know what we got you?

JESSIE: You got me dusting powder, Loretta got me a new housecoat, pink probably, and Dawson got me new slippers, too small, but they go with the robe he'll say.

[MAMA *cannot speak.*]

Right?

[*Apparently* JESSIE *is right.*]

Be back in a minute.

[JESSIE *takes the gun box, puts it on top of the stack of towels and garbage bags, and takes them into her bedroom.*]

FIGHTING OVER BEVERLEY
BY ISRAEL HOROVITZ

CHARACTERS
BEVERLEY *(70) came to America as the war bride of Zelly over fifty years ago, and now she has been pursued here by Archie, the boyfriend of her youth.* CECILY *(40) is* BEVERLEY's *daughter with Zelly, whose own marriage to Gerald is currently in crisis.*

SCENE
Beverley's home in Gloucester, Massachusetts.

TIME
Afternoon. Winter, 1998.

[CECILY *dials another number, talks to another answering machine.*]

CECILY: Gerald, it's me. I'm still at my parents. I know why I'm crazy, Gerald . . . Hullo? . . .

[*New tone, suddenly. She is no longer talking to an answering machine.*]

Gerald? Hiiii! . . . Are you still sleeping? . . . I'm sorry! . . . No, no, no, go back to sleep . . . What? . . . Is somebody there? . . . No, I just thought I heard somebody . . . Fine. No, no, it's fine . . . Bye, Gerald.

[CECILY *switches portable phone off. She is terribly sad.* BEVERLEY *enters, carrying tea tray.*]

BEVERLEY: Did someone call?

CECILY: No. I called someone.

[*Tries not to say more; then does.*]

I called Gerald.

BEVERLEY: That's a good idea.

[*Puts tea tray down.*]

And how is Gerald?

CECILY: In bed with somebody.

BEVERLEY: Somebody? . . . Oh. I see. He told you this?

CECILY: I could hear.

BEVERLEY: Did you ask him?

CECILY: Mother, I could hear.

BEVERLEY: Sometimes, when you're overwrought, dear, the imagination plays tricks . . .

CECILY: Mum, *please!*

[CECILY *fights back tears. She goes to window; looks out at the storm. Suddenly, tears overwhelm her.* BEVERLEY *watches her daughter weep. She keeps her distance. When she speaks, she speaks quietly.*]

BEVERLEY: Are you alright, darling?

CECILY: I'm fine, Mum.

BEVERLEY: Is Gerald treating you badly?

CECILY: Yes. No. Yes.

BEVERLEY: Do you want to end your marriage?

CECILY: No. Yes. Those two things: No and Yes.

BEVERLEY: Is little Gerald difficult?

CECILY: That's not it.

BEVERLEY: *What's* it, dear?

CECILY: Why do we let them get away with it, Mum?

[*Pauses; explains.*]

Men. They can't bear any success we have, can they?

BEVERLEY: Things were different in my day, I suppose. Women didn't seem to want so much.

CECILY: You *didn't,* Mum? You always wanted to spend your life waiting for your husband to come home stinking of fish and female fish-packers? Waiting for him to come in from his homo nights out with The Boys, stinking of bar bimbos and beer? . . .

BEVERLEY: You have such an unpleasant way of putting things, dear!

CECILY: Yuh, well, maybe I do. Maybe I'm not telling you the honest-to-God truth, Mum. Maybe it's not just Daddy. Maybe it's that I'm terrified of ending up like you.

BEVERLEY: That's charmingly put as well, love.

CECILY: You know what I mean, Mum! Not you, personally! You, personally, are my *ideal!* You're beautiful, witty, composed, clear-headed . . . It's you, *married,* that terrifies me. I see what they're like, Mum . . . and I see what I'm like . . . what *we're* like. We're weak in their presence. We . . .

[*Suddenly sobs; turns away from* BEVERLEY.]

Shit!

BEVERLEY: Are you alright, dear?

CECILY: Never better.

[*Goes to Kleenex box; dries eyes, blows nose.*]

I know women who used to be vital, brilliant thinkers . . . leaders . . *world-beaters.* They had everything, except a husband and kids. So they got married, got the husband, got the kids, got the big house closed the door behind them and never saw daylight, again! I can' do this.

BEVERLEY: That's not necessarily been my life, thus far, Cecily.

CECILY: What has necessarily been your life, thus far, Mum? Staying alone in this goddamn house, day after day, waiting for him to come and go, when and if he wants? . . . What kind of life are you having?

[*There is a pause.*]

BEVERLEY: I had you . . . Your father let me go to school . . .

CECILY: Your husband *let you* go to school? You needed his *permission*

BEVERLEY: It took money.

CECILY: Salem Teachers College took money? How much money. Five hundred a year? A thousand? Two thousand? Ten thousand?

BEVERLEY: That wasn't the issue, Cecily.

CECILY: What wasn't the issue?

BEVERLEY: Whether I worked and earned money, or whether I went to school and earned no money. Your father wanted me to go to school. He was proud of me.

CECILY: You believe that?

BEVERLEY: Yes, I do believe that.

CECILY: Did he ever actually "let you" *teach* school? Did he ever actually "let you" go out of this house for fifteen minutes without your having to make a full report? Did he ever actually "let you" take a breath of air without asking his *permission*?

BEVERLEY: We're different people, you and I. I tend to look on the brighter side of things. No marriage is easy, Cecily. Your father and I have had some lovely times together.

CECILY: He bullies you. He badgers you. He treats you like you're dumb and useless. He talks down to you. He expects you to listen to the same stupifyingly boring stories, over and over again, ten thousand times! . . . He expects you to clean up after his endless mess. And he expects you to put up with the unspeakable . . .

BEVERLEY: I must ask you to stop, now . . .

CECILY: *And he expects you to put up with the unspeakable . . .*

BEVERLEY: *Cecily, stop talking! You are insulting me! . . .*

[BEVERLEY *sobs.* CECILY *goes to her, kneels at her feet, holds* BEVERLEY*'s hand.*]

CECILY: Come away with me, Mum.

BEVERLEY: Pardon?

CECILY: I want you to come away with me.

BEVERLEY: On a holiday?

CECILY: On a *life*! . . . I want you to come back to California with me.

BEVERLEY: What are you saying, Cecily?

CECILY: I'm not going back to Gerald. I want you to come live with me, Mum. I make a lot of money. A *wick'id awful* lot of money. Plenty for both of us and then some!

[*Pauses.*]

California is warm. People are happy there . . . polite. They smile at you. They stop their cars at crosswalks!

[*Pauses.*]

It's like the walking dead here, Mum. Everything's frozen, covered with ice. There's no work. People are dead broke, depressed. Gloucester's a dead place. You're married to a fisherman who doesn't fish. He limps around here, shouting orders at you, like you're some dumb lumper workin' his crew. He's *got* no crew. He's got no *hope.* He's just waiting to die. You're young enough to live still, Mum. In ten more years, who knows? . . . Leave with me, Mum. Do the exciting thing for yourself. Leave him. Come live with *me*!

BEVERLEY: Why do you have to hate your father so?

CECILY: Because I have been in psychoanalysis for fifteen years, trying to sort through my nightmares . . . trying to find a way to stop believing that every man I meet isn't really, deep-down, a woman-hating murderer come to kill me.

BEVERLEY: Oh, darling Cecily! Surely, you can't blame your father!

CECILY: I can and I do! Come away with me, Mum. We're both still young enough. *You're* still young enough! . . . You can't seriously consider either one of them, Mum! They're mean and they're old . . . In five years' time, they'll both be wearing pacemakers and colostomy bags! And you'll be wearing a nurse's uniform! Come with me, mum! *Live* with me!

THE GNADIGES FRAULEIN

BY TENNESSEE WILLIAMS

CHARACTERS

POLLY *and* MOLLY *(no age specified—but could be 50s or 60s) are residents of Cocaloony Key, a fictional place of great comedy and tragedy.* POLLY *is the society columnist for the local gazette, and she is out looking for a story.* MOLLY, *who runs a bunkhouse for "permanent transients," has a million stories, but she just wants a nice mention in* POLLY's *column.*

SCENE

Outside a rickety bunkhouse in Cocaloony Key, off the southern tip of Florida.

TIME

Morning. The present. There's a fierce wind.

[*The exterior of a frame cottage on the Key is visible.*]

POLLY: [*Crossing to the porch steps.*] Whatcha moppin' up, Molly?

[*They shout at each other above the wind.*]

MOLLY: Blood.

POLLY: The best time to mop up blood is before daybreak.

MOLLY: It wasn't shed before daybreak.

POLLY: Well, the next best time to mop it up's after dark.

MOLLY: That's not the policy of a good housekeeper.

POLLY: There's been some violence here?

MOLLY: Yep. I chopped the head off a chicken.

POLLY: On the front porch, Molly?

MOLLY: Nope. In the backyard, Polly.

[*The wind subsides.*]

POLLY: It sure did make a long run, all the way round the house and up the front steps and right on into the parlor, yep. I know a chicken can run with its head cut off, but I never known it to make such a long run as that with such a good sense of direction. Molly, this explanation that you are mopping up chicken blood don't hold water. There's been some violence here and the victim wasn't a chicken, that I know, as well as I happen to know that you ain't had a live or dead piece of poultry on these premises since that old Rhode Island Red hen that you were fattenin' up for Thanksgivin' died of malnutrition before Hallowe'en.

MOLLY: Yeah, well, why don't you go over to your desk at the *Cocaloony Gazette* and work on your gossip column, Polly, and let me finish this mopping up operation without the nasal monotone of your voice to distract me and annoy me to distraction! Huh, Polly?

POLLY: How long has it been since you got a favorable mention in my society column?

MOLLY: Never read it. When a lady's sure of her social position as I am, she don't concern herself with gossip columns.

POLLY: You're asking for a bad write-up.

MOLLY: Couldn't care less, pooh for you.

POLLY: You don't mean that.

MOLLY: Yes, I do.

POLLY: I see you got a "vacancy" sign in your window.

MOLLY: What about it?

POLLY: You got a "vacancy" sign in your window and you're mopping up blood on your porch.

MOLLY: No connection, none at all whatsoever.

POLLY: *Aw?*

[*She laughs skeptically.*]

MOLLY: They's always a "vacancy" sign in that window since I knocked out the walls of the private bedrooms to make the big dormitory. Because in a big dormitory they's always rooms for one more. I do a quantity business. Also a quality business but the emphasis is on quantity in the big dormitory because it's furnished with two- and three-decker bunks. It offers accommodations for always one more.

POLLY: Yeah, well, this type of material is okay for the classified ads but not for the gossip column and the society page, so I reckon I'll toddle on. Toodle-oo!

[*She has opened her Pan-Am zipper bag and removed a suspiciously thin cigarette.*]

MOLLY: [*With covetous interest.*] Whatcha took outa of your Dorothy bag, Polly, a Mary Jane?

POLLY: Ta-ta, toddle-oo, see you someday . . . maybe.

MOLLY: Polly, sit down in this rocker and rock. I guarantee you material for your column.

POLLY: That's mighty nice of you, Molly—

[*She lights the cigarette.*]

—but I really go have to be going, I have to cover—well something—somewhere . . .

MOLLY: Polly, I promise you, sweetheart, that in the course of thi late afternoon no matter how the sky changes through light and shadow, I'll give you material for the Goddamnest human and inhuman interest story you ever imagined, Polly. Besides, you ankles look swollen, set down in a comfortable rocker and let' rock together while we turn on together. Huh, honey?

[*She pushes her into the rocker.*]

Wait! Let's synchronize rockers! Hold yours still till I count to three Okay?

POLLY: Count away!

MOLLY: ONE! TWO! THREE! *ROCK!*

[*They rock with pelvis thrusts as if having sex.*]

POLLY: WHEEE!

MOLLY: Now we're rocking in beautiful unison, Polly!

POLLY: In tune with the infinite, Molly!

MOLLY: In absolute harmony with it!

TOGETHER: HUFF, HUFF, HUFF, WHEE!

MOLLY: I love to rock. It reminds me of my girlhood romances Polly!

POLLY: One of your girlhood romances is still in traction, ain't he?

MOLLY: That's a lie, he gets around fine!—on crutches.

[*They cackle together.*]

Now, Polly, about the big dormitory, Polly!

POLLY: [*Throwing up her legs gaily.*] Huff, huff, huff, WHEEE!

MOLLY: I said about THE BIG DORMITORY, Polly!

POLLY: WHEEE!

MOLLY: [*Through the megaphone.*] THREE, TWO, ONE! STOP ROCKERS!

[*She stops* POLLY*'s rocker so abruptly that* POLLY *is nearly thrown to the floor.*]

Let's have a little propriety and some decorum on the front porch, Polly, you're not out back of the woodshed! I was saying: about the big dormitory. The overhead, the operating expenses such as free limousine service, are astronomical, Polly.

POLLY: Oh?

MOLLY: So!—I can't afford to buy advertising space in the *Cocalooney Gazette,* and in the light of this situation which is a mighty dark situation, I could use and would surely appreciate the use of a knockout feature story in your next Sunday supplement, Polly, a two-page spread with photos of personages and caption without a word of profanity in them. How does that strike you, Polly?

POLLY: It didn't strike me, Molly, it whistles over my head like a cocalooney.

MOLLY: I'm dead serious, Polly.

POLLY: It's natural to be serious when you're dead, WHEEE!

[*She resumes rocking.* MOLLY *stops the rocker so forcibly that* POLLY *slides on the front porch.*]

OW!

MOLLY: COW!—Get back in your rocker and listen to what I tell you. You'd go a long way out of your way to find a richer gold mine of material in the class category than I got here in the big dormitory under the rooftree of God, I've got REAL PERSONAGES here!

POLLY: Including that wino?

MOLLY: That's, uh, that's an old family domestic I keep on th premises for sentimental, uh—reasons.

[*She picks up a megaphone and calls through it.*]

WILLIAM? I want the Rolls to roll me to vespers at sunset.

[*She snaps her fan open. The wino takes two steps backward, with a hiccough, and then staggers off.*]

I was saying? Oh, personages, yaiss! Take the Gnadiges Fraulein, on instant for an instance, there's a personage for you, internationall celebrated for yea many years on this earth if not on other planets yes, I've got the Fraulein to mention only a few of the more or les permanent guests of the big dormitory of the rooftree of God.

POLLY: What about Indian Joe?

MOLLY: Yes, how about Indian Joe, that's a personage, Polly, a blond Indian with Caribbean-blue eyes, moving in beauty like the nigh of cloudless climes, and so forth.

POLLY: I catch this inimitable and ineffable aroma somewhere in the near distance: is it outside or in? If I turn around, I'm afraid i would make me giddy, I might lose concentration.

MOLLY: Sit back down in your rocker but don't rock.—What wa I saying?—Oh, the big dormitory. Don't be misguided by the "vacancy" sign. On weekends, Polly, as God's my judge, I hang out the SRO sign for standing room only in the big dormitory!

POLLY: You sell standing room in the big dormitory, Molly?

MOLLY: You bet your sweet ass I do. You take a permanent transien that's ever in his existence had a run-in with the law and show me a permanent that hasn't. It's four a.m. No intelligent permanent transient prefers to stay on the street at that desperate hour when even the Conch Gardens closes. Not in a state of the Union where they's eighteen different kinds of vagrancy charges that a lone man at the streets at night might be charged with. All right. The SRO sign looks mighty good to a permanent transient, it shines to him like the Star of Bethlehem shone to the kings that came from the East.

POLLY: And do they sleep standing up?

MOLLY: Unless they can find a voluntary bed-partner.

POLLY: Flamingoes can sleep standin' up on one leg, even.

MOLLY: Anything havin' a leg to stand on can sleep standin' up if it had to.

POLLY: Don't they fall down, Molly?

MOLLY: They fall down and get back up.

POLLY: Well, Molly, when one of your standing-up sleepers falls down, don't it disturb the sleep of the horizontal sleepers?

MOLLY: Polly, a permanent transient is a wonderful sleeper. He sleeps heavy and late in the calm and security of the big dormitory, as God is my witness in heaven.

POLLY: What is the check-out time?

MOLLY: They wake up to music which is provided by the Gnadiges Fraulein.

POLLY: It'll be fun to watch 'em coming out, Molly.

MOLLY: They have to go out the back way because it's daylight and they make a better public appearance by starlight on a starless night because of embarrassing subtractions from their wardrobe, like some of them can't find their shoes when they go to get up in

the morning and some of them can't find their shirts or their pant
when they go to get up in the morning and some of them can'
find a Goddamn bit of their wardrobe when they go to get up in
the morning, including their lingerie, Polly. And some of them
can't find their equilibrium or concentration or will to continu
the struggle for survival when they go to get up in the morning
and some of them don't get up in the morning, not even when th
Gnadiges Fraulein sings the reveille song.

POLLY: Obstinate?

MOLLY: Nope, dead, Polly.

[POLLY *breathes out a sound like the wind in the pines, rolling her
eyes above a wicked grin.*]

MOLLY: Yep, the Dark Angel has a duplicate key to the big dormitor
and faithfully every night he drops by to inspect the sleepers and
check their dog tags. He wanders among the two- and three
decker bunks and never leaves without company, nope, neve
leaves unattended and no one grieves when he leaves.

POLLY: [*Lisping.*] Between the dark and the daylight—

MOLLY: When the gloom of doom is in flower—

TOGETHER: Comes a pause in the night's occupation. Which i
known as the Angel's Dark Hour.

THE OLD SETTLER

BY JOHN HENRY REDWOOD

HARACTERS

IZABETH *(55) and her sister,* QUILLY *(53), are trying to make
ds meet in 1943 Harlem. Then* ELIZABETH *decides to take in a
arder, the much younger Husband, who has come to the city looking
his girlfriend, Lou Bessie. But* ELIZABETH *wants Husband for
rself, and eventually the two of them make plans to elope.*

CENE

*e living room of the apartment of Elizabeth Borny in Harlem,
w York City.*

IME

nday, 9:30 a.m. Spring, 1943.

[QUILLY *is in the living room standing in front of the mirror
putting on her hat.* ELIZABETH *enters in slippers and robe with a
kerchief in her hand.*]

JILLY: Happy Mother's Day.

IZABETH: I ain't nobody's mama.

JILLY: You sure about that?

IZABETH: [*Sitting.*] Don't be starting no stuff with me the first
thing this morning, Quilly. I ain't up to it. Can't get no sleep.

Did you hear little Charles doing all that screaming? Delores mus[t] have been spanking him in the room right next to me. Sounde[d] like he was right in my bedroom.

QUILLY: She should spank his little behind in every room in tha[t] apartment, as spoiled as that child is.

ELIZABETH: She don't have to spank him every day.

QUILLY: He's bad every day, ain't he? She wasn't doing nothing t[o] that boy anyway . . . and he over there screaming bloody murde[r] He ought to be mine. I'd set his little hind-pots on fire. H[e] wouldn't be able to sit down for a week. That's right. Spare the ro[d] and spoil the child. That's what's wrong with these kids today . .

ELIZABETH: You sure shouldn't be going to no church this mornin[g] as evil as you is.

QUILLY: At least I'm going, shoot. When's the last time you bee[n] Not since that boy moved . . .

ELIZABETH: How did Sister Wallace and her children make out?

QUILLY: When I got to the Mother's Day program last night, Reveren[d] Osborne told us that Sister Wallace and those children finally di[d] get on another train. But it was the same thing . . . only two car[s] for the colored folks. Sat, the people was standing on top of on[e] another in the aisles. Some people was sitting on their suitcase[s] They couldn't move . . . couldn't even turn around it was so tight.

[*Proudly.*]

But you know what happened, Bess? Say, the men who was sittin[g] all got up and turned the seats around so you had two seats facin[g] one another. Then the men let the women and small children si[t] in three of the seats and a man sat in the fourth seat. And ever[y] half-hour, the man who was sitting, would get up and let a ma[n] who was standing take his seat. Some of the women wanted to tak[e] turns standing, but the men wouldn't hear it. No woman or chil[d] had to stand. I tell you, Bess, those colored men sure make me feel proud to be a Negro. I wanted to call some of the members this morning, but Miss-Mile-a-Minute-Mouth was at it again. You know we can ask the telephone company to put us on another line with somebody else. I guess I'll hear something more when I get to church.

ELIZABETH: Why didn't you wake me up this morning in time to go?

QUILLY: I barely got up myself. I didn't get to bed until after twelve and didn't get to sleep until after you came in . . . which was about three. So I didn't think you would be able to get up and go to church.

ELIZABETH: That sure enough is right. I've got the biggest headache. I had some champagne last night.

QUILLY: Champagne? You don't drink. What you doing drinking champagne?

ELIZABETH: We went to eat, then went to the movies to see Herb Jeffries in *The Bronze Buckaroo*. And then . . .

QUILLY: That's an old movie.

ELIZABETH: So what, Quilly? I hadn't seen it. Goodness! Then Husband took me to Small's Paradise where we had a glass of champagne to celebrate him giving me the ring.

QUILLY: How he going to pay for that ring . . . a dollar down and dollar when they catch him? He ain't got no job.

ELIZABETH: He paid for it outright. And he paid for the champagne outright. And we didn't eat no pimp steak.

QUILLY: You stop going to church. You start wearing tight-fitting clothes. You start staying out half the night finger-popping and cutting the fool. You used to not drink, now you drink champagne and sit up in beer gardens. Soon all kinds of filth will be coming out of your mouth just like that Lou Bessie. That's what you're doing . . . trying to be a Lou Bessie for him.

ELIZABETH: Quilly, it was only one glass of champagne to celebrate

QUILLY: Yeah, that's just like all those other people who talk about drinking only to be sociable.

ELIZABETH: [*Getting up.*] If I wanted to hear preaching, I would be hurrying to get dressed so I could go to church with you.

[*She crosses to exit into the hallway. She then turns and crosses back to* QUILLY.]

If you wasn't happy for me, why did you lie and hug me last night?

QUILLY: Because I wanted to be happy for you.

ELIZABETH: And? . . . And?

QUILLY: I've already missed Sunday School. I don't want to be late for church too.

ELIZABETH: It's not just that he's younger than I am.

QUILLY: Yeah, he's younger. He's walking a long ways behind you in age.

ELIZABETH: But it's more than that, isn't it?

[*Pause.*]

What is it?

[*Pause.*]

If it was a man with a woman half his age, you wouldn't be making such a fuss, would you?

QUILLY: You're not a man . . . and neither is he. That's a mama's boy looking for another mama and you fit the bill. Even that old cricket-brain Lou Bessie ain't what the chickens left, but, as sad as it is, she's the woman in his life. You're just the new mama.

ELIZABETH: [*Holding up her finger.*] Who has the ring . . . Lou Bessie or me?

QUILLY: Yeah, you got the ring, but did you get it the same way Lou Bessie gets what she wants from him?

ELIZABETH: What's that supposed to mean?

QUILLY: You know good and well what I'm talking about.

ELIZABETH: Let me get one thing straight. I told Husband that I don't believe in laying down with no man before marriage and he respects that.

QUILLY: What you going to do when boy's nature get up, Bess? That's a young, healthy, strong, country boy. What you going to do when his nature gets up two and three times a night . . . and day? You haven't used it in so long . . . if you've ever used it at all, that you don't even know if it works. And if you can't cut the mustard, you're going to have to pick the jar.

ELIZABETH: Why you got to be talking all up under people's clothes like that?

QUILLY: Because it's life. You too old to have any babies.

ELIZABETH: Don't you think he knows that.

QUILLY: So, what's going to happen when he starts wanting a son? You think you're going to be like Abraham's wife Sarah in the Bible? You think God's going to touch your belly and out going to pop a little Husband?

ELIZABETH: We've already talked about that, I told you.

QUILLY: It's one thing to talk about it, but it's another thing to be faced with it. When he gets the yearning and you keep saying you're too tired . . . When he wants to continue his name and you can't provide him with a way to do that . . . not even a daughter that's where a Lou Bessie comes in.

ELIZABETH: Oh, will you shut up! Shut up! Why are you so mean? I come up here and worked and sent Mama money so she could buy you shoes and clothes for school. When Mama died, I went down there and brought you back up here to live with me. I fed you and put clothes on your back until you started working at a job I got for you. And after you tore my heart out and shamed me before the whole world, then didn't talk to me for eight years, I still loved you and swallowed my pride and came looking for you to make peace. Because you was my sister. We came out of the same body . . . shared the same mother. Because there was nobody else in this whole world with the same blood as mine running through their veins, and it wasn't right for us not to be talking to each other . . . loving each other. Because if I couldn't give you anything else, love was the one thing I could give you every day of my life . . . and I tried. What terrible thing have I done to you . . . other than love you, to make you treat me so mean? You hurt me.

QUILLY: You're finally getting to it, ain't you, Bess? . . .

ELIZABETH: . . . Stole from me!

QUILLY: I couldn't have stolen what wasn't really yours.

ELIZABETH: You knew I loved Herman and . . .

QUILLY: But Herman didn't love you, Bess!

ELIZABETH: He did until you came up here with your fast self!

QUILLY: He didn't love you and he told you so. You just didn't listen like you won't listen now. He even told you that before I came up here . . . before he even saw or knew me. Didn't he?

ELIZABETH: That's why you know so much about Lou Bessie, because you was just like her.

QUILLY: Didn't he?

ELIZABETH: And then you want to flaunt that picture of you and him together in the house I took you into . . . again.

QUILLY: Didn't he tell you he didn't love you? Tell the truth, Bess. You know he didn't love you.

ELIZABETH: [*Screaming.*] *You was my sister!*

[*Pause.*]

It didn't matter if he loved me of not! You was my sister and you knew I loved him! That meant you should have kept your hands off.

[*Pause.*]

If you hadn't come along, I would have made him love me. Maybe that's why you're so against me and Husband. Maybe you're jealous and want him too. Well, this is one you're not going to get. We're going to leave here in a couple of weeks after we get all of our business taken care of. We're going to take the train to Elkton, Maryland, and get married and then get back on the train and stop in Halifax so I can take care of some more business, then head on down to his place in Frogmore. So you'll only have to put up with Husband and me for two more weeks, then the place is yours . . . and you can put that picture of you and Herman anyplace you want.

[*She begins to cross out of the room.*]

QUILLY: You're going to leave me. You're going to leave me up here alone.

[*Pause.*]

You've known since we were little girls that I was always afraid of being alone. First it was you, me and Mama; then it was Mama and me; then Mama died and I came to live with you, then I married Herman and after Herman, I came back to live with you. I ain't never been alone. I don't know why, but I'm scared of being alone. I don't want to die alone.

ELIZABETH: Quilly, you left me alone. After Mama died, the one thing I loved in the whole world, other than the Lord and you, was Herman, and you came up here and stole him away from me. And you never once said you was sorry. Never!

[*After a beat of silence,* QUILLY *turns and crosses to the door to exit, then stops.*]

QUILLY: Maybe you'll feel better knowing that I didn't kick Herman out like I said. We're separated all right, but Herman walked away from me with the young girl from the apartment across the hall. I came home from an all-day retreat with the Ladies of the Golden Scepter and they were gone.

[ELIZABETH *turns her back on* QUILLY. *After a beat* QUILLY *comes back to* ELIZABETH.]

QUILLY: I know I never said it, but, honest to God, I've tried to show it. I'm sorry for what I did to you, Bess. I'm truly sorry for the hurt.

[*After a beat of no response from* ELIZABETH, QUILLY *exits.*]

ELIZABETH: The good don't die alone, Quilly. God always sends someone from the other side to greet us.

MARVIN'S ROOM
BY SCOTT MCPHERSON

CHARACTERS
BESSIE *(40) is a woman who has been the caretaker for her dying father, Marvin, for the past twenty years; she also looks after her aunt* RUTH *(70), who has several collapsed vertebrae, for which she wears an electrode pack on her waist to control her constant pain (but it also tends to open the garage door when she uses the bathroom). But* BESSIE's *health is also in crisis—she has recently been told that she has leukemia, for which she's now being treated.*

SCENE
Bessie's hospital room in Florida.

TIME
Lunchtime.

[BESSIE *in her hospital bed, wearing a wig and eating lunch.* RUTH *sits in a chair beside her.*]

RUTH: Being confined to your bed is nothing to be afraid of.

BESSIE: I'm not confined to my bed. I'm just a little tired today.

RUTH: I was confined to my bed most of my life. You find things to do.

BESSIE: Like what?

RUTH: Oh my . . . well . . . you can sleep, or you can lay there awake . . .

BESSIE: Do you want any of this?

RUTH: No, no. That's all for you. You should eat that and be strong. Have you made a stinky today?

BESSIE: Yes.

RUTH: That's good. That's important. Do you want your rice pudding?

BESSIE: Do you want it?

RUTH: Not if you were going to have it.

BESSIE: You can have it.

RUTH: I didn't really have time for a lunch.

BESSIE: This is too far for you to come, Ruth. I don't think you should visit me again.

RUTH: You visited me every day when I was in for my cure. It's nice for me to visit you.

BESSIE: It's too hard on you.

RUTH: It's such a lovely walk.

BESSIE: Besides, you're needed at home now.

RUTH: I wish we could do something about that garage door. I feel like the whole street knows my business.

BESSIE: How is Dad?

RUTH: Oh, he's fine.

BESSIE: Does he miss me?

RUTH: Well, I haven't actually told him you're gone.

BESSIE: What?

RUTH: I didn't know what to say.

BESSIE: Doesn't he wonder where I am?

RUTH: When he asks, I say you're just in the other room busy with something. Then he falls asleep for a while, and when he wakes up I say he just missed you.

BESSIE: Ruth.

RUTH: It would upset him.

BESSIE: Who does he think that nurse is living with you?

RUTH: Well, I pretend not to notice her.

BESSIE: What do you mean?

RUTH: If she comes in the room while I'm there I pretend she's not real. That she doesn't exist.

BESSIE: Then what does Dad think?

RUTH: I think he thinks he's hallucinating.

BESSIE: What?

RUTH: I never told him he was hallucinating. He came up with that himself. I didn't know what to do. I was going to try and tell him you were in the hospital, and—and she walked in before I was ready, so I didn't. I—I pretended she wasn't there.

BESSIE: You have to tell him.

RUTH: But he's used to it now. The only time it seems to bother him is when she carries him to the bath. And I say, "Oh, look, Marvin, you're flying. Bessie will want to see this." And then I go into the other room to get you.

BESSIE: He must think he's losing his mind.

RUTH: But it's better than telling him. You don't know. He would be so upset. He's still your father. What am I supposed to tell him? That his little girl is . . . ? How can I tell him? Then he'll really think he's losing his mind. He'll be so upset. It would be so upsetting to him. He's your father.

BESSIE: All right. All right.

RUTH: I wouldn't know what to say.

BESSIE: Tell him I'm going to be fine and I'll be home soon and there's no reason to be upset.

RUTH: You want me to tell him?

BESSIE: Yes. Because there is no reason to be upset. I'm going to be fine, Ruth. I know I am.

RUTH: Nothing happens that God doesn't have a reason for.

BESSIE: I'm sure He does.

RUTH: He tries to teach us things. He tries to reach down and shake us out of our ignorance.

BESSIE: I'm sure that's it.

RUTH: I know He made me crippled for a reason. He wants me to learn something. It may be patience or it may be forbearance or it may be how to dress without standing up. He doesn't tell you what it is, you just have to learn it.

BESSIE: I don't think it's how to dress.

RUTH: Oh, it wouldn't surprise me. I often ask Him why I'm crippled. I also ask Him why He let Marvin buy this house down here to take care of me, then struck Marvin with a stroke. Why? And then have him lose his colon to cancer. Why? And then lose the sight in one eye and the use of one kidney and yet keep a full head of hair. Why?

BESSIE: I don't know.

RUTH: But God knows. He has his reasons. And I'm not upset.

BESSIE: Then tell Dad his nurse is not a hallucination and that I am not in the other room.

RUTH: I think he's starting to enjoy flying.

BESSIE: And I don't want you to visit me again. It's too hard on you.

[*Pause.*]

It's almost time for your show. Don't you want to watch?

RUTH: I didn't think you would want to.

BESSIE: I kind of want to see if Lance proposes to Coral.

RUTH: Have you been watching?

BESSIE: I've seen it since I've been in here.

RUTH: [*Sits on the bed with* BESSIE.] Isn't it wonderful? I think she'll say yes. They really do love each other.

BESSIE: But now, is he the same guy who raped her at one point?

RUTH: Oh, that was months ago. He's really a nice boy.

[BESSIE *clicks on the TV with the remote. She and* RUTH *both look to the corner of the room where it would be. The soap opera theme swells as the lights fade.*]

PART III

SCENES FOR TWO MEN

DEATH AND THE MAIDEN

BY ARIEL DORFMAN

CHARACTERS

GERARDO ESCOBAR *(45) is a lawyer who wants to be part of the coalition replacing the now-ousted dictator of this country;* ROBERTO MIRANDA *(50) is a doctor who* GERARDO's *wife (Paulina) suspects was one of her torturers when the government arrested her fifteen years ago.*

SCENE

The dining room of the Escobars' beach house in Chile (or any country that is attempting a democracy after a period of dictatorship).

TIME

The present.

[*It is lunchtime.* GERARDO *and* ROBERTO *sit at a wooden table across from each other. There are bowls of soup in front of both.* ROBERTO *is tied to the chair with rope, his hands in front. Paulina is offstage, on the balcony; she can see the men but cannot hear them.* ROBERTO *and* GERARDO *remain for several silent moments looking at the food.*]

GERARDO: You're not hungry, Doctor Miranda?

ROBERTO: Roberto. My name is Roberto. Please treat me with the same familiarity that you—please.

GERARDO: I'd rather speak to you as if you were a client, Doctor Miranda. That will help me out. I think you should eat something.

ROBERTO: I'm not hungry.

GERARDO: Let me . . .

[GERARDO *fills a spoon with soup and feeds* ROBERTO *as if he was a baby. Throughout the following scene,* GERARDO *is continually feeding* ROBERTO *as well as feeding himself.*]

ROBERTO: She's mad. You'll have to excuse me for saying this, Gerardo, but your wife . . .

GERARDO: Bread?

ROBERTO: No thanks.

[*Brief pause.*]

She should be receiving some sort of psychiatric treatment for—

GERARDO: To put it brutally, you are her therapy, doctor.

[*He cleans* ROBERTO'*s mouth with a napkin.*]

ROBERTO: She's going to kill me.

GERARDO: Unless you confess, she'll kill you.

ROBERTO: But what can I confess? What can I confess if I . . . ?

GERARDO: You may be aware, doctor, that the secret police used some doctors as—consultants in torture sessions . . .

ROBERTO: The medical association gradually learned of these situations, and looked into them wherever possible.

GERARDO: She is convinced that you are that doctor who . . . And unless you have a way of denying it . . .

ROBERTO: How could I deny it? I'd have to change my voice, prove that this is not my voice—if it's only voice which damns me, if there's no other evidence, nothing that—

GERARDO: And your skin. She mentioned your skin.

ROBERTO: My skin?

GERARDO: And your smell.

ROBERTO: Fantasies of a diseased mind. She could have latched on to any man who came through that door. . . .

GERARDO: Unfortunately, you came through that door.

ROBERTO: Look, Gerardo, I'm a quiet man. Anyone can see that I'm incapable of violence—violence of any sort sickens me. I come to my beach house, I wander on the beach, I watch the waves, I hunt for pebbles, I listen to my music—

GERARDO: Shubert?

ROBERTO: Shubert, there's no reason to feel ashamed. I also like Vivaldi and Mozart and Telemann. And I had the stupid idea of bringing Shubert to the beach yesterday. But it was much more stupid to stop for me—Gerardo, I'm only in this mess because I felt sorry for some lunatic waving his arms next to his broken-down car—Look, it's up to you to get me out of here.

GERARDO: I know.

ROBERTO: My ankles hurt, my hands, my back. Couldn't you untie me a little, so—

GERARDO: Roberto, I want to be honest with you. There is only one way to save your life . . .

[*Brief pause.*]

I think we have to—indulge her.

ROBERTO: Indulge her?

GERARDO: Humor her, placate her, so she feels that we—that you are willing to cooperate . . .

ROBERTO: I don't see how I can cooperate, given my rather peculiar position . . .

GERARDO: Indulge her, make her believe that you . . .

ROBERTO: Make her believe that I . . .

GERARDO: She promised me that if you—confessed she would be ready to—

ROBERTO: I haven't got anything to confess!

GERARDO: I think you'll have to invent something then, because the only way she'll pardon you is if—

ROBERTO: She's got nothing to pardon me for. I did nothing and there's nothing to confess. Do you understand? Instead of proposing dishonorable solutions to me, you should be out there convincing that madwoman of yours to cease this criminal behavior before she ruins your career and ends up in jail or in an insane asylum. Tell her that. Or can't you impose a little order in your own house?

THE SPEED OF DARKNESS

BY STEVE TESICH

CHARACTERS

JOE *(40s) is a successful businessman and hero of the Vietnam War;*
LOU *(40s) is his war buddy who is homeless and spends his time
following around the mobile Vietnam Wall Memorial.*

SCENE

*South Dakota, living room of Joe's home. (NOTE: Anne is Joe's wife,
Mary is their daughter.)*

TIME

3 a.m. on a night in the late 1980s.

[JOE *and* LOU *are sitting and smoking. All of* LOU's *stuff is next
to him.*]

LOU: That's what I call a full moon. Sitting right there on top of the
mesa like some crystal ball.

JOE: Yeah, it's nice.

LOU: Boy, I've had me some day today. It was one of those days. I
even got a little baby boy named after me. Did Mary tell you? His
name's Lou.

JOE: She did, yeah. Lou Junior.

LOU: How about that? Always a godfather. Never a god.

JOE: We were gonna pick up where we left off. Do you remember where that was?

LOU: Something about me going. You can relax, Joe. That's what I plan to do. I'll be leaving in a few minutes.

JOE: Don't be stupid. You're not gonna leave in the middle of the night.

LOU: It's like this. When you show up, you can show up any old way, but when you leave, you have to leave right. After what your Mary did for me, I don't think I could say good-bye to her without lying and saying, "I'll see you soon," or something like that. I don't want to lie to her.

JOE: It's none of my business, Lou, but maybe you shouldn't keep on hanging around these traveling war memorials.

LOU: I know.

JOE: Let them go.

LOU: Maybe I will. You never did come to Washington, did you? When they unveiled, or whatever they call it, the real one.

JOE: No.

LOU: I looked for you that day.

JOE: I had no desire to see it.

LOU: All the vets were there.

JOE: Good for them.

LOU: Like big stone pages from some book, that's what it looked like. Page after page. I was hoping to find my name on one of them.

OE: What are you talking about? You're not a crazy man, are you?

LOU: I didn't think so. But I made the papers the next day. I got so upset when I couldn't find my name there, I tried to scratch it in stone with my can opener. These two Marine guards dragged me away. They didn't hurt me or nothing. Very nice boys and kind of sorry they had to be doing what they were doing. "I'm an M.I.A., boys, missing in America. Give me an address." "We can't let you do that, sir." "Sir," they called me. Wonderful boys. Perfect Marines. "We can't let you do that, sir. The Wall's only for those who died. Not for those who survived, sir." "Boys," I told them, "I swear to you on my word of honor, I didn't survive. If you don't believe me, just ask some of these vets here who knew me when I was alive. They'll tell you." Anyway, I made the papers. No picture. Just a little story. "Disturbed vet tries to desecrate the memorial." It hurt when I read that.

[*He stands.*]

I guess I better get going.

OE: C'mon, Lou. It's three in the morning. Wait a bit.

LOU: I might change my mind if I wait. You saved my life. I can't betray you. And I can't do anything without betraying you.

[*He reaches for his things, stops.*]

Tell me, Joe. Maybe you understand it. How do they do it?

OE: Do what?

LOU: You know, how do they decide? It's like they all get together and decide. From now on, let's treat the vets like garbage. Just when you get used to it, they change their minds. From now on, let's treat them like heroes. I know they'll change their minds again. There's an edge to things already. We've given you a monument in Washington and a parade on Wall Street, what else do you want? You don't know what's next, do you, Joe?

JOE: No.

> [LOU *picks up his things, starts to go.*]

Here's something to . . .

> [*He takes out an envelope from his back pocket, offers it to* LOU.]

LOU: [*Takes the envelope, looks inside.*] Boy, the longer I stay, the more money I'm offered. If I could stick around for a few more days, I'd be a rich guy.

AFTER CRYSTAL NIGHT

BY JOHN HERMAN SHANER

CHARACTERS

SEYMOUR GOLDSTEIN *(45) is a successful businessman who has always been haunted by fears of confrontation;* JERRY GOLDSTEIN *(48),* SEYMOUR*'s older brother, is an out-of-work tax consultant who follows all the New Age trends. (NOTE: Jacob is his birth name.)*

SCENE

The uncluttered living room of the expensive Goldstein home in Beverly Hills, California.

TIME

A Sunday morning, 1983.

[*A Neo-Nazi group will be holding a rally later today in downtown Los Angeles.* SEYMOUR *is furious about it and wants to show his opposition; but he is scared to do so and to be shown up in front of his fourteen-year-old son. Also his wife, Joyce, opposes his participation. Nevertheless, he has put on his old work boots and is preparing for battle.*]

SEYMOUR: Please, my wife and I are going to have a terrible fight. Go to your Swami Vuctananda. Let him turn the other cheek, he can afford it.

JERRY: What other cheek? He says punch 'em in the mouth.

SEYMOUR: Then come down. I'm scared to go alone.

JERRY: He says punch 'em in the mouth. I don't. He's only my guru for certain things.

SEYMOUR: What the hell do you think Nazis are? They're intellectual heirs of Hitler. Can't you get it through your head they mean what they say? If they can pull it off, they mean the ovens.

JERRY: Leave me alone, I don't want to hear that. Go—fight with your wife.

[*He pushes his brother toward the bedroom.*]

SEYMOUR: What the hell's wrong with us? I don't understand the Jews! A non-Jew goes outside, and he sees a dark cloud. He figures it's going to rain. He goes inside for an umbrella. Not a Jew. A Jew's got to catch pneumonia first. Self-defense is the first law of any living organism—if it doesn't adapt to that simple principle of nature, it doesn't deserve to go on.

JERRY: What self-defense? You're provoking them.

SEYMOUR: We have a right to counter-demonstrate.

JERRY: That's bullshit. Nobody'll control themselves. That's like two scorpions in a bottle.

SEYMOUR: It's honor, it's self-defense.

JERRY: Stop with the self-defense. Where do you know from self-defense?

SEYMOUR: Don't do that, Jacob!

JERRY: All right. Okay. You're right. I've got to stop that.

[*He rubs his temples, realizes what he's been doing.*]

God.

[*Distraught, he paces the room.*]

I'm going to stop that, I promise. You know the biggest influence on my life? Not teachers or Elvis or college or John F. Kennedy. Adolf Hitler. It was Adolf Hitler. Remember those newsreels of the Nuremburg rallies? They absolutely fascinated me. Hitler speaking, the violence, the rage—at me. God, I hated him, but I was morbidly fascinated too, isn't that terrible?—all at the same time. Talk about mixed-up. Sometimes I believed I'd done something terrible, but what was it? I couldn't figure it out. Maybe I was guilty about something, but what? Why do we always have to apologize for our existence? Why? Nobody else has to! Is it any wonder that I'm crazed and demented?

SEYMOUR: You'd have been crazed and demented no matter what.

ERRY: That's true.

[*He starts to exit to the kitchen.*]

God, what happened to the sixties? Everything was so quiet and peaceful then . . .

[*He exits to kitchen.*]

A WAY WITH WORDS

BY FRANK D. GILROY

CHARACTERS

FRED *(45), a successful businessman;* ARTIE *(45), his longtime friend.*

SCENE

A corner table in a Manhattan restaurant.

TIME

The present, midday.

[ARTIE *and* FRED *sit across from each other, drinks by their elbows.*]

FRED: I don't believe it. I do not fucking believe it.

ARTIE: I'm sorry.

FRED: Spare me.

ARTIE: I had no idea you'd take it like this.

FRED: What did you expect?

ARTIE: You look like I hit you.

FRED: That's how I feel.

ARTIE: I should have told you when it happened.

FRED: What stopped you?

ARTIE: I figured once she had her fling, she'd come back. Why make waves.

FRED: And later? When you knew it wasn't a fling?

ARTIE: I was embarrassed.

FRED: So you kept lying.

ARTIE: I never thought of it as lying.

FRED: Every year I come to New York and we have lunch and I always ask how Louise is and you always say "fine" . . .

ARTIE: Which she is.

FRED: . . . Until today when you announce that you and she aren't together anymore . . .

ARTIE: It makes you feel better—I lied.

FRED: . . . "That's too bad," I say. "When did it happen?" And you say . . . Say it.

ARTIE: I said it.

FRED: Say it again so I'm sure I heard it right.

ARTIE: Louise left me thirteen years ago.

FRED: Thirteen?

ARTIE: Thirteen.

FRED: Artie, if this is a joke—

ARTIE: It's on me.

FRED: How could you not tell me?

ARTIE: We see each other once a year.

FRED: You lied because it was easy?

ARTIE: We always talk about when we were kids. Good times. didn't want to spoil it.

FRED: Bullshit.

ARTIE: You're right.

FRED: Why then?

ARTIE: Promise not to laugh.

FRED: Artie—please.

ARTIE: Because you thought she and I were still together made i seem true for a few hours.

FRED: Jesus.

ARTIE: Sometimes after our lunches I was so into it I expected to find her there when I got home.

FRED: Thirteen years and you're still carrying a torch?

ARTIE: Never changed the lock on the door or the phone numbe in case she—

FRED: I get the picture. The Christmas cards with both you signatures?

ARTIE: Forged.

FRED: And that's why whenever I phoned I got you.

ARTIE: You didn't phone that often.

FRED: The phone works both ways.

ARTIE: You can only talk so much about boyhood memories.

FRED: We went separate ways—okay. But I always felt I could rel on you in an emergency.

ARTIE: I feel the same.

FRED: Your wife walking out wasn't an emergency?

ARTIE: What could you have done?

FRED: Provided a sympathetic ear at least.

ARTIE: I felt sorry enough for myself without encouragement.

FRED: Why did she do it?

ARTIE: I guess she wasn't happy.

FRED: You guess?

ARTIE: I came home from work. She's at the door, bags packed, cab waiting. Hands me a list of household things that need doing. Says it will be best for both of us in the long run. The next thing I know the cab is turning the corner and I'm waving with a smile on my face like she's going to visit her mother in case any neighbors are watching.

EYES FOR CONSUELA
BY SAM SHEPARD

CHARACTERS
HENRY *(late 40s) is a man in escape mode from the failure of h*
marriage, his life; AMADO *(40s) is a Latino man who is living*
shadow life, clever and crafty.

SCENE
A second-floor room in a boardinghouse in Mexico on the edge o
the jungle.

TIME
Evening. The present.

[AMADO, *wearing a sombrero, approaches* HENRY. AMADO ha.
a machete swinging at his side. He also carries a knife.]

AMADO: Light the lamp.

HENRY: Look—I'm just down here on a kind of—vacation. I don't—

AMADO: Be silent! Light the lamp!

[HENRY *lights a kerosene lamp, filling the room with a glow.*]

I have no interest in you. I don't care why you're here or who you are
I only care about one thing. Just one. Making my woman happy

Right now, she is not happy. She is sad. Her sadness is my doing. It is my duty to change that.

[AMADO *paces slowly.* HENRY *stands still.*]

HENRY: I wish I could help you.

AMADO: Your wish is to run. To be far away. Don't lie to me.

HENRY: I just—don't understand.

AMADO: Sit down. By the lamp. Sit!

[HENRY *moves to the chair by the table, removes the sombrero from it, sits.*]

Turn your face to the light.

[HENRY *does this,* AMADO *moves toward him with the knife.*]

Open your eyes.

[HENRY *follows instructions.* AMADO *moves closer and peers into* HENRY's *eyes.*]

HENRY: Why can't you see they're not blue? They're not blue eyes. I don't know how many times you have to look.

[AMADO *looks intensely, the knife held up. Suddenly he turns away, pacing.*]

AMADO: Do you have a woman?

HENRY: I—yes. Yes, I do.

AMADO: Only one?

HENRY: Yes. Of course.

AMADO: [*Laughs.*] "Of course!" Of course.

HENRY: My wife.

AMADO: Aah—How long? How long, your wife and you?

HENRY: You mean—together?

AMADO: Yes. Together. How long?

HENRY: Well—it's been off and on now for over twenty years.

AMADO: Off and on? Off and on. What does this mean, "Off and on"?

HENRY: We haven't exactly—seen things—eye to eye over the years.

AMADO: Are you making fun of me?

HENRY: No. No, not at all.

AMADO: [*Pacing again.*] And which way are you now? You and your wife. "Off" or "on"?

HENRY: We—We're separated now.

AMADO: Separated. Apart?

HENRY: Yes.

AMADO: Then—that's "off," no?

HENRY: Yes.

AMADO: And you—you're suffering from this? Your wife is suffering?

HENRY: Well—

AMADO: Be a man. You must know these things. You must know them by heart.

HENRY: Yes. Sometimes.

AMADO: Sometimes suffering? Sometimes not?

HENRY: Yes.

AMADO: It comes and goes, this suffering?

HENRY: Yes.

AMADO: Why is that?

HENRY: I—I don't know.

AMADO: You don't—wonder about it?

HENRY: What?

AMADO: This suffering! "Off and on." On and off. It doesn't puzzle you?

HENRY: I never—I never actually thought about it much.

AMADO: Ah, so you just suffer like a dog? A whipped dog.

HENRY: No, I—

AMADO: Tell the truth? What have you got to lose?

THE KENTUCKY CYCLE
BY ROBERT SCHENKKAN

CHARACTERS

This dialogue occurs in the sixth play of the cycle, Tall Tales. *JT WELLS (40) is a traveling storyteller and confidence artist; JED ROWEN (52), who owns a family farm, thinks he's a pretty sharp fellow—a delusion that* JT *is only too happy to take advantage of.*

SCENE

A wooden-plank dinner table with a recently completed meal on it inside the Rowen farmhouse in the rolling hills of eastern Kentucky.

TIME

A summer evening in 1885.

JT: You know, you folks been so kind to me 'n' all, I'd sure like to be able to do somethin' for you in return. I mean, when you see a family like this one, so close, so full of love for each other 'n' all, it just makes you think: What if . . . ?

[*Beat.*]

JED: What if?

JT: What if, God forbid, somethin' should happen to one of you. I mean, we can't all be as lucky as Baucis and Philomen and count on the Lord callin' us at the same time, can we? And in the unpleasant event of your absence, you'd sure want your wife and child looked over proper now, wouldn't you?

JED: Well, sure.

JT: Course you would. But how's a man to do that? You sure wouldn't want to rely on the Jacksons or the rest of your neighbors now, would you?

JED: No, sir.

JT: It's a problem for sure. But one for which, I'm happy to say, there is a solution.

JED: What's that?

JT: I have been empowered by certain parties to purchase the mineral rights from farsighted Christian gentlemen like yourself.

[*Beat.*]

JED: My mineral rights?

JT: Yes sir.

JED: Oh. Well . . . uh . . . what exactly are we talkin' about here, JT?

JT: Well, "mineral rights" is just a twenty-five-cent word for rocks, actually.

JED: Rocks? You mean somebody wants to buy the rocks offa my land?

JT: That's it exactly. The people I represent will pay you *fifty cents an acre* for the right to haul off all mineral and metallic substances and combinations of the same. In your case, countin' your three-hundred-odd acres—

JED: Three hunert and fifty-seven acres.

JT: [*Smiling.*] That'd be about a hundred and seventy-nine dollars in cold, hard American cash.

[*Stunned silence.*]

JED: Let me get this straight, JT—I been breakin' my back diggin' rocks outta my damn fields so I could plow for nigh onto forty years, and now there are people willin' to pay me money for the same privilege?

JT: What can I tell you, Jed, 'cept there's a fool born every day. Here, you read it for yourself, it's all down there in black and white.

[*He pulls out a contract from his jacket and hands it to* JED, *who inspects it awkwardly, too embarrassed to admit he can't read.*]

JT: [*Gently.*] Light's kinda bad in here—maybe you'd like me to go over it for you.

JED: Can't do nothin' with these old eyes of mine.

JT: Essentially, this says that for the sum in question, you, the owner, pass over the title to the minerals underlying your land with all the usual and ordinary mining rights. It says all that a lot longer, but that's what it boils down to.

JED: And that's all there is to it?

JT: That's all.

JED: Well, that sounds easy, don't it! Where am I supposed to sign?

JT: Right here.

[JED *picks up the pen.* JED *looks the document over again.*]

JED: Just outta curiosity, JT, what exactly are those "usual and ordinary mining rights" you were talking about?

JT: [*Picking his way carefully.*] That means they can excavate for the minerals . . . uh, build a road here and there, if necessary—long as they don't disturb you, of course. Use some of the local water . . .

JED: Hold it right there! You never said anything before about cuttin' across my land or taking my water!

JT: That was understood, Jed. I figured a man of your experience knew how these things worked.

JED: Nope! No way! Ain't no way anybody's gonna build a road over my land!

JT: Look, Jed, I promise you, I swear to God, you'll hardly know they're there! They gonna be real careful with your land.

JED: You want my mineral rights, that's one thing. But I just can't see my way to all that other stuff. Roads and water—no, sir!

[*Beat.*]

'Less you're willin' to go a whole 'nother quarter an acre.

JT: What?!

JED: A dollar an acre and she's yours!

JT: Hell, Jed, you can practically *buy* land in these parts for that!

JED: Then you do it! Course I thought you wanted the mineral rights to a *particular* piece of land. *Mine.*

JT: You tryin' to cut my throat, Jed?!

JED: [*Innocently.*] Why no, JT—but you did start out by sayin' how you wanted to do me and mine a favor.

[*Beat. Both men are breathing a little hard. JT finally manages a smile.*]

JT: Jed Rowen, I hope you won't take this the wrong way if I tell you I ain't never met anybody like you. You, sir, are one tough son of a bitch.

JED: [*Smiling.*] I'd consider that a compliment. We doin' business?

JT: Yeah, we're doin' business.

JED: Dollar an acre?

JT: Dollar an acre.

JED: Where do I sign?

[*He picks up the pen and then puts it down again.*]

JT: I ain't goin' any higher, Jed.

JED: [*Embarrassed.*] Ain't the money, JT. I don't know how to sign my name.

JT: [*Relieved.*] All you do is touch the pen and make your mark. An X or whatever.

[JED *signs.*]

JT: An' here's a bank draft for—

JED: Three hundred and fifty-seven dollars!

JT: Now, you just take this draft to the bank—any bank, anywhere. That little paper's as good as gold.

[JED *examines the paper with great respect.* JT *leans over the table.*]

JT: I'm gonna ask you a favor, Jed, man to man. I'd appreciate it if you wouldn't mention this price to your neighbors—least not til after I been a round and had a crack at 'em. Make my job a little easier, you know?

JED: I understand, JT. When it comes to business, everybody got his own lookout.

T: Ain't that the truth.

[*Beat.*]

Well, I sure want to thank you folks for your hospitality, but I better be goin'.

ED: Sure wouldn't be any trouble.

T: No, I better be movin'.

ED: Suit yourself.

T: Jed? Take care of yourself.

THE PRICE
BY ARTHUR MILLER

CHARACTERS
VICTOR FRANZ *(50) is a police sergeant trying to sell off the estate of his late father, as the storage building is being torn down.* GREGORY SOLOMON *(90) is the wily Russian Jewish antique dealer who* VICTOR *called to come take a look.*

SCENE
The attic in midtown Manhattan where Victor's father's things have been stored.

TIME
Early afternoon.

SOLOMON: Tell me, if you don't mind, how did you get my name?

VICTOR: In the phone book.

SOLOMON: You don't say! The phone book.

VICTOR: Why?

SOLOMON: No-no, that's fine, that's fine.

VICTOR: The ad said you're a registered appraiser.

SOLOMON: Oh yes, I am registered, I am licensed, I am even vaccinated.

[VICTOR *laughs.*]

Don't laugh, the only thing you can do today without a license is you'll go up the elevator and jump out the window. But I don't have to tell you, you're a policeman, you know this world. I'm right?

VICTOR: I suppose.

[SOLOMON *surveys the furniture, one hand on his thigh, the other on the chair arm in a naturally elegant position.*]

SOLOMON: So.

[*He glances about again, and with an uncertain smile.*]

That's a lot of furniture. This is all for sale?

VICTOR: Well, ya.

SOLOMON: Fine, fine. I just like to be sure where we are. Frankly, in this neighborhood I never expected such a load. It's very surprising.

VICTOR: But I said it was a whole houseful.

SOLOMON: Look, don't worry about it, we'll handle everything very nice.

[*He gets up from the chair and goes to one of the pair of chiffoniers, which he is obviously impressed with. He looks up at the chandeliers. Then straight at* VICTOR.]

I'm not mixing in, officer, but If you wouldn't mind—what is your connection? How do you come to this?

VICTOR: It was my family.

SOLOMON: You don't say. Looks like it's standing here a long time, no?

VICTOR: Well, the old man moved everything up here after the '29 crash. My uncles took over the house and they let him keep this floor.

SOLOMON: I see.

[*He walks to the harp.*]

VICTOR: Can you give me an estimate now, or do you have to—?

SOLOMON: [*Running a hand over the harp frame.*] No-no, I'll give you right away, I don't waste a minute, I'm very busy.

[*He plucks a string, listens. Then bends down and runs a hand over the sound board.*]

He passed away, your father?

VICTOR: Oh, long time ago—about sixteen years.

SOLOMON: It's standing here sixteen years?

VICTOR: Well, we never got around to doing anything about it, but they're tearing the building down, so . . . It was very good stuff, you know—they had quite a little money.

SOLOMON: Very good, yes . . . I can see.

[*He leaves the harp with an estimating glance.*]

I was also very good; now I'm not so good. Time, you know, is a terrible thing.

[*He is a distance from the harp and indicates it.*]

That sounding board is cracked, you know. But don't worry about it, it's still a nice object.

[*He goes to an armoire and strokes the veneer.*]

It's a funny thing—an armoire like this, thirty years you couldn't give it away; it was a regular measles. Today all of a sudden, they want it again. Go figure it out.

[*He goes to one of the chests.*]

VICTOR: [*Pleased.*] Well, give me a good price and we'll make a deal.

SOLOMON: Definitely. You see, I don't lie to you.

[*He is pointing to the chest.*]

For instance, a chiffonier like this I wouldn't have to keep it a week.

[*Indicating the other chest.*]

That's a pair, you know.

VICTOR: I know.

SOLOMON: That's a nice chair, too.

[*He sits on a dining-room chair, rocking to test its tightness.*]

I like the chairs.

VICTOR: There's more stuff in the bedroom, if you want to look.

SOLOMON: Oh?

[*He goes toward the bedroom.*]

What've you got here?

[*He looks into the bedroom, up and down.*]

I like the bed. That's a nice carved bed. That I can sell. That's your parents' bed.

VICTOR: Yes. They may have bought that in Europe, if I'm not mistaken. They used to travel a good deal.

SOLOMON: Very handsome, very nice. I like it.

[*He starts to return to the center chair, eyes roving the furniture.*]

Looks a very nice family.

VICTOR: By the way, that dining-room table opens up. Probably seat about twelve people.

SOLOMON: [*Looking at the table.*] I know that. Yes. In a pinch even fourteen.

[*He picks up the foil.*]

What's this? I thought you were stabbing your wife when I came in.

VICTOR: [*Laughing.*] No, I just found it. I used to fence years ago.

SOLOMON: You went to college?

VICTOR: Couple of years, ya.

SOLOMON: That's very interesting.

VICTOR: It's the old story.

SOLOMON: No, listen—What happens to people is always the main element to me. Because when do they call me? It's either a divorce or somebody died. So it's always a new story. I mean it's the same, but it's different.

[*He sits in the center chair.*]

VICTOR: You pick up the pieces.

SOLOMON: That's very good, yes. I pick up the pieces. It's a little bit like you. I suppose. You must have some stories, I betcha.

VICTOR: Not very often.

SOLOMON: What are you, a traffic cop, or something . . . ?

VICTOR: I'm out in Rockaway most of the time, the airports.

SOLOMON: That's Siberia, no?

VICTOR: [*Laughing.*] I like it better that way.

SOLOMON: You keep your nose clean.

VICTOR: [*Smiling.*] That's it.

[*Indicating the furniture.*]

So what do you say?

SOLOMON: What I say?

[*Taking out two cigars as he glances about.*]

You like a cigar.

VICTOR: Thanks, I gave it up long time ago. So what's the story here?

SOLOMON: I can see you are a very factual person.

VICTOR: You hit it.

SOLOMON: Couldn't be better. So tell me, you got some kind of paper here? To show ownership?

VICTOR: Well, no, I don't. But . . .

[*He half-laughs.*]

I'm the owner, that's all.

SOLOMON: In other words, there's no brothers, no sisters.

VICTOR: I have a brother, yes.

SOLOMON: Ah-hah. You're friendly with him. Not that I'm mixing in, but I don't have to tell you the average family they love each other like crazy, but the minute the parents die is all of a sudden a question who is going to get what and you're covered with cats and dogs—

VICTOR: There's no such problem here.

SOLOMON: Unless we're gonna talk about a few pieces, then it wouldn't bother me, but to take the whole loan without a paper is a—

VICTOR: All right, I'll get you some kind of statement from him: don't worry about it.

SOLOMON: That's definite; because even from high-class people you wouldn't believe the shenanigans—lawyers, college professors, television personalities—five hundred dollars they'll pay a lawyer to fight over a bookcase it's worth fifty cents—because you see, everybody wants to be a number one, so . . .

VICTOR: I said I'd get you a statement.

[*He indicates the room.*]

Now what's the story?

SOLOMON: All right, so I'll tell you the story.

[*He looks at the dining-room table and points to it.*]

For instance, you mention the dining-room table. That's what they call Spanish Jacobean. Cost maybe twelve, thirteen hundred dollars. I would say—1921, '22. I'm right?

VICTOR: Probably, ya.

SOLOMON: [*Clears his throat.*] I see you're an intelligent man, so before I say another word, I ask you to remember—with used furniture you cannot be emotional.

VICTOR: [*Laughs.*] I haven't opened my mouth!

SOLOMON: I mean you're a policemen, I'm a furniture dealer, we both know this world. Anything Spanish Jacobean you'll sell quicker a case of tuberculosis.

VICTOR: Why? That table's in beautiful condition.

SOLOMON: Officer, you're talking reality; you cannot talk reality with used furniture. They don't like that style; not only they don't like it, they hate it. The same thing with that buffet there and that . . .

[*He starts to point elsewhere.*]

VICTOR: You only want to take a few pieces, is that the ticket?

SOLOMON: Please, officer, we're already talking too fast—

VICTOR: No-no, you're not going to walk off with the gravy and leave me with the bones. All or nothing or let's forget it. I told you on the phone it was a whole houseful.

SOLOMON: What're you in such a hurry? Talk a little bit, we'll see what happens. In a day they didn't build Rome.

[*He calculates worriedly for a moment, glances again at the pieces he wants. He gets up, goes and touches the harp.*]

You see, what I had in mind—I would give you such a knockout price for those few pieces that you—

VICTOR: That's *out.*

SOLOMON: Out.

VICTOR: I'm not running a department store. They're tearing the building down.

SOLOMON: Couldn't be better! We understand each other, so—so there's no reason to be emotional.

[*He goes to the records.*]

These records go?

[*He picks up one.*]

VICTOR: I might keep three or four.

SOLOMON: [*Reading a label.*] Look at that! Gallagher and Shean!

VICTOR: [*With only half a laugh.*] You're not going to start playing them now!

SOLOMON: Who needs to play? I was on the same bill with Gallagher and Shean maybe fifty theaters.

VICTOR: You were an actor?

SOLOMON: An actor? An acrobat; my whole family was acrobats. You never heard The Five Solomons—may they rest in peace? I was the one on the bottom.

VICTOR: Funny—I never heard of a Jewish acrobat.

SOLOMON: What's the matter with Jacob, he wasn't a wrestler?— wrestled with the Angel?

[VICTOR *laughs.*]

SOLOMON: Jews been acrobats since the beginning of the world. I was a horse them days: drink, women, anything—on the go, on the go, nothing ever stopped me. Only life. Yes, my boy.

[*Almost lovingly putting down the record.*]

What do you know, Gallagher and Shean.

VICTOR: So where are we?

SOLOMON: [*Glancing off, he turns back to* VICTOR *with a deeply concerned look.*] Tell me, what's with crime now? It's up, hey?

VICTOR: Yeah, it's up, it's up. Look, Mr. Solomon, let me make one thing clear, heh? I'm not sociable.

SOLOMON: You're not.

VICTOR: No, I'm not; I'm not a businessman, I'm not good at conversations. So let's get to a price, and finish. Okay?

SOLOMON: You don't want we should be buddies.

VICTOR: That's exactly it.

SOLOMON: So we wouldn't be buddies!

[*He sighs.*]

But just so you'll know me a little better—I'm going to show you something.

[*He takes out a leather folder, which he hands to* VICTOR.]

There's my discharge from the British Navy. You see? "His Majesty's Service."

VICTOR: [*Looking at the document.*] Huh! What were you doing in the British Navy?

SOLOMON: Forget the British Navy. What does it say the date of birth?

VICTOR: "Eighteen . . ." You're almost ninety?

SOLOMON: Yes, my boy. I left Russia sixty-five years ago, I was twenty-four years old. And I smoked all my life. I drinked, and I loved every woman who would let me. So what do I need to steal from you?

VICTOR: Since when do people need a reason to steal?

SOLOMON: I never saw such a man in my life!

VICTOR: Oh yes, you did. Now you going to give me a figure or—?

SOLOMON: How can I give you a figure? You don't trust one word I say!

VICTOR: I never saw you before, what're you asking me to trust you?!

SOLOMON: [*With a gesture of disgust.*] But how am I going to start to talk to you? I'm sorry; here you can't be a policeman. If you want to do business a little bit you gotta believe or you can't do it. I'm . . . I'm . . . Look, forget it.

[*He gets up and goes to his portfolio.*]

VICTOR: [*Astonished.*] What are you doing?

SOLOMON: I can't work this way. I'm too old; every time I open my mouth you should practically call me a thief.

VICTOR: Who called you a thief?

SOLOMON: [*Moving toward the door.*] No—I don't need it. I don't want it in my shop.

[*Wagging a finger into* Victor's *face.*]

And don't forget it—I never gave you a price, and look what you did to me. You see? I never gave you a price!

VICTOR: Well, what did you come here for, to do me a favor? What are you talking about?

SOLOMON: Mister, I pity you! What is the matter with you people! You're worse than my daughter! Nothing in the world you believe, nothing you respect—how can you live? You think that's such a smart thing? That's so hard, what you're doing? Let me give you a piece of advice—it's not that you can't believe nothing, that's not so hard—it's that you still got to believe it. *That's* hard. And if you can't do that, my friend—you're a dead man.

[*He starts toward the door.*]

COME AGAIN, ANOTHER DAY

BY CARY PEPPER

CHARACTERS
IVAN FOLEY *(40), a businessman, receives a very unexpected visit from* MARTIN *(50). Well-dressed. A gentleman. But not welcome.*

SCENE
The living room of Ivan Foley.

TIME
The present.

[IVAN *comes in, dressed in a suit, which he immediately begins to take off as he moves about the room, muttering angrily.*]

IVAN: Goddamn bastards! Stupid pricks! For two months you give 'em your best while they sit there and sip it through a straw! . . . Then they narrow it down to you and some other bimbo, and throw you against each other for another month while they make up their minds . . . Finally, they name a day when they'll tell you who beat out the other, then they cancel the final interview, say they need more time, and they'll call in an hour! Sure! What do they care! They're safe and secure behind their desks! They've got a job! What do they care about what you're going through!? How many times do they expect you to pour yourself through a tube? How many times do you think you can!? . . . They'll call in an hour! . . . Suppose I wasn't here to get the call? Then what? . . . Would they panic? Would they sit by their phone all day, dialing and dialing until they got me in? Or would they just call the other guy? "What the hell, one's as good as the other!" . . . Goddamn, inefficient, inconsiderate, insensitive . . .

MARTIN: [*Stepping from the shadows.*] Sleazebags.

[IVAN *jumps at the sound of* MARTIN*'s voice and wheels around, very frightened.*]

IVAN: Jesus!

[IVAN *shudders as he regards* MARTIN. MARTIN *smiles at him.*]

Who the hell are you!

MARTIN: Martin.

IVAN: Martin . . . Martin who?

MARTIN: Just . . . Martin.

IVAN: Just Martin . . . How'd you get in here?

[IVAN *can barely contain himself as he virtually hops around in fear, not wanting to remain in any one place for too long, yet not sure just where he will be safe.*]

MARTIN: There are ways.

IVAN: Well, what do you want?

MARTIN: To talk. Would you care to sit down?

IVAN: Yes! I would care to sit down! . . . No, I don't want to sit down! And I still don't know who you are.

[MARTIN *starts to answer.*]

And just "Martin" doesn't do it! Or is that your last name?

MARTIN: Just Martin.

IVAN: All right, "just Martin," what do you want?

MARTIN: To talk.

IVAN: About what!?

MARTIN: You. What you're like. Who you are.

IVAN: Why?

MARTIN: Because there's time.

IVAN: Oh, really? Time for what?

MARTIN: To talk. There's some extra time.

IVAN: Extra time before what?!

MARTIN: Before I have to kill you.

IVAN: WHAT?

MARTIN: I'm here to kill you. And there's some extra time before I have to do it. I thought we'd talk.

[*Pause.*]

IVAN: You're here . . . to . . . kill me? . . . What is that supposed to mean?

MARTIN: I really don't know how to make it much clearer.

IVAN: You're here to kill me . . .

[MARTIN *nods.*]

WHY?

MARTIN: I don't know . . . I never ask.

IVAN: Ask? Ask who?

MARTIN: The people paying me.

IVAN: You're being paid to kill me?

[MARTIN *nods.*]

ME?

[MARTIN *nods.*]

By who?

MARTIN: I never divulge the name of a client.

IVAN: They've got the wrong person.

MARTIN: Ivan Foley . . . ?

IVAN: Yeah . . .

MARTIN: 373 E. 33rd Street . . . ?

IVAN: Yeah . . .

MARTIN: Apartment #23 . . . Social Security # 170-46-3782 . . .

IVAN: What are you, from the IRS?

MARTIN: Born: July 7, 1956 . . . Father: Henry . . . Mother: Susan . . Black hair, brown eyes . . . height: 5 feet, 6 inches . . . weight: 145 pounds . . . Birthmark on the inner right thigh . . .

IVAN: You from my doctor? . . . So I'm Ivan Foley, birthmark and all. So why does someone want me dead?

MARTIN: I imagine it must be something you've done.

IVAN: What?! . . . To who?

MARTIN: I never divulge the name of a client.

IVAN: Well then, fuck you! And as a matter of fact, get the hell out of here!

MARTIN: I'm the one in control here, Ivan.

IVAN: The fuck you are!

[IVAN *goes to the door and throws it open.*]

Get out!

[IVAN *takes a few steps back into the room, coming close to* MARTIN, *only to find* MARTIN *has drawn a gun, which is equipped with a silencer. Drawn up short,* IVAN *freezes at the sight of the weapon and stares at it.*]

IVAN: Jesus . . . Christ!

[*Pause while* IVAN *continues to stare.*]

God . . . damn!

MARTIN: Close the door, Ivan.

IVAN: Hey, wait a minute . . . let's talk about this.

MARTIN: That's what I want to do . . . talk.

IVAN: Yeah, yeah . . . let's talk.

MARTIN: But first, close the door.

IVAN: The door?

MARTIN: Yes. The door.

IVAN: The door . . .

MARTIN: The door.

IVAN: The door.

MARTIN: Close it. And please don't do anything stupid, or I'll be forced to kill you right now.

IVAN: [*In a daze.*] Uh-huh . . . uh-huh . . .

[IVAN *goes to the door, closes it, and comes back into the room.*]

MARTIN: Sit down, Ivan.

IVAN: [*Dutifully sitting.*] What the hell is going on here?

MARTIN: Someone has put out a contract on you. I'm carrying it out.

IVAN: Why? . . . Don't I have a right to know what I did?

MARTIN: You know. You just can't remember.

IVAN: They've got the wrong man.

MARTIN: The description matched.

IVAN: Maybe the description matched, but that still doesn't mean I did it. Maybe I was there, and someone saw me . . . But I still didn't do it . . . Or maybe I did it. But they don't have to kill me for it. I mean, how bad could it have been . . . whatever it was I did? But I never did it!

MARTIN: If they say it's you, it's you. They're very thorough.

IVAN: Who is? Who are they? Don't I have a right to know that?

MARTIN: What difference does it make? If someone puts out a contract on you, what's the difference if it's the Mafia, the government, or the Parking Violations Bureau?

IVAN: It's right that I should know! It just is!

MARTIN: Maybe . . . That's what everyone else asks.

IVAN: And you never answer?

MARTIN: I never divulge the name of a client.

IVAN: Well, you've got a hell of a nerve!

MARTIN: I do a job. Just like you.

IVAN: I don't have a job!

MARTIN: Sorry.

VAN: Is this someone I owe money to?

MARTIN: Do you owe money to anyone?

VAN: No.

MARTIN: Well then, it couldn't be that, could it?

VAN: So what the hell can it be?

MARTIN: I told you, I don't know.

VAN: Well, how can you kill someone without knowing why? Aren't you just the least bit curious?

MARTIN: Not really . . . It's got nothing to do with me. It's nothing personal.

VAN: Oh, so it's like going to the supermarket and picking out a can of peas!

MARTIN: It's a job.

VAN: Well, mister, if there is a hell, you are sure going to spend some hard time down there. And someday it's going to be reversed . . . I'd like to see how smug you are when that happens.

MARTIN: That will depend on who's holding the gun. A person, or a sleazebag.

VAN: Which are you?

MARTIN: A person.

VAN: I think you're a sleazebag!

MARTIN: That's because I'm going to kill you. If we met under other circumstances, you might like me.

VAN: You want to give it a try?

MARTIN: Personally, I wouldn't mind. But this isn't a personal matter.

IVAN: Somehow, I keep forgetting that.

[*Pause.*]

So what happens now? You just pull the trigger, and that's it?

MARTIN: If you like . . . But there's still some time.

[*Long pause.*]

IVAN: And . . . ?

MARTIN: I thought we'd talk.

IVAN: Talk about what?

MARTIN: You.

IVAN: Why? It's nothing personal.

MARTIN: It's very rare that I get to talk to any of my . . . assignments

IVAN: Must be a lonely job.

MARTIN: It can be.

IVAN: So what's going on here that's special?

MARTIN: You came home early. You weren't due back until three.

IVAN: What is this? They know my schedule?

MARTIN: They're very thorough.

IVAN: So if my interview wasn't canceled, I'd come walking in here at three, like I was supposed to, and you'd have just opened fire?

MARTIN: Something like that.

IVAN: So am I supposed to be grateful?

MARTIN: I am. It's given us this chance to talk.

IVAN: What is this thing you have with talking?

MARTIN: I love to learn about people.

IVAN: Why? So you can kill them better? . . . Sleazebag!

MARTIN: I'm not a sleazebag. I use what I know to make it easier for others when I do my job. If I used what I know to torture people, I'd be a sleazebag.

IVAN: Hey, look, really, are you just crazy, and it's simply a matter of time until the drugs wear off? Or is there some way we can talk this over and find a way out?

MARTIN: We should talk . . . But there's no way out that I can see.

IVAN: But we can try.

MARTIN: See what a good idea talking was?

IVAN: I sure do . . . Okay . . . Tell me more about this difference between people and sleazebags.

MARTIN: People know how to live together in a tough world and not hurt each other. Sleazebags are greedy and selfish. They'll do anything they have to, to get what they want.

IVAN: Uh-huh . . . Which is the biggest group? Or are they both about the same size?

MARTIN: Sleazebags are biggest, by far.

IVAN: And I guess they should be eliminated, right?

MARTIN: Right!

IVAN: But the good ones, the people, they should live, is that it?

MARTIN: Right!

IVAN: Well, Martin, I'm not a sleazebag!

[*A short pause, while* MARTIN *regards* IVAN.]

MARTIN: Sorry . . . a deal is a deal.

IVAN: Well, how much are you being paid? Maybe I can meet it. Maybe I can do better!

MARTIN: I don't do things that way.

IVAN: At least give me a chance to beat their price! That's only fair!

MARTIN: You should have called me before they did.

IVAN: I didn't know any of this was going on!

MARTIN: Neither did I until I got their call.

IVAN: Okay . . . But if they can hire you, I can hire you back, right? And everything is even. You could make a good living not killing anyone . . . just going back and forth, and letting everybody buy you off!

MARTIN: That would be breaking a contract.

IVAN: So what?!

MARTIN: Breaking a contract makes you a sleazebag.

IVAN: I don't care if you're a sleazebag or not! I'll pay you not to kill me!

MARTIN: I don't do business that way.

IVAN: [*To himself.*] This is great . . . I'm locked in a room with an overly principled psychotic!

[*To* MARTIN.]

So what am I supposed to do now?

MARTIN: Talk.

IVAN: All right . . . Let's talk about not killing me.

MARTIN: I had something a little different in mind.

IVAN: So you think of a topic.

[IVAN *gets up and begins to randomly wander around the room.*]

MARTIN: If you're looking for something to throw at me, don't do it.

IVAN: [*All "innocence."*] I wasn't looking for something to throw at you.

MARTIN: Yes, you were. But it won't do you any good. I'm very fast.

IVAN: Oh, people have tried that before, huh?

MARTIN: It's a common ploy.

IVAN: But it doesn't work.

MARTIN: Never.

IVAN: Tell me, what else do people try?

MARTIN: Lots of things. But I'd much rather talk about you.

IVAN: You want a drink? Some coffee? Anything to eat?

MARTIN: No, thank you very much . . . People try that, too. And I'd prefer you don't leave this room.

IVAN: I can't believe this is happening to me!

MARTIN: We all have to die at some point.

IVAN: That's so easy for you to say! You're just gonna do your job and walk, and I'm just gonna be lying here and never know another thing, ever!

MARTIN: You're right. It's very scary.

IVAN: Thanks a lot. Sleazebag!

MARTIN: I'm not a sleazebag.

IVAN: No, you're just a prick! Go around killing people you don't even know . . . The world certainly needs a lot more of you!

MARTIN: You don't know me.

IVAN: How can anybody ever get to know you? You always kill them first! Tell you what . . . I'll get to know you—all you like. You want a friend, I'll be your friend. You want to talk, you can come over every night, we'll talk. We'll do anything you want.

MARTIN: Anything?

IVAN: Oh, Jesus! . . . Yeah, anything.

MARTIN: Ivan . . . what is it you think I want?

IVAN: Martin . . . I don't know.

MARTIN: Then what makes you think you can do it?

IVAN: You're right . . . You're right . . . Maybe I can't do it . . . But then we can't be sure, because I don't know what it is.

[*Pause.* MARTIN *regards* IVAN *in silence.*]

But you can tell me! You can tell me what it is, and then we'll know if I can do it. Okay?

AN ENEMY OF THE PEOPLE

BY HENRIK IBSEN,
ADAPTED BY ARTHUR MILLER

CHARACTERS

The town in which this play is set has built a huge bathing complex that is central to the town's economy. DR. THOMAS STOCKMANN *(mid-40s) has found that the springs are contaminated. But the town has reacted to* DR. STOCKMANN*'s report with anger and denial. Chief among those dissenting voices is the doctor's older brother, businessman* PETER STOCKMANN *(late 40s).*

SCENE

The living room of Dr. Stockmann's residence, which has been attacked with rocks by angry townspeople, breaking all the windows.

TIME

Morning. (The play was written in 1882.)

[PETER STOCKMANN *enters, says nothing, looking at the damage in the room.*]

DR. STOCKMANN: Keep your hat on if you like, it's a little drafty in here today.

PETER STOCKMANN: Thanks, I believe I will.

[*He puts his hat off.*]

I think I caught cold last night—that house was freezing.

DR. STOCKMANN: I thought it was kind of warm—suffocating a a matter of fact. What do you want?

PETER STOCKMANN: May I sit down?

[*He indicates a chair next to the window.*]

DR. STOCKMANN: Not there. A piece of the solid majority is liable to open your skull. Here.

[*They sit on the couch.* PETER STOCKMANN *takes out a large envelope.*]

DR. STOCKMANN: Now don't tell me.

PETER STOCKMANN: Yes.

[*He hands the doctor the envelope.*]

DR. STOCKMANN: I'm fired.

PETER STOCKMANN: The Board met this morning. There was nothing else to do, considering the state of public opinion.

DR. STOCKMANN: [*After a pause.*] You look scared, Peter.

PETER STOCKMANN: I—I haven't completely forgotten that you're still my brother.

DR. STOCKMANN: I doubt that.

PETER STOCKMANN: You have no practice left in this town Thomas.

DR. STOCKMANN: Oh, people always need a doctor.

PETER STOCKMANN: A petition is going from house to house Everybody is signing it. A pledge not to call you anymore. I don't think a single family will dare refuse to sign it.

DR. STOCKMANN: You started that, didn't you?

PETER STOCKMANN: No. As a matter of fact, I think it's all gone a little too far. I never wanted to see you ruined, Thomas. This will ruin you.

DR. STOCKMANN: No, it won't.

PETER STOCKMANN: For once in your life, will you act like a responsible man?

DR. STOCKMANN: Why don't you say it, Peter? You're afraid I'm going out of town to start publishing about the springs, aren't you?

PETER STOCKMANN: I don't deny that. Thomas, if you really have the good of the town at heart, you can accomplish everything without damaging anybody, including yourself.

DR. STOCKMANN: What's this now?

PETER STOCKMANN: Let me have a signed statement saying that in your zeal to help the town you went overboard and exaggerated. Put it any way you like, just so you calm anybody who might feel nervous about the water. If you'll give me that, you've got your job. And I give you my word, you can gradually make all the improvements you feel are necessary. Now, that gives you what you want . . .

DR. STOCKMANN: You're nervous, Peter.

PETER STOCKMANN: I am not nervous!

DR. STOCKMANN: You expect me to remain in charge while people are being poisoned?

[*He gets up.*]

PETER STOCKMANN: In time you can make your changes.

DR. STOCKMANN: When, five years, ten years? You know your trouble, Peter? You just don't grasp—even now—that there are certain men you can't buy.

PETER STOCKMANN: I'm quite capable of understanding that. But you don't happen to be one of those men.

DR. STOCKMANN: [*After a slight pause.*] What do you mean by that now?

PETER STOCKMANN: You know damned well what I mean by that. Morten Kiil is what I mean by that.

DR. STOCKMANN: Morten Kiil?

PETER STOCKMANN: Your father-in-law, Morten Kiil.

DR. STOCKMANN: I swear, Peter, one of us is out of his mind. What are you talking about?

PETER STOCKMANN: Now don't try to charm me with that professional innocence!

DR. STOCKMANN: What are you talking about?

PETER STOCKMANN: You don't know that your father-in-law has been running around all morning buying up stock in Kirsten Springs?

DR. STOCKMANN: Buying up stock?

PETER STOCKMANN: Buying up stock, every share he can lay his hands on!

DR. STOCKMANN: Well, I don't understand, Peter. What's that got to do with—

PETER STOCKMANN: [*Walking around agitatedly.*] Oh, come now, come now, come now!

DR. STOCKMANN: I hate you when you do that! Don't just walk around gabbling "Come now, come now!" What the hell are you talking about?

PETER STOCKMANN: Very well, if you insist on being dense. A man wages a relentless campaign to destroy confidence in a corporation. He even goes so far as to call a mass meeting against it. The very next morning, when people are still in a state of shock about it all, his father-in-law runs all over town, picking up shares at half their value.

DR. STOCKMANN: [*Realizing, turns away.*] My God!

PETER STOCKMANN: And you have the nerve to speak to me about principles!

DR. STOCKMANN: You mean you actually believe that I . . . ?

PETER STOCKMANN: I'm not interested in psychology! I believe what I see! And what I see is nothing but a man doing a dirty, filthy job for Morten Kiil. And let me tell you—by tonight every man in this town'll see the same thing!

DR. STOCKMANN: Peter, you, you . . .

PETER STOCKMANN: Now go to your desk and write me a statement denying everything you've been saying, or . . .

DR. STOCKMANN: Peter, you're a low creature!

PETER STOCKMANN: All right then, you'd better get this one straight, Thomas. If you're figuring on opening another attack from out of town, keep this in mind: the moment it's published I'll send out a subpoena for you and begin a prosecution for conspiracy. I've been trying to make you respectable all my life; now if you want to make that big jump, there'll be nobody there to hold you back. Now do we understand each other?

DR. STOCKMANN: Oh, we do, Peter!

[PETER STOCKMANN *starts for the door.*]

Get the girl—what the hell is her name—scrub the floors, wash down the walls, a pestilence has been here!

EYES FOR CONSUELA

BY SAM SHEPARD

CHARACTERS

HENRY *(40s) is a man in escape mode from the failure of his marriage, his life;* AMADO *(40s) is a Latino man who wears a machete on his hip and is living a shadow life, clever and crafty.*

SCENE

A second-floor room in a boardinghouse in Mexico on the edge of the jungle.

TIME

Evening. The present.

HENRY: Now, look—I can—I can empathize with your situation. Women can be very—persuasive in certain areas. Very—I mean a man can find himself doing things he never dreamed—Things he never imagined. And—suddenly you see that you're in—a pickle.

AMADO: A "pickle"? What is a "pickle"?

HENRY: A—conundrum. A dilemma. I mean—Take me, for instance—uh—I'm uh—having some difficulties myself. I mean, my situation might be very similar in some ways to your own.

AMADO: You have no idea about me.

HENRY: No—No, I don't. It's true, but I can see certain—

AMADO: You have never seen me before in your life.

HENRY: No. No, I haven't.

AMADO: You will never see me again. After this.

HENRY: I—

AMADO: I have just appeared to you. Out of nowhere.

HENRY: [*Pacing.*] I don't—I don't want any trouble. I—I came down here just to get away for a while. Just to—

AMADO: You have left your wife?

HENRY: Yes—Well, we both agreed it would be better to be apart.

AMADO: Better for who?

HENRY: For us both. It was mutual.

AMADO: You don't know your heart.

HENRY: No—I suppose that's true. I suppose you're right about that. I keep thinking—It's funny, you know—

AMADO: What is funny?

HENRY: I just realized—I mean, you know how you can be going along, kind of thinking everything is perfectly normal—perfectly sane—and—I—I keep having these little dialogues with her. Out loud.

AMADO: Your wife?

HENRY: Yes. These little running commentaries. As though she's right here with me. Right here now. I talk out loud to her. Argue with her. Reason with her. Out loud. To myself.

AMADO: But she is not here.

HENRY: No. She's not. That's what I'm trying to say. She's not here at all. She's somewhere else. And I—Well, that's what I was trying to say before—How there might be certain similarities in our predicament. I mean—I thought—What I thought was, that I would come down here to get away from her. Maybe that would help. Something—You know, I would be in a warm place. The sun on my back. Surrounded by parrots and—I might forget all about her. Find a new life.

AMADO: Parrots?

HENRY: Yes. You know—sounds. Tropical sounds. They would take me away. Spanish. Palm trees. Tequila. A whole new environment. It would distract me. I could start all over.

AMADO: Tequila? Do you have tequila?

HENRY: Yes. As a matter of fact, I do. I have some right here. Would you like some tequila?

AMADO: I would like some, yes.

HENRY: [*Goes to his bag and pulls out a bottle of tequila, half-full. He gets a glass from the table and pours a drink.*] Good. That's good. I've been carrying it around with me. It was a gift. Unfortunately, I only have one glass. This hotel is not much on service.

AMADO: You take the glass.

HENRY: [*Offers glass to* AMADO.] No, no, please. I insist.

AMADO: You take the glass. I will take the bottle.

HENRY: Of course.

[AMADO *takes the bottle and drinks from it, a long thirsty drink.* HENRY *watches, then sips from his glass.*]

I'M NOT RAPPAPORT
BY HERB GARDNER

MIDGE *and* NAT, *both about eighty years old.* MIDGE *is black and* NAT *is white. And that is the only thing about them that is simple.*

SCENE
A bench near a path at the edge of the lake in Central Park, New York City.

TIME
Early October, 1982.

[MIDGE *and* NAT *are seated at either end of the center bench; they sit several feet apart, an old briefcase between them.* MIDGE *wears very white bifocals and an old soft hat; he is reading* The Sporting News. NAT *wears a beret and has a finely trimmed beard, a cane with an elegant ivory handle rests next to him against the bench. The two men do not look at each other.*]

NAT: Okay, where was I?

[*No response. He smacks himself on the forehead.*]

Where the hell was I? What were we talking about? I was just about to make a very important point here.

[*To* MIDGE.]

What were we talking about?

MIDGE: [*No response, he continues to read his newspaper for a moment.*] We wasn't talking. *You* was talking.

[*Turns page.*]

I wasn't talking.

NAT: Okay, so what was I saying?

MIDGE: I wasn't listening either. You was doing the whole thing by yourself.

NAT: Why weren't you listening?

MIDGE: Because you're a Goddamn liar. I'm not listening to you anymore. Two days now I ain't been listening.

NAT: Stop pretending to read. You can't see anything.

MIDGE: Hey, how 'bout you go sit with them old dudes in fronta the Welfare Hotel, them old butter brains—

[*Pointing about the lake.*]

—the babies at the carousel, them kids in the boat—or some o' them junkie folk yonder, whyn't you go mess with them? 'Cause I'm not talking to you anymore, mister. Puttin' you on notice of that. You may's well be talking to that tree over there.

NAT: It's a lamppost.

MIDGE: Sittin' here a week now, ain't heard a worda truth outa you. Shuckin' me every which way till the sun go down.

NAT: [*Slapping the bench.*] I am not!

MIDGE: Okay, and your name ain't Hernando—

NAT: Absolutely not!

MIDGE: So it's a lie—

NAT: It's a cover story!

[*Pause.*]

My line of work, they give you a cover story.

MIDGE: Are you sayin'—?

NAT: All I'm saying, and that's *all* I'm saying, is that in my particular field you gotta have a cover story. More than that I can't divulge at the present time.

MIDGE: Honey bun, you sayin' you're a spy?

NAT: I'm not saying my name is Hernando and I'm an escaped Cuban terrorist.

MIDGE: But what kinda weirdo, bullshit cover story—?

NAT: You don't think I *said* that to them? That's what *I* said to them. I said to them, an eighty-one-year-old Lithuanian is a Cuban Hernando? That's right, they said, tough luck, sweetheart; yours is not to reason why. That's how they talk. Of *course* you don't believe it! You think *I* believe it? Such dopes. But it's a living. I beg you not to inquire further.

MIDGE: But why'd they pick an old—

NAT: Do *I* know? You tell *me*. A year ago I'm standing in line at the Medicaid, a fellah comes up to me—boom, I'm an undercover.

MIDGE: [*Impressed.*] Lord . . .

NAT: Who knows, maybe they got something. They figure an old man, nobody'll pay attention. Could wander through the world like a ghost, pick up some tidbits.

MIDGE: [*Nodding thoughtfully.*] Yeah . . .

NAT: So maybe they got everything, even though, I grant you, they screwed up on the cover story. All I know is every month a thousand bingos is added to my Social Security check.

MIDGE: Bingos?

NAT: Bingos. Dollars. Cash. It's a word we use in the business. Please don't inquire further.

[*Silence.*]

Please, I'm not at liberty.

[*Longer silence.*]

Okay, they also gave me a code name, "Harry."

MIDGE: "Harry"?

NAT: Harry Schwartzman.

MIDGE: What's your real name?

NAT: Sam Schwartzman.

[*Outraged.*]

Can you believe it? Can you *believe* it? That's some imaginative *group* they got up there, right? That's some bunch of geniuses!

[*Then, shrugging.*]

What the hell, a thousand bananas on your Social Security every month you don't ask fancy questions.

MIDGE: Best not, best not.

[*Leaning closer.*]

So, do ya . . . do ya ever pick up any information for them?

NAT: Are you kidding? Sitting on a bench all day with a man who can't tell a tree from a lamppost? Not a shred.

[*Glances about, leans closer.*]

Fact is, I think they got me in what they call "deep cover." See, they keep you in this "deep cover" for years; like five, maybe ten years they keep you there, till you're just like this regular person in the neighborhood . . . and then, boom, they pick you out for the big one. Considering my age and general health, they're not too bright.

[*Reaches into briefcase.*]

Okay, snack time.

MIDGE: [*Nodding.*] Yeah. Deep cover. I hearda that . . .

NAT: [*Taking foil-wrapped sandwich from briefcase.*] Here. Tuna salad with lettuce and tomato on whole wheat toast. Take half.

MIDGE: [*Accepting sandwich.*] Thank ya, Sam; thank ya.

NAT: Yeah, comes three o'clock, there's nothing like a nice, fresh tuna salad sandwich.

MIDGE: [*Chewing.*] Uh-huh.

NAT: [*Chewing.*] Crisp.

[*Silence for several moments as their old jaws work on the sandwiches.*]

MIDGE: [*Suddenly.*] Bullshit!

[*Sits upright.*]

Bullshit! Lord, you done it to me *again*! You done it!

[*Throws the sandwich fiercely to the ground.*]

Promised myself I wouldn't let ya, and ya done it again! Deep cover! Harry Schwartzman! Bingos! You done it again!

NAT: [*Smiling to himself as he continues eating.*] That was nice . . . a nice long story, lasted a long time . . .

MIDGE: [*Shouting, poking* NAT *sharply.*] That's *it*! That's it, no more conversin'! Conversin' is *over* now, mister! No more, ain't riffin' *me* no more!

NAT: Please control yourself—

MIDGE: *Move* it, boy; *away* with ya! This here's *my* spot!

NAT: Sir, I was—

MIDGE: This is *my* spot. I come here first!

NAT: I was merely—

MIDGE: Get offa my spot 'fore I lay you out!

NAT: *Your* spot? Who made it *your* spot? Show me the plaque. Where does it say that?

MIDGE: Says right here . . .

[*Remains seated, slowly circling his fists in the air like a boxer.*]

You read them hands? Study them hands, boy. Them hands wore Golden Gloves, summer of Nineteen and Twenty-Four. This here's *my* spot, *been* my spot six months now, my good and peaceful spot till you show up a week ago start playin' Three Card Monte with my head. Want you *gone,* Sonny!

[*Continues circling his fists.*]

Givin' ya three t'make dust; comin' out on the count o'three. *One*—

[MIDGE *rises, moving to his corner of the "ring."*]

NAT: Wait, a brief discussion—

MIDGE: Sound of the bell, I'm comin; out. *You* won't hear it but I *will. Two*—

NAT: How you gonna hit me if you can't *see* me?

MIDGE: Dropped Billy D'Amato in the sixth round with both eyes swole shut. I just keep punchin' till I hear the crunchin'. *Three!*

NAT: [*Rising with dignity.*] Please, sir—this is an embarrassing demonstration—

MIDGE: [*Moving in* NAT'*s general direction, a bit of remembered footwork, jabbing.*] Okay, comin' out, comin' out; at ya, boy, comin' at ya—

NAT: [*Moving behind bench for protection.*] Sir, you . . . you have a depressing personality and a terrible attitude!

MIDGE: Prepare yourself, mister, prepare yourself, get your—

[MIDGE *suddenly lunges, bumping against the bench, stumbling—he struggles to keep his balance, grabbing desperately at the air—then falls flat on his back in the path. He lies there silently for several moments.*]

MIDGE: [*Quietly, frightened.*] Oh, shit . . .

NAT: [*Aware that* MIDGE *is in danger, whispering.*] Mister . . . ?

[*No response. He leans forward urgently.*]

Mister, mister . . . ?

[*Silence. He moves towards* MIDGE *as quickly as possible.*]

Don't move, don't move . . .

MIDGE: [*Trembling.*] I know . . .

NAT: Could be you broke something . . .

MIDGE: [*Softly.*] I know. Oh, shit. Never fall down, *never* fall down . . .

DINNER WITH FRIENDS
BY DONALD MARGULIES

CHARACTERS

GABE *and* TOM *(both early 40s) were once best friends—but are they still? Not long ago they and their families spent every weekend together, their children grew up together, they and their wives (Karen and Beth, respectively) were inseparable. But now* TOM *has dumped Beth for Nancy, and so many things have changed in his life. Where does that leave him and* GABE?

SCENE

A bar in Manhattan.

TIME

Afternoon.

[GABE *is drinking Pellegrino. He has the self-conscious look of someone drinking alone who is trying not to appear self-conscious; he is waiting for* TOM, *who is late. He glances at his watch, sips, reads the* Times, *looks around, checks his datebook.* TOM, *looking fit in a smart summer suit, breezes in and joins him.*]

TOM: Gabe!

GABE: There you are.

[*The men embrace;* TOM*'s hug is more fervent than* GABE*'s.*]

TOM: Good to see you. God, I miss you.

GABE: Miss you, too.

TOM: Been here long?

GABE: A few minutes.

TOM: Sorry about that. This meeting . . .

GABE: [*Shrugs it off, offers a drink.*] Want some?

TOM: Please.

[GABE *fills his glass.*]

It's been weeks!

GABE: Months.

TOM: Karen still pissed with me?

GABE: You could say that.

TOM: Boy, she really holds a grudge, doesn't she?

GABE: Well, this is sort of a biggie, though, you gotta admit.

[*A beat.*]

When'd you get into town?

TOM: This morning. Nancy came *with* me.

GABE: Oh yeah?

TOM: She loves New York. Thought we'd hang out, see a couple of shows . . .

GABE: Uh-huh. So, you're going up to see the kids?

TOM: No, not this weekend; I have them *next* week. This is *her* week; I'm not gonna mess with *that,* believe me.

GABE: Oh.

TOM: God forbid there's any change of plan . . . It's like Nuremberg.

GABE: [*A chuckle.*] Uh-huh. You look great.

TOM: Thanks, I feel great. I'm running again.

GABE: Oh yeah?

TOM: I lost a little weight . . .

GABE: More than a little.

TOM: Nancy and I, we get up at six . . .

GABE: Wow. Six!

TOM: . . . run four, five miles . . .

GABE: How do you do it?

TOM: . . . come back, make love in the shower . . .

GABE: Uh-huh.

TOM: Then off to work. That's my new regimen. And let me tell you: It's totally changed my perspective on my day.

GABE: Must be those invigorating showers.

TOM: [*Leaning forward.*] The things she's got me doing, Gabe . . . !

GABE: Lucky you.

TOM: Nancy has more imagination, more daring, more wisdom . . . I mean, it just goes to show you that age is totally irrelevant. I'm a boy toy at forty-three!

GABE: Uh-huh.

TOM: She is so at home in her own body. See, I've never known what that was like. A lover teaches you that, it's something you learn together. Beth and I never had that; she was never comfortable in her own body . . .

GABE: Really? Gee, I always thought . . .

TOM: [*Continuous.*] So how could I expect her to be comfortable with *mine*? Nancy and I'll be strolling along and she'll put her hand on my ass or something, just like that, without even thinking about it. With Beth, sex was always up to me. It was never about her *wanting* me, it was never about desire, it was all about obligation. And then once the kids came . . . Well, *you* know how that is.

GABE: Uh-huh.

TOM: Sex became one more thing on my list of things to do. You know? Nancy and I, we are totally in sync. She just has to stroke my *fingers* and I get hard, or give me a look, or laugh a certain way.

GABE: Do you two ever . . . talk?

TOM: Oh yeah. Are you kidding? We talk all the time. Remember what that's like when a relationship is new? All that talk, all that sex, all that laughter? Nancy really hears me. She hears me.

GABE: Uh-huh.

TOM: She saved my life, Gabe. She really did; she breathed life back into me.

GABE: [*Nods, then.*] Good. That's great. I'm glad.

[*He sips his drink.* TOM *looks at him.*]

What.

TOM: What are you thinking?

GABE: What do you mean?

TOM: Come on, I know *you,* I know that *look* . . .

GABE: I'm just listening. You don't want me to say anything, right?

TOM: [*Over "*. . . *right?*"*] Oh, Christ . . .

GABE: No, isn't that what you told me?

TOM: I said that to you . . . when I was still very raw . . .

GABE: Oh. And you're not so raw anymore? Well, what are the rules, then? You've gotta fill me in here, pal, I've gotta know the rules so I don't step out of bounds.

TOM: Gabe . . .

GABE: Okay, you want to know what I'm thinking? I'm thinking: I hear you talking, Tom, I hear those *words* coming out, and you sound like a fucking *moonie* to me, Tom, you really do . . .

TOM: [*Over ". . . you really do . . ."*] I'm trying to tell you . . . I was dying! You don't understand that, do you? I was losing the will to live, wasn't that dying? The life I was leading had no relationship to who I was or what I wanted. It was deadening. The constant logistics of "You pick up Sam and take him to lollypop tennis, I'll take Laurie to hockey practice . . ."

GABE: But, that's . . .

TOM: This is what we'd talk about! No, really. This would pass for conversation in our house.

GABE: I know, but . . .

TOM: The dog finished me off. Oh man, that dog. Sarge. It wasn't enough that we had two cats and fish and a guinea pig, no, Beth felt the kids had to have a dog because *she* had a dog. I'd spent my entire adult life cleaning up one form of shit or another, now I was on to *dog* shit. I should've gone into waste management. How do you keep love alive when you're shoveling shit all day?

GABE: We've all made sacrifices to our kids. It's the price you pay for having a family.

TOM: Yeah, but you have to really want that.

GABE: What do you mean?

TOM: You and Karen: You really wanted it. That's what I realized: I never really did.

GABE: What are you talking about?

TOM: I don't know what I was thinking. It was completely against my nature.

GABE: What was?

TOM: Settling down, having kids. It was just one more thing I did because it was expected of me, not because I had any real passion for it. Like law: It was my foregone conclusion since the age of ten I'd be a lawyer like my father. I always felt, I don't know, *inauthentic* living this life.

GABE: What, you were a party boy trapped in the body of a family man? Tommy, I could swear I actually saw you *enjoy*ing yourself on a number of occasions in the past decade or so.

TOM: Well, sure. But honestly? Most of the time I was just being a good sport.

GABE: A good sport?!

TOM: You know what I mean . . .

GABE: [*Continuous.*] Wait a minute. You were faking it?! You mean to tell me that all those years—all those years, Tom!—the four of us together, raising our kids together, the dinners, the vacations, the hours of videotape, you were just being a good sport?

TOM: No . . .

GABE: Then what, Tom, I don't get it. I was there, as well as you. This misery you describe, the agony. Gee, I thought we were all just living our lives, you know? Sharing our humdrum little existences. I *thought* you were there, wholeheartedly there. And now you're saying you had an eye on the clock and a foot out the door?!

TOM: You've got to stop taking this so personally.

GABE: How would *you* take it? You say you were wasting your life, that's what you've said.

TOM: [*Over ". . . that's what you've said."*] I don't mean you and Karen. I don't mean *you,* I'd never mean *you;* you're my best friend, I've got to be able to say this stuff to you. I'm talking about my marriage.

GABE: But it's not that simple, Tom. We were there. Karen and Danny and Isaac and I, we were all there, we were all a big part of that terrible life you had to get the hell away from. Isaac's totally freaked out by this, by the way. So when you repudiate your entire adult life . . .

TOM: That's not what I've done . . .

GABE: That's *essentially* what you've done. And I can understand how you might find it necessary to do that: It must be strangely exhilarating blowing everything to bits.

TOM: Gabe . . .

GABE: I mean it. You build something that's precarious in even the best of circumstances and you succeed, or at least you make it *look* like you've succeeded, your *friends* think you have, you had *us* fooled, and then, one day, you blow it all up! It's like, I watch Danny and Isaac sometimes, dump all their toys on the floor Legos and blocks and train tracks, and build these elaborate cities together. They'll spend hours at it, they'll plan and collaborate and squabble and negotiate, but they'll do it. And then what do they do? They wreck it! No pause to revel in what they accomplished no sigh of satisfaction, they just launch into a full-throttle attack bombs bursting, and tear the whole damn thing apart.

[*Pause.*]

TOM: I just want you to be my friend. That's all. I want you to be happy for me.

THE VALUE OF NAMES
BY JEFFREY SWEET

CHARACTERS

BENNY SILVERMAN *and* LEO GRESHEN *are both around seventy. Many years ago, they were in a theater group called The New Labor Players. Then the House Un-American Committee went on their witch-hunt for Communists, and* LEO *gave testimony against* BENNY *so he would be allowed to direct his first movie.* BENNY *was blacklisted for several years as a result, though eventually he outlived the ban and achieved success on a TV sitcom. Now circumstances have brought* BENNY *together with* LEO *again. Should* BENNY *forgive him?*

SCENE

The patio of Leo Silverman's house in Malibu, overlooking the Pacific Ocean.

TIME

Day. 1981.

[*The scene takes place on the patio.*]

BENNY: Sounds like you've got this all thought out.

LEO: It's not like I haven't had the time.

BENNY: Just one problem, Leo. When you called me up that night, you didn't call me because you thought you were right. You called me because you felt lousy about what you were going to do.

LEO: Benny, I never claimed to feel good about it.

BENNY: But you did it.

LEO: Only a fool fights the drop.

BENNY: You want to translate?

LEO: You've seen enough cowboy movies. If the bad guys have got the drop on you, it's crazy to draw on them. You're only going to get gunned down. Can't fight if you're dead.

BENNY: So now we're cowboys?

LEO: Thank you for taking what I have to say seriously.

BENNY: Seriously, okay: Leo, not only did you not fight the drop, you helped the bad guys gun down some good guys. What would the kids in the balcony say if Roy Rogers shot Gabby Hayes?

LEO: Bad guys, good guys . . .

BENNY: It's your analogy.

LEO: I said nothing about good guys.

BENNY: Oh, I see: there were no good guys?

LEO: Present company excepted, of course.

BENNY: No good guys. Well, that makes it nice and convenient, doesn't it? If everybody's equally scummy, then the highest virtue is survival. That must make you pretty goddamn virtuous. You should write a book about your philosophy, Leo. Really. I've got the title for you: *Charles Darwin Goes to the Theatre.*

LEO: Being a victim doesn't automatically entitle you to a white hat, Benny. It's that old liberal impulse—romanticize the persecuted.

BENNY: What the hell would you know about liberal impulses.

LEO: Hey, I've got my share of them.

BENNY: You—a liberal? Don't make me laugh.

LEO: I sure wouldn't want to do that, Benny—make you laugh.

BENNY: Maybe you're a checkbook liberal. You send in contributions to those ads with pictures of kids starving in South America, a couple bucks to the ACLU . . .

LEO: More than a couple of bucks, but never mind . . .

BENNY: More than a couple? Well, hey, that changes my opinion completely.

LEO: I'll tell you where I part company with a lot of them, though. I won't romanticize. Just because someone's a martyr doesn't make him wise and good and pure. Sure, I sent in money to Joan Little's defense fund, but that doesn't mean I'd trust her to babysit my grandchildren.

BENNY: Joan Little was on trial for killing someone, for Christ's sake. The guys the Committee went after—only thing they did was make the mistake of believing in something unpopular. And the ones who wouldn't buckle under to the Committee—out with the garbage.

LEO: Which is exactly what they did to each other when they were members of the Party. Those bastards were always browbeating each other, excommunicating each other for not embracing "the correct revolutionary line." Do you remember when the Party endorsed Henry Wallace for president? Lenny Steinkempf got up in a meeting, said he thought it was a crappy idea. So what did the Party do? They threw him the fuck out. And after *they* threw him out, his *wife*, Elaine, being a loyal Party member, *she* threw him out. As far as I was concerned, facing the Committee was an exercise in déjà vu. Believe me, Nixon and Mundt could hav taken lessons from some of those old Commies. I wasn't about to put my dick on the block for any of those guys. Why should I keep faith with them when they couldn't keep faith with themselves?

BENNY: The point wasn't to keep faith with *them*. Leo, don't you remember anything about how or why we put together the New Labor Players?

LEO: Oh, for Christ's sake!

BENNY: For Christ's sake what?

LEO: [*Laughing.*] Benny, you aren't seriously going to hit me with the New Labor Players?

BENNY: And why not?

LEO: All that agitprop bullshit, the slogans, screaming our lungs raw . . .

BENNY: Worthless?

LEO: Not worthless, exactly . . .

BENNY: Then *what,* exactly?

LEO: All we ever did was play to people who felt exactly like we did. Invigorating—sure. Fun—absolutely. And a great way to meet girls. But don't try to tell me we ever accomplished any great social good. I doubt that we ever changed anybody's mind about anything.

BENNY: That's how you measure it?

LEO: You measure it differently?

BENNY: Seems to me there's some value in letting people know— because they laughed or maybe cheered at the same time as a bunch of other people—letting them know they aren't alone. That there are other people who feel like they do.

LEO: Maybe we should have broken out some pom-poms while we were at it.

BENNY: Pom-poms?

LEO: Hey, if you're going to cheerlead, you should have pom-poms. "Give me a P, give me an R, give me an O, give me an L!"

BENNY: Leo . . .

LEO: "Whattaya got? Proletariat! Whattaya got? Class struggle! Whattaya got? Dialectical materialism! Rah, rah, rah!

BENNY: Some terrific joke, Leo. Very funny.

LEO: What's funny is you telling me this stuff.

BENNY: What's funny about that?

LEO: You think I don't know my own spiel when I hear it?

BENNY: Your spiel?

LEO: Of course my spiel. "Class consciousness is the first step. Through theater we give dramatic form to our lives and hopes and so create our identity and the identity of our community." You like it? I've got another three or four hours of this. Rousing stuff, huh?

BENNY: Yeah, I thought so.

LEO: Oh, I convinced myself pretty good, too. But I'm not a twenty-two-year-old kid anymore, and neither are you. And I'm not going to let you get away with pretending that "Capitalist Heaven" and the rest of it was any great golden age of drama. Face it, Benny, it was amateur night.

BENNY: I'm not talking about how sophisticated or how professional, Leo, what I'm saying is that when we started, all right, we may not have had much polish or technical expertise, but we did have sense of purpose. There was a *reason* I started acting. There was *reason* Mort Kessler started writing. There was a *reason* you started directing. And then came a point you gave up your reason so you could keep on directing.

LEO: Maybe directing *was* my reason.

BENNY: What—directing anything.

LEO: Of course not.

BENNY: You say of course not, but I don't take it for granted that there are things you wouldn't direct. Before the Committee—yes. But after?

LEO: So all of a sudden I'm a whore. Of course, it isn't whoring to do some dumb-ass sitcom. What was it called—*Rich and Happy?*

BENNY: *Rich but Happy.*

LEO: I stand corrected. Truly edifying, uplifting stuff. My God, in the old days, if somebody had told you that's what you'd end up doing! *Rich but Happy.* I mean, back then just the *title* would have made you gag!

BENNY: I had to live.

LEO: So did I, Benny. So did I.

BENNY: But if I did crap—and God knows I'm not holding up *Rich but Happy* as an example of high culture—but if I did crap, I didn't destroy other people to do it.

LEO: I know where this is heading: If a guy's politics aren't approved, aren't correct, then he can't be any good as an artist. I bet you're one of those people who think God took away Frank Sinatra's voice as a punishment for voting Republican.

BENNY: I'm not talking party affiliation . . .

LEO: I know what you're talking about: In order to be an artist, you've got to be a certified good guy.

BENNY: Being a *mensch* enters into it, yes.

LEO: And if he isn't, you feel cheated. Short-changed. Well, if art by bastards upsets you so much, you should drop everything right now, go into your library and toss out anything you have by Robert Frost. Now there was a world-class shit! And how about Ezra Pound? And let's not bring up Wagner!

BENNY: I don't have any Wagner in my house.

LEO: No? Well, now *there's* a brave stand! My hat's off to you, Benny! Keep those doors guarded. Be vigilant! Hey, you can't be *too* careful. I mean, you never know when somebody might try to sneak the fucking *Ring Cycle* into your house without knowing, right?

BENNY: This I'm enjoying—you linking arms with Wagner!

LEO: Tell me something, if you found out that Charles Dickens fucked ten-year-old boys, would that make him any less of a writer?

BENNY: Well, it sure as hell would make a difference in how I read *Oliver Twist.*

LEO: Whatever you or anybody else thinks of me as a person, I did good work, Benny. Not just before. After, too.

BENNY: I wouldn't know about after. I didn't see most of it.

LEO: Well, you missed some good stuff. If you don't want to take my word for it, you can take it from the critics. You can look on my fucking mantle in New York at the prizes and the plaques . .

BENNY: I'm sure they would blind me.

LEO: They mean something, Benny, even if it's fashionable to sneer at them. They mean that a lot of people thought that the work was good.

BENNY: And that's important to you.

LEO: Yes, it is.

BENNY: You like having the good opinion of others.

LEO: Is that a crime?

BENNY: No, I don't think it's a crime. I like it, too. I'm just sorry to have to tell you that you haven't got *my* good opinion, Leo.

LEO: And I'm sorry to have to tell you I don't give a damn.

BENNY: Then why are you here?

LEO: Because I don't want your goddamn daughter walking out of my goddamn play.

BENNY: Fine, you told her that. So why are you still here?

LEO: Because I'm a masochistic idiot!

BENNY: What, you expected me to throw my arms open?

LEO: No.

BENNY: Then what?

LEO: Damn it, Benny—thirty years! It's been more than thirty years! We're going to start *dying* soon!

[*A beat.*]

While there's still a chance.

[*For a moment, there is little in this world that* BENNY *wants more than to respond to* LEO.]

THAT CHAMPIONSHIP SEASON

BY JASON MILLER

CHARACTERS

On the twentieth anniversary of their victory in the Pennsylvania state championship game, four members of the starting team from this Catholic high school have come to the coach's home to celebrate. GEORGE SITKOWSKI *and* TOM DALEY *(both approaching 40) are the first two to arrive.* GEORGE *is the local town's inept mayor, while* TOM *is an unsuccessful and embittered writer who has only recently returned to the town.*

SCENE

The coach's house in Scranton, Pennsylvania. A large and expansive living room in the Gothic-Victorian tradition.

TIME

Evening. 1972.

[*On the dining room table sits a huge silver trophy.* TOM DALEY *stands at the gun racks. He suddenly takes a shotgun from the wall rack.*]

GEORGE: [*Offstage.*] Hey, Tom, Scotch and water on the rocks?

TOM: [*Holding gun.*] No ice.

GEORGE: Scotch and water comin' up.

TOM: Bring in the bottle, no one's going to need it. Hey, George, you know he keeps these guns loaded?

GEORGE: Yeah, I know. Hey, put it down, I'm out of season! Those guns have their triggers.

TOM: I got the safety on.

GEORGE: Only my laundry man will know how scared I was.

[*Pause.*]

You've been missed around here, Tom.

TOM: It's only been, what, a couple of years?

GEORGE: Three years, Tom. You've missed three reunions. Remember the time you put the winter-green in my jock? I thought my balls were on fire. Those were the days, the good old days. I am sincerely more proud of winning the championship than I am of being mayor of this town. Do you believe that?

TOM: No.

GEORGE: Dirty bastard. I'll never forget you. You were a great guard. Brilliant playmaker.

TOM: [*Deadpan.*] You were a great guard too, George.

GEORGE: I mean it. Bottom of my heart. This is me talking, no politician. Tremendous ball handler . . . I wonder what's keeping them.

TOM: They'll be here.

GEORGE: [*Pops a pill.*] Feena-mint. Pressure is murderous. Tense. Get a little constipated now and then. Mostly now.

TOM: When do you start your campaign?

GEORGE: I campaign every day of my life. The real grind begins . . . one week.

TOM: I never thought Sharmen would end up a politician.

GEORGE: Everybody ends up a politician. I'll beat his ass. He can't touch me in this town. Sharmawitz was his real name. That was his family's original name. The coach and me did some research on Mr. Sharmen. The only thing a Jew changes more than his politics is his name.

[*Pause.*]

He wants this town. Yeah. He wants to take it away from me.

TOM: Ready for another one, your honor?

GEORGE: James is going to be pissed at me if you're high when he gets here.

TOM: Brother James wouldn't dare get pissed at you.

GEORGE: After the election I'm going to endorse him for superintendent of schools. Too valuable a man to waste his time being a junior high school principal.

TOM: That's patronage, George.

GEORGE: I know. Is there any other way?

TOM: What did they find when they opened him up?

GEORGE: Who, the coach? Nothing. An ulcerated stomach. That's all. He'll live forever. I love that man, as we all do. I owe my whole life, success to that man. He convinced me that I could be mayor of this town. He ran me. Do you know how goddamn close that first election was? Any idea?

TOM: I don't remember.

GEORGE: Thirty-two votes. I beat Hannrin by thirty-two votes. I looked it up. Closest election in the history of Pennsylvania politics.

TOM: The coach sent me a mass card when I was in the hospital. Mass card . . . I thought I was dead when I saw it.

GEORGE: How the hell long does it take to pick up fried chicken?

TOM: How's Marion?

GEORGE: She's my conscience for God's sake. My severest critic. She knows the political scene . . . she's almost as sharp as I am.

[*Pause.*]

You know, after the baby, she was . . . very depressed, not quite herself. She's coming around now, thank God.

TOM: That's good.

GEORGE: Hey, do you know what would make this reunion truly memorable?

TOM: Martin would come walking in that door.

GEORGE: Magic on the court, wasn't he?

TOM: Unbelievable.

GEORGE: Greatest high school basketball player I ever saw.

TOM: Unbelievable.

[*Pouring.*]

Bless me, Father, for I have sinned.

[*Drinks.*]

GEORGE: Make that the last, huh?

TOM: It's only six o'clock, George.

GEORGE: Six. It's nine. Where the hell have you been?

TOM: I drink on Pacific Coast time. That way I'm three hours behind everybody else.

GEORGE: [*Seriously.*] Do you have a drinking problem, Tom?

TOM: No problem. I get all the booze I want.

GEORGE: Look at you, you're underweight, restless, your memory's going, you forget people's names.

TOM: Almost forty, George.

GEORGE: Forty, yeah, it's like half time.

TOM: Hey, I remember somebody. I saw her standing by the library yesterday. Mary . . . what's-her-name?

GEORGE: Who?

TOM: The epileptic. Mary . . . you know, the one we banged in your garage . . . we were freshmen or something.

GEORGE: I don't remember.

TOM: We humped her in your garage. She took fits or something.

GEORGE: Don't even breathe a word . . . she wasn't an epileptic. She was only retarded. Not a word. It could ruin me. She was raped here about two years ago. Scandal. Remember Mike Pollard?

TOM: No.

GEORGE: The guy with the glass eye. Yeah. He raped her in the cemetery. The one and only serious crime I had in four years. Dumb bastard. Where the hell is everybody? The coach loves to drive Phil's Caddie. That's why they're not here. Phil's got three cars now. Got a German car goes like a rocket. I cancel at least five speeding tickets for him a month. He's going out with this seventeen-year-old, believe that, up in Scranton. Had to take her to Philadelphia for an abortion.

TOM: He gave me a big hug and kiss.

GEORGE: Oh, hugs and kisses everybody. Italians are like that. Can't keep their hands off you. Hey, what's air pollution? Five hundred Italian paratroopers.

TOM: What has an I.Q. of 100?

GEORGE: Poland. See, I'm Polish, but I don't mind that, don't mind at all. But Phil gets pissed. Moody bastard. You can never tell what he's thinking. But right now I'm waiting for Phil to kick in thirty thousand for my campaign.

TOM: Thirty thousand . . .

GEORGE: But in return, Phil keeps all the strip land he's leased from the city. Sharmen wants to break that lease. Mr. Sharmen is an ecology nut. The fashionable issue, right? If he gets elected mayor, you won't be able to piss in your toilet. And I'm going to whip Sharmen's ass all over this town. Not this town. Not here. This town is not going to change hands. I love this town, Tom, love the people. Sure we have problems, but if we pull together I can make it the greatest little city in the country. That's one of my campaign slogans. "Greatest Little City in the Country."

TOM: Original.

GEORGE: Yeah. We have some information for Phil that's going to knock him on his ass. He's holding back. He knows we need him. See, Phil's not bright, really. James has often said that about Phil. Marion went up to see Phil last month about the contribution. He stalled. She doesn't trust him either.

THE OIL WELL
BY HORTON FOOTE

CHARACTERS
WILL THORNTON *(mid-60s) and* GEORGE WEEMS *(late 60s)*
*are both hardworking farmers, with little to show in the bank for all
their labors. But now the oil executives have come to town, looking
for new wells. Will this be the best or the worst thing that's ever
happened?*

SCENE
The front porch of a ranch near Harrison, Texas.

TIME
Morning. 1953.

[*An old man is seated in a cane-bottom chair, smoking a cigar.*
WILL THORNTON, *a tall, angular, nervous man in his middle
sixties, comes striding up to him. He is dressed in a blue serge suit.
The old man,* GEORGE WEEMS, *is in an old shirt and pants.*]

GEORGE: Morning, Will.

WILL: Howdy, Mr. George . . .

GEORGE: What are you doing all dressed up? Going to a funeral?

WILL: Nope. Just come over to talk to you.

GEORGE: You need to dress up in a blue serge suit to come over and talk to me?

WILL: No, sir. Put that on for my own benefit.

GEORGE: Start your plowing today?

WILL: No, sir.

GEORGE: You better get started. This good weather won't last forever.

WILL: I am aware of that.

GEORGE: Have a chair?

WILL: No, thank you.

GEORGE: I've never seen better weather for plowing. Have you?

WILL: No, sir. I don't believe I have, Mr. George.

GEORGE: Then why ain't you at it? I've been up since five and as soon as I take a nap I'm going back to it until sundown.

WILL: Mr. George. Have any men been over here trying to buy your land?

GEORGE: Yep. Matt Drew. H. T. Mavis. And two fellows come around to see about leasing today.

WILL: What did you say to them?

GEORGE: I said I wasn't interested.

WILL: We've got oil in our land, Mr. George.

GEORGE: Now, Will, I hate to dispute you . . .

WILL: I know we have. I've been saying it for twenty-eight years, and I know it's so. We're going to be rich men before we die. I couldn't sleep last night for thinking about it. It's the justification of my faith as I see it. I've held on to my land in spite of debt and fire and flood. Sometimes I'd be so tired I couldn't stand the thought of looking at another row of cotton, but every day when I went out to plow or to plant I'd say, don't give up. Hold on. There's oil here and you're gonna be rich.

GEORGE: That so?

WILL: You know that's so, Mr. George.

GEORGE: I've heard you say it often enough.

WILL: Well, it's so. And you're gonna live to see it's so. That's why I'm not planting this year, Mr. George, or plowing either. I'm leasing my land for the first decent offer I get, and I'm gonna sit this spring and this summer out on my porch and watch the men come and put the wells up and I'm . . .

[*He turns his head away. He is crying. His voice breaks.*]

Excuse me, Mr. George. I just get overcome when I think about it.

[*A pause.*]

I was getting scared. I'm sixty-five and I was getting scared that I wasn't going to live to see it. Then yesterday when Matt Drew and H. T. Mavis come around and offered to buy my farm, I knew. I knew clear as day it was going to happen. That my faith was going to be justified, and I was going to die a rich man.

GEORGE: What are you going to do with all that money when you get it?

WILL: I don't know, Mr. George. I don't dare to think about it. I started thinking last night and I had to stop. I got so excited my heart got to pounding and my breath caught short on me. If I hadn't made myself start thinking about it, I swear I might have had a heart attack, and then I wouldn't live to be a rich man at all.

[*A pause.*]

There's so many things I want to do. Buy a new gas range for Loula, take Thelma Doris out of her job at the courthouse. Set my boy up in a business of his own. Get myself a television set, and a man to drive me around the country when I want to get up and go.

[*A pause.*]

What are you going to do?

GEORGE: Nothing.

WILL: Nothing. You mean you're gonna leave all that money in the bank? Just let it set there . . .

GEORGE: Nope. I'm not seeing my land tore up. I'm plowing, remember? And that's what you'll do if you've got any sense. There's no oil here, Will.

WILL: Don't say that.

GEORGE: There's no oil here. There's three or four fools with nothing to do with their time and money than to go looking around and buying up what they can't use, but there's no oil here . . .

WILL: There is. Oh, yes. There is. I've seen it in my dreams at night, gushing up out of the earth. Those dreams weren't for nothing. They was the substance of my faith, and you and Loula and all the doubters in the world ain't getting me to turn my back on my dreams and my birthright.

GEORGE: Go back and plant your crop, Will. Don't be a fool.

WILL: A fool? You're the fool. I'll be riding to California with my chauffeur while you're out here breaking your back riding a tractor. Don't be a fool. I'm gonna be rich. I'm gonna be rich and it'll take more than you and your gloomy words to stop me.

[*He turns and strides out.* GEORGE *shakes his head sadly.*]

"MASTER HAROLD" . . . AND THE BOYS

BY ATHOL FUGARD

CHARACTERS

WILLIE *and* SAM *(both 40s) are servants, black men who work for Master Harold, a seventeen-year-old South African schoolboy. They are dependent on him for their livelihoods and for their very survival under the apartheid form of government.*

SCENE

The St. George's Park Tea Room in Port Elizabeth, South Africa.

TIME

A wet and windy afternoon in 1950.

[*Leaning on the solitary table, his head cupped in one hand as he pages through one of the comic books, is* SAM. *A black man in his mid-forties. He wears the white coat of a waiter. Behind him on his knees, mopping down the floor with a bucket of water and a rag, is* WILLIE. *Also black and about the same age as* SAM. *He has his sleeves and trousers rolled up.*]

WILLIE: [*Singing as he works.*]

She was scandalizin' my name,

She took my money

She called me honey

But she was scandalizin' my name.

Called it love but was playin' a game . . .

[*He gets up and moves the bucket. Stands thinking for a moment, then, raising his arms to hold an imaginary partner, he launches into an intricate ballroom dance step. Although a mildly comic figure, he reveals a reasonable degree of accomplishment.*]

Hey, Sam.

[SAM, *absorbed in the comic book, does not respond.*]

Hey, Boet Sam!

[SAM *looks up.*]

I'm getting it. The quickstep. Look now and tell me.

[*He repeats the step.*]

Well?

SAM: [*Encouragingly.*] Show me again.

WILLIE: Okay, count for me.

SAM: Ready?

WILLIE: Ready.

SAM: Five, six, seven, eight . . .

[WILLIE *starts to dance.*]

A-n-d one two three four . . . and one two three four . . .

[*Ad-libbing as* WILLIE *dances.*]

Your shoulders, Willie . . . your shoulders! Don't look down! Look happy, Willie! Relax, Willie!

WILLIE: [*Desperate but still dancing.*] I am relax.

SAM: No, you're not.

WILLIE: [*Falters.*] Ag no man, Sam! Mustn't talk. You make me make mistakes.

SAM: But you're stiff.

WILLIE: Yesterday I'm not straight . . . today I'm too stiff!

SAM: Well, you are. You asked me and I'm telling you.

WILLIE: Where?

SAM: Everywhere. Try to glide through it.

WILLIE: Glide?

SAM: Ja, make it smooth. And give it more style. It must look like you're enjoying yourself.

WILLIE: [*Emphatically.*] I wasn't.

SAM: Exactly.

WILLIE: How can I enjoy myself? Not straight, too stiff and now it's also glide, give it more style, make it smooth . . . Haai! Is hard to remember all those things, Boet Sam.

SAM: That's your trouble. You're trying too hard.

WILLIE: I try hard because it *is* hard.

SAM: But don't let me see it. The secret is to make it look easy. Ballroom must look happy, Willie, not like hard work. It must . . . Ja! . . . it must look like romance.

WILLIE: Now another one. What's romance?

SAM: Love story with happy ending. A handsome man in tails, and in his arms, smiling at him, a beautiful lady in evening dress!

WILLIE: Fred Astaire, Ginger Rogers.

SAM: You got it. Tap dance or ballroom, it's the same. Romance. In two weeks' time when the judges look at you and Hilda, they must see a man and a woman who are dancing their way to a happy ending. What I saw was you holding her like you were frightened she was going to run away.

WILLIE: Ja! Because that is what she wants to do! I got no romance left for Hilda anymore, Boet Sam.

SAM: Then pretend. When you put your arms around Hilda, imagine she is Ginger Rogers.

WILLIE: With no teeth? You try.

SAM: Well, just remember, there's only two weeks left.

WILLIE: I know, I know!

[*To the jukebox.*]

I do it better with music. You got sixpence for Sarah Vaughan?

SAM: That's a slow fox-trot. You're practicing the quickstep.

WILLIE: I'll practice slow fox-trot.

SAM: [*Shaking his head.*] It's your turn to put money in the jukebox.

WILLIE: I only got bus fare to go home.

[*He returns disconsolately to his work.*]

Love story and happy ending! She's doing it all right, Boet Sam, but is not be she's giving happy endings. Fuckin' whore! Three nights now she doesn't come practice. I wind up gramophone, I get record ready, and I sit and wait. What happens? Nothing. Ten o'clock I start dancing with my pillow. You try and practice romance by yourself, Boet Sam. Struesgod, she doesn't come tonight I take back my dress and ballroom shoes and I find me new partner. Six twenty-six. Shoes size seven. And now she's also making trouble for me with the baby again. Reports me to Child Wellfed, that I'm not giving her money. She lies! Every week I give her money for milk. And how do I know is my baby? Only his hair looks like me. She fucking around all the time I turn my back. Hilda Samuels is a bitch!

[*Pause.*]

Hey, Sam!

SAM: Ja.

WILLIE: You listening?

SAM: Ja.

WILLIE: So what you say?

SAM: About Hilda?

WILLIE: Ja.

SAM: When did you last give her a hiding?

WILLIE: [*Reluctantly.*] Sunday night.

SAM: And today is Thursday.

WILLIE: [*He knows what's coming.*] Okay.

SAM: Hiding on Sunday night, then Monday, Tuesday, and Wednesday she doesn't come to practice . . . and you are asking me why?

WILLIE: I said okay, Boet Sam!

SAM: You hit her too much. One day she's going to leave you for good.

WILLIE: So? She makes me the hell-in too much.

SAM: [*Emphasizing his point.*] *Too* much and *too* hard. You had the same trouble with Eunice.

WILLIE: Because she also make the hell-in, Boet Sam. She never got the steps right. Even the waltz.

SAM: Beating her up every time she makes a mistake in the waltz?

[*Shaking his head.*]

No, Willie! That takes the pleasure out of ballroom dancing.

WILLIE: Hilda is not too bad with the waltz, Boet Sam. Is the quickstep where the trouble starts.

SAM: [*Teasing him gently.*] How's your pillow with the quickstep?

WILLIE: [*Ignoring the tease.*] Good! And why? Because it got no legs. That's her trouble. She can't move them quick enough, Boet Sam. I start the record and before halfway Count Basie is already winning. Only time we catch up with him is when gramophone runs down.

[SAM *laughs.*]

Haaikona, Boet Sam, is not funny.

SAM: [*Snapping his fingers.*] I got it! Give her a handicap.

WILLIE: What's that?

SAM: Give her a ten-second start and then let Count Basie go. Then I put my money on her. Hot favorite in the Ballroom Stakes: Hilda Samuels ridden by Willie Malopo.

WILLIE: [*Turning away.*] I'm not talking to you no more.

SAM: [*Relenting.*] Sorry, Willie . . .

WILLIE: It's finish between us.

SAM: Okay, okay . . . I'll stop.

WILLIE: You can also fuck off.

SAM: Willie, listen! I want to help you!

WILLIE: No more jokes.

SAM: I promise.

WILLIE: Okay. Help me.

SAM: [*His turn to hold an imaginary partner.*]

Look and learn. Feet together. Back straight. Body relaxed. Right hand placed gently in the small of her back and wait for the music. Don't start worrying about making mistakes or the judges or the other competitors. It's just you, Hilda, and the music, and you're going to have a good time. What Count Basie do you play?

WILLIE: "You the cream in my coffee, you the salt in my stew."

SAM: Right. Give it to me in strict tempo.

WILLIE: Ready?

SAM: Ready.

WILLIE: A-n-d . . .

[*Singing.*]

You the cream in my coffee.

You the salt in my stew.

You will always be my necessity.

I'd be lost without you . . .

[SAM *launches into the quickstep. He's obviously a more accomplished dancer than* WILLIE.]

I'M NOT RAPPAPORT

BY HERB GARDNER

CHARACTERS

MIDGE *and* NAT, *both about eighty years old;* MIDGE *is black and* NAT *is white. That's the only thing that can be said about them that is simple.*

SCENE

A bench near a path at the edge of the lake in Central Park, New York City.

TIME

Early October, 1982.

[*Park bench in Central Park.* MIDGE *and* NAT *are smoking pot.*]

MIDGE: [*Glancing anxiously upright.*] Man say three miles, he sure takin' it slow.

NAT: Maybe he dropped dead.

[*On the inhale, handing joint to* MIDGE.]

A lot of these running people; boom.

MIDGE: [*On the inhale.*] You fellah like him?

NAT: They're the first ones; the young ones. Boom. They're running they're smiling; boom. You should be here in the evening, the drop like flies . . .

[*Chuckling, taking joint from* MIDGE.]

Boom, boom, boom . . .

[MIDGE *chuckles along with him,* NAT *studies the joint fondly for a moment.*]

All my life I fought for socialized medicine . . .

MIDGE: Stopped smoking dope when I turned seventy . . .

NAT: [*Peering up at* LAURIE.] That girl just went from very prett to beautiful . . .

MIDGE: Scared of goin' foolish. My daddy went foolish five year before he died, didn't know his own name. Sad to see. Hope I ain' the only one hearin' that music.

NAT: [*Moving towards bench, squinting up at Laurie.*] Now she' Hannah Pearlman . . .

MIDGE: Who?

NAT: [*Sits on bench; softly.*] Hannah Pearlman. She worked as finisher, stitched linings for yachting caps, Shiffman's Chapeaux on West Broadway. Nineteen Twenty-One.

MIDGE: [*Joins* NAT *at bench; squints up at Laurie for a moment.*] No ain't her. Tell you who you got there; that's Ella Mae Tilden . . .

[*Both looking up at Laurie as they talk, getting more and more stoned; the gentle carousel music continuing, bringing the past with it on the breeze. Now, in this delicate, dappled, late-afternoon light, Laurie truly seems to have the glow that* NAT *described.*]

NAT: Very shy, shyer even than me. She would sit on her stoop in th early evening, a fine, fine face like an artist would paint . . .

MIDGE: Ella Mae; best wife I had, number three. Five all told. It's Ella Mae give me John, it's John give me Billy and it's Billy give me these teeth . . .

NAT: I passed that stoop a million times; I couldn't say hello. Funny-looking fingers from the stitching, she sat on the stoop with the hands hidden, like so . . .

MIDGE: Eight grandchildren professionals and Billy's the dentist. Billy gave me this smile.

[*He demonstrates.*]

Put the teeth in, smiled, and left Ella Mae. Smile needed a new hat, and the hat made me walk a new way, which was out . . .

NAT: Also she was married. Yeah, went to work so her greenhorn husband could go to law school, become an American Somebody. Comes June, Arnold Pearlman graduates, suddenly finds out he's an attorney with a Yiddish-speaking wife which finishes yachting caps. Boom; he leaves her for a smooth-fingered Yankee Doodle he met at school. Four months later Hannah took the gas; a popular expression at that time for putting your head in an oven . . .

MIDGE: Poor Ella Mae cryin', me hearin' my new mouth say good-bye. She was near seventy then, but when my mind moves to her she is fresh peach prime . . .

NAT: September, a month before she took the gas, I see her in the Grand Central Library, second-floor reading room. A special place, quiet, not even a clock; I'm at the main table with *Macbeth,* I look up, there's Hannah Pearlman. She doesn't see me; her head is buried in a grammar book for a ten-year-old. She looks up, she knows me, she smiles. My heart goes directly into my ears, bang, bang, bang, I'm deaf. I don't speak. I can't speak. She puts her hands under the table, goes back to her book. After a while she leaves. I didn't *speak* . . .

MIDGE: [*Bangs his fist on the bench.*] Goddamn smile got me two more wives and nothin' but trouble! Damn these teeth and damn my wanderin' ways . . .

[*Takes out huge handkerchief, the carousel music fades.*]

NAT: I didn't *speak,* I didn't *speak* . . .

MIDGE: [*Blowing his nose.*] There's dope makes you laugh and dope makes you cry. I think this here's cryin' dope.

NAT: [*Bangs his cane on the ground.*] Stop, stop! Nostalgia, I hate it. The dread silence of old people! Kills more of us than heart failure!

MIDGE: [*Drying his eyes.*] When's the last time you made love to a woman?

NAT: Listen to him, more nostalgia! My poor schmeckle, talk about nostalgia! It comes up once a year, like Ground Hog Day. The last time I made love was July tenth, Nineteen Seventy-One.

MIDGE: Was your wife still alive?

NAT: I certainly hope so.

MIDGE: No, I meant—

NAT: I know what you meant. With Ethel is wasn't always easy to tell.

[*Smacks his forehead.*]

Shame on me! A good woman, a fine woman, was it *her* fault would always be in love with Hannah Pearlman?

MIDGE: See, last time for me I was bein' unfaithful. Damn my fickle soul, I cheated on them all. Daisy, I was seventy-six, stil had somethin' on the side; somethin' new.

NAT: Carter, this is the most courageous thing I ever heard abou you.

MIDGE: No courage to it, it's a curse. "Don't do it, Midge; don't *do* it," I kept sayin' while I did it. *Damn* my cheatin' soul.

NAT: No, no, you were *right*! You dared and did, I yearned and regretted. I *envy* you. You were always what I have only recently become.

MIDGE: A dirty old man.

NAT: A *romanticist*! A man of hope! Listen to me, I was dead once so I know things—it's not the sex, it's the romance. It's all in the head. Now, finally, I know this. The schmeckle is out of business, but still the romance remains, the adventure. That's all there *ever* was. The body came along for the ride. Do you understand me, Carter?

MIDGE: I'm thinkin' about it . . .

NAT: Because, frankly, right now I'm in love with this girl here.

MIDGE: [*After a moment.*] Well, fact is, so am I. I got to admit.

[*Peers up at Laurie for a few seconds.*]

Son of a gun . . . First time I ever fell in love with a white woman.

NAT: The first? Why the first?

MIDGE: Worked out that way.

NAT: All the others were black? Only black women?

MIDGE: Listen, you ran with a wild, Commie crowd; where *I* come from you stuck with your own. Bein' a black man, I—

NAT: A what?

MIDGE: A black man. Y'see, in *my* day—

NAT: Wait. Stop. Excuse me . . .

[*A beat; then* NAT *takes his bifocals out of his jacket pocket, puts them on, leans very close to* MIDGE. *He studies him for a few moments; then, quietly.*]

My God, you're right. You *are* a black man.

[*Silence for a moment. Then* NAT *bursts into laughter, pointing at* MIDGE.]

MIDGE: [*After a moment, catching on to the joke, a burst of laughter.*] Sly devil, you sly ol' devil . . .

NAT: [*Laughing happily, pointing at* MIDGE.] Hey, had ya goin', had ya *goin'* there for a minute, didn't I . . . ?

MIDGE: [*Clasps his hands, delighted laughter building.*] Had me goin', had me *goin'*, yeah . . . Lord, Lord . . .

NAT: [*Hitting his knees roaring.*] I love it, I love it, I love it—

[*Fresh gales of stoned laughter; they rock on the bench.*]

MIDGE: Stop, stop, I'm gonna die . . .

NAT: I'm gonna drop dead right here . . .

[*Suddenly stops laughing.*]

Wait a minute, Carter; is it *this* funny?

MIDGE: [*Stops laughing. Considers it. Bursts into laughter again.*]

Yes, it is. It is, definitely . . .

[*They point at each other, laughing at each other's laughter, laughing now at the fact that they* are *laughing; they fall on each other, shaking with mirth, threatening to roll off the bench.* MIDGE *suddenly leans back on the bench and abruptly falls asleep, snoring loudly.*]

NAT: Carter, what are you doing? We're right in the middle.

[MIDGE *keeps snoring.*]

How do you like that? One joint, look at this.

PLAY SOURCES, PERMISSIONS, AND ACKNOWLEDGMENTS

Albee, Edward © 1966. *A Delicate Balance*. Published in 2013 by Overlook Duckworth, Peter Mayer Publishers, Inc., New York, NY. www.overlookpress .com. All rights reserved. Direct inquiries to rights@overlookny.com.

Albee, Edward © 1975, 1976, 1977. *Counting the Ways*. Published in *The Collected Plays of Edward Albee, Volume 2* by Edward Albee in 2005 by Overlook Duckworth, Peter Mayer Publishers, Inc., New York, NY. www.overlookpress .com. All rights reserved. Direct inquiries to rights@overlookny.com.

Albee, Edward © 1975. *Seascape*. Published in *The Collected Plays of Edward Albee, Volume 2* by Edward Albee in 2005 by Overlook Duckworth, Peter Mayer Publishers, Inc., New York, NY. www.overlookpress.com. All rights reserved. Direct inquiries to rights@overlookny.com.

Alvarez, Lynn © 1987. *Hidden Parts*. Published by Smith and Kraus Publishers, Inc., in the collection *Lynne Alvarez: Collected Plays, Volume 1* in 1998. Direct inquiries to the author's agent, Susan Gurman, at rights@gurmanagency.com.

Anderson, Jane © 1994. *The Last Time We Saw Her*. Published by Samuel French, Inc., in the collection *Ten Minute Plays from the Actors Theatre of Louisville, Volume 3*, edited by Michael Bigelow Dixon and Michele Volansky. Direct inquiries to the author's agent's assistant, Aislinn Frantz, at afrantz@bretadamsltd.net.

Busch, Charles © 1999. *The Tale of the Allergist's Wife*. Published by Samuel French, Inc., in 2001. Direct inquiries to the author's agent, Jeffrey Melnick, at Eighth Square Entertainment, 4565 S. Ogden Drive, Los Angeles, CA 90036.

Dorfman, Ariel © 1992. *Death and the Maiden*. Used by permission of Viking Books, an imprint of Penguin Publishing Group, a division of Penguin Random House LLC. Direct inquiries to Sarah Laskin at slaskin@penguinrandomhouse .com. UK rights by permission of Nick Hern Books Ltd, The Glasshouse, 49a Goldhawk Road, London W12 8QP UK. www.nickhernbooks.co.uk. Direct inquiries to info@nickhernbooks.co.uk.

Fife, Stephen © 2013. *Break of Day*. Published by Samuel French, Inc., in 2014. Direct inquiries to the author at slfife@aol.com or www.stealfireproductions.com.

Fife, Stephen, adaptor, © 1992, 1998. *God of Vengeance* by Sholem Asch. Published by CUNE Press in 2004 as an Appendix in *Best Revenge: How the Theater Saved My Life and Has Been Killing Me Ever Since* by Stephen Fife. Direct inquiries to the author at slfife@aol.com or www.stealfireproductions.com.

Foote, Horton © 1957. *The Oil Well*. Published by Dramatists Play Service, Inc., in *Young Lady of Property: Six Short Plays* by Horton Foote. Reprinted by permission of ICM Partners. Direct inquiries to the author's agents at ICM Partners. www.icmpartners.com.

Fugard, Athol © 1981. "*Master Harold*" . . . *and the Boys*. Published by Samuel French, Inc. Reprinted by permission of ICM Partners. Direct inquiries to the author's agents at ICM Partners. www.icmpartners.com.

Gardner, Herb © 1984. *I'm Not Rappaport*. Published by Applause Theatre & Cinema Books in *The Collected Plays of Herb Gardner* in 2000. Reprinted by permission of ICM Partners. Direct inquiries to the author's agents at ICM Partners. www.icmpartners.com.

Gilroy, Frank D © 1993. *A Way with Words*. Published by Samuel French, Inc. in *A Way with Words: Five One Act Plays* by Frank D. Gilroy in 1993. Direct inquiries to the author's agent, Jonathon Lomma, at WME Entertainment jlomma@wmeentertainment.com.

Gotanda, Phillip Kan © 1995. *Ballad of Yachiyo*. Published by Dramatists Play Service Inc., in 1997. Direct inquiries to the author at www.philipkangotanda.com.

Guare, John © 1996. *The House of Blue Leaves*. Published in *The House of Blue Leaves and Chaucer in Rome: Two Plays by John Guare* in 2002 by Overlook Duckworth, Peter Mayer Publishers, Inc., New York, NY. www.overlookpress .com. All rights reserved. Direct inquiries to rights@overlookny.com.

Gurney, A. R. © 1994. *Later Life*. Published in *Later Life and Two Other Plays: The Snow Ball and the Old Boy* by A. R. Gurney in 1994 by Penguin Random House. Used by permission of Plume, an imprint of Penguin Publishing Group, a division of Penguin Random House LLC. UK rights by permission of William Morris Endeavor Entertainment, LLC. Direct Inquiries to the author's agent Jonathan Lomma at WME Entertainment, LLC, 1325 Ave. of the Americas, NYC, 10019. Caution: Professionals and amateurs are hereby warned that *Later Life* is subject to a royalty. It is fully protected under the copyright laws of the United States of America and of all countries covered by the International Copyright Union (including the Dominion of Canada and the rest of the British Commonwealth), the Berne Convention, the Pan-American Copyright Convention and the Universal Copyright Convention as well as all countries with which the United States has reciprocal copyright relations. All rights, including professional/amateur stage rights, motion picture, recitation, lecturing, public reading, radio broadcasting, television, video or sound recording, all other forms of mechanical or electronic reproduction, such as CD-ROM, CD-1, information storage and retrieval systems and photocopying, and the rights of translation into foreign languages, are strictly reserved. Particular emphasis is laid upon the matter of readings, permission for which must be secured from the Author's agent in writing.

Horovitz, Israel © 1993. *Fighting Over Beverley*. Published by Doubleday & Co., Inc., in 1995. Direct inquiries to the author's agent, Chris Till, at the Creative Artists Agency. chris.tillasst@caa.com.

Howe, Tina © 1982. *Painting Churches*. Published by Samuel French, Inc., in 2011. Reprinted by permission of ICM Partners. Direct inquiries to the author's agents at ICM Partners. www.icmpartners.com.

Hwang, David Henry © 1983. *The House of Sleeping Beauties*. Published in *Trying to Find Chinatown and Other Plays*. Copyright © 2000 by David Henry Hwang. Published by Theatre Communications Group. Used by permission of Theatre Communications Group. Direct inquiries to Zach Chotzen-Freund at zcfreund@tcg.org.

Hwang, David Henry © 1983. *The Sound of a Voice*. Published in *Trying to Find Chinatown and Other Plays*. Copyright © 2000 by David Henry Hwang. Published by Theatre Communications Group. Used by permission of Theatre Communications Group. Direct inquiries to Zach Chotzen-Freund at zcfreund@tcg.org.

Letts, Tracy © 2008. *August: Osage County*. Published by Theatre Communications Group in 2008. Used by permission of Theatre Communications Group. Direct inquiries to Zach Chotzen-Freund at zcfreund@tcg.org.

Letts, Tracy © 2006. *The Man From Nebraska*. Published by Northwestern University Press in 2006. All rights reserved. Direct inquiries to Liz Hamilton, Permissions at emhamilton@northwestern.edu.

Lindsay-Abaire, David © 2011. *Good People*. Published by Theatre Communications Group in 2011. Used by permission of Theatre Communications Group. Direct inquiries to Zach Chotzen-Freund at zcfreund@tcg.org.

Machado, Eduardo © 1991. *In the Eye of the Hurricane*. Published by Samuel French, Inc., in 2009. Direct inquiries to the author's agent, Chris Till, at the Creative Artists Agency. chris.tillasst@caa.com.

Margulies, Donald © 2000. *Dinner with Friends*. Published by Theatre Communications Group in 2011. Used by permission of Theatre Communications Group. Direct inquiries to Zach Chotzen-Freund at zcfreund@tcg.org.

Margulies, Donald © 2010. *Time Stands Still*. Published by Theatre Communications Group in 2011. Used by permission of Theatre Communications Group. Direct inquiries to Zach Chotzen-Freund at zcfreund@tcg.org.

McPherson, Scott/Scout Productions, Inc. © 1990. *Marvin's Room*. Published by Dramatists Play Service, Inc., in 1991. Direct inquiries to the author's agent, James J. Bagley, at 350 North Palm Drive, Suite 104, Beverly Hills, CA 90210.

Meyerson, Henry © 2009. *Shtick*. Published by Samuel French, Inc., in 2009. Caution: Professionals and amateurs are hereby warned that *Shtick* being fully protected under the copyright laws of the United States of America, the British Commonwealth countries, including Canada, and the other countries of the Copyright Union, is subject to a royalty. All rights, including professional, amateur, motion picture, recitation, public reading, radio, television and cable broadcasting, and the rights of translation into foreign languages, are strictly reserved. Any inquiry regarding the availability of performance rights, or the purchase of individual copies of the authorized acting edition, must be directed to Samuel French, Inc., 235 Park Avenue South, Fifth Floor, New York, NY 10003 with other locations in Hollywood and London. Direct inquiries to Caitlin Bartow, Business Affairs at Samuel French. cbartow@samuelfrench.com.

Miller, Arthur © 1949, renewed 1977. *The Death of a Salesman*. Used by permission of Viking Books, an imprint of Penguin Publishing Group, a division of Penguin Random House LLC. Direct inquiries to Sarah Laskin at slaskin @penguinrandomhouse.com. UK rights by permission of the Wylie Agency. All rights reserved. Direct inquiries to permissions@wylieagency.com.

Miller, Arthur. *The Price*. Copyright © Arthur Miller and Ingeborg M. Miller, Trustee. Used by permission of Viking Books, an imprint of Penguin Publishing Group, a division of Penguin Random House LLC. Direct inquiries to Sarah Laskin at slaskin@penguinrandomhouse.com. UK rights by permission of the Wylie Agency. All rights reserved. Direct inquiries to permissions@wylieagency.com.

Miller, Arthur, adaptor © 1950, 1951, renewed 1979. *The Enemy of the People* by Henrik Ibsen, adapted by Arthur Miller. Used by permission of Viking Books, an imprint of Penguin Publishing Group, a division of Penguin Random House LLC. Direct inquiries to Sarah Laskin at slaskin@penguinrandomhouse.com. UK rights by permission of the Wylie Agency. All rights reserved. Direct inquiries to permissions@wylieagency.com.

Miller, Jason © 1972. *That Championship Season*. Published by Dramatists Play Service, Inc., in 1973. Direct inquiries to the author's agent, Earl Graham, at the Graham Agency. grahamacynyc@aol.com.

Norman, Marsha © 1983. *'Night Mother*. Published by Hill and Wang, 1983. Reprinted by permission of Hill and Wang, a division of Farrar, Straus and Giroux, LLC. Direct inquiries to fsg.rights@fsgbooks.com, attn.Victoria Fox. UK rights by permission of William Morris Endeavor Entertainment, LLC. Direct Inquiries to John Buzzetti at WME Entertainment, LLC, 1325 Ave. of the Americas, NYC, 10019. Caution: Professionals and amateurs are hereby warned that *'Night, Mother* is subject to a royalty. It is fully protected under the copyright laws of the United States of America and of all countries covered by the International Copyright Union (including the Dominion of Canada and the rest of the British Commonwealth), the Berne Convention, the Pan-American Copyright Convention and the Universal Copyright Convention as well as all

countries with which the United States has reciprocal copyright relations. A
rights, including professional/amateur stage rights, motion picture, recitatio
lecturing, public reading, radio broadcasting, television, video or soun
recording, all other forms of mechanical or electronic reproduction, such as CI
ROM, CD-1, information storage and retrieval systems and photocopying, an
the rights of translation into foreign languages, are strictly reserved. Particula
emphasis is laid upon the matter of readings, permission for which must b
secured from the Author's agent in writing.

Oates, Joyce Carol. *The Key*. From *Twelve Plays* by Joyce Carol Oates, copyrigh
© 1991 by The Ontario Review, Inc. Used by permission of New America
Library, an imprint of Penguin Publishing Group, a division of Penguin Randor
House LLC. Direct inquiries to Sarah Laskin at slaskin@penguinrandomhous
.com. UK rights by permission of John Hawkins & Associates, Inc. Reprinte
by permission of John Hawkins & Associates, Inc. Direct inquiries to Liz Fre
at free@jhalit.com.

O'Neill, Eugene © 1956. *Long Day's Journey into Night*. Published by Yal
University Press in 1956. Reprinted by permission of ICM Partners. Direct a
inquiries to ICM Partners. www.icmpartners.com.

Pepper, Cary © 1990. *Come Again, Another Day*. Published by Applause Theatre 8
Cinema Books in *The Best American Short Plays 2011–2012*. Direct inquirie
to the author at pepperplays@carypepper.com.

Rebeck, Theresa © 1990. *Sex with the Censor*. Published by Smith and Krau
Publishers, Inc., in *Theresa Rebeck: Complete Plays Volume III, Short Play
1989–2005*. Reprinted by permission of ICM Partners. Direct inquiries t
the author's agents at ICM Partners. www.icmpartners.com.

Rebeck, Theresa © 1999. *Walk*. Published by Smith and Kraus Publishers, Inc., i
Theresa Rebeck: Complete Plays Volume III, Short Plays 1989–2005. Reprinte
by permission of ICM Partners. Direct inquiries to the author's agents at ICM
Partners. www.icmpartners.com.

Redwood, John Henry © 1998. *The Old Settler*. Published by Dramatists Pla
Service, Inc., in 1998. Direct inquiries to the author's agent, Ross Weiner, a
rweiner@paradigmagency.com.

Rivera, José © 1983. *The House of Ramon Iglesia*. Published by Samuel French
Inc., in 1983. Direct inquiries to the author's agent, Jonathon Lomma, a
WME Entertainment. jlomma@wmeentertainment.com.

Ross, Melissa © 2011. *Thinner Than Water*. Published by Smith and Kraus Publishers, Inc., in *New Playwrights: The Best Plays 2011*, edited by Larry Harbison. Direct inquiries to the author's agent, Jessica Amato, at the Gersh Agency in New York City. jamato@gershny.com.

Schenkkan, Robert © 1991. *The Kentucky Cycle (Tall Tales)*. Published by Dramatists Play Service, Inc., in 1994. Direct inquiries to the author's agent, Derek Zasky, at WME Entertainment. dzasky@wmeentertainment.com.

Shaner, John Herman © 1986. *After Crystal Night*. Published by Samuel French, Inc., in 1986. Direct inquiries to the author at John Herman Shaner, 735 North Orlando Ave., Los Angeles, CA 90064. (323) 655-1250. johnhshaner@att.net.

Shepard, Sam © 2002. *Eyes for Consuela*. Published in the volume *The Late Henry Moss, Eyes for Consuela, When the World Was Green: Three Plays* by Sam Shepard. Used by permission of Vintage Books, an imprint of the Knopf Doubleday Publishing Group, a division of Penguin Random House LLC. All rights reserved. Direct inquiries to Emory Johnson at emjohnson@randomhouse.com.

Sterner, Jerry © 1989. *Other People's Money*. Published by Samuel French, Inc., in 1989. Direct inquiries to Caitlin Bartow, Business Affairs at Samuel French. cbartow@samuelfrench.com.

Strindberg, August, trans. by Arvid Paulson. *The Father*. From *Seven Plays by August Strindberg*, translated by Arvid Paulson. Translation copyright © 1960 by Bantam Books, a division of Penguin Random House LLC. Used by permission of Bantam Books, a division of Penguin Random House LLC. Any third party use of this material, outside of this publication, is prohibited. Interested parties must apply directly to Penguin Random House LLC for permission. Direct inquiries to Alicia Dercole at Permissions at Penguin Random House. adercole@penguinrandomhouse.com.

Sweet, Jeffrey © 1983. *The Value of Names*. Published by Dramatists Play Service, Inc., in 1986. Direct inquiries to the author at dgsweet@aol.com.

Tesich, Steve © 1989. *The Speed of Darkness*. Published by Samuel French, Inc., in 1990. Reprinted by permission of ICM Partners. Direct inquiries to the author's agents at ICM Partners. www.icmpartners.com.

Valdez, Luiz © 1986. *I Don't Have to Show You No Stinking Badges!*. Published by Arte Publico Press-The University of Houston in *Zoot Suit and Other Plays* by Luis Valdez in 1992. Reprinted by permission of Arte Publico Press-University of Houston. Direct inquiries to Arte Publico Press, Permissions Dept., University of Houston, 4902 Gulf Parkway, Bldg. 19, Room 100. Houston, TX 77204. (713) 743-2843. www.artepublicopress.com.

Wasserstein, Wendy © 1993. *The Sisters Rosensweig*. Published by Dramatists Play Service, Inc., in 1997. Direct inquiries to the author's agent, Phyllis Wender, at the Gersh Agency, 41 Madison Avenue, 33rd floor, New York, NY 10010.

Wilder, Thornton © 1955, 1957. *The Matchmaker*. Earlier version under the title *The Merchant of Yonkers*, copyright © 1939 by The Wilder Family LLC. Reprinted by arrangement with The Wilder Family LLC and The Barbara Hogenson Agency, Inc. All rights reserved. Published by Samuel French, Inc., in 2010 (among many other publishers). Direct inquiries to the author's estate's agent, Barbara Hogenson, at the Barbara Hogenson agency. bhogenson@aol.com.

Williams, Tennessee. *The Gnadiges Fraulein*. Copyright © 1965, 1967 by Two Rivers Enterprises, Inc. From *The Theatre of Tennessee Williams, Volume VII*, copyright © 1981 by The University of the South. Previously published by New Directions in the collection *Dragon Country: Selected One Act Plays by Tennessee Williams* in 1970. Reprinted by permission of New Directions Publishing Corp. Direct inquiries to permissions@ndbooks.com, attn. Christopher Wait. UK rights by permission of Georges Borchardt, Inc. Reprinted by permission of Georges Borchardt, Inc., on behalf of the Tennessee Williams Estate.

Wilson, August © 1986. *Fences*. Published by Plume in 1987 (among other publishers). Used by permission of New American Library, an imprint of Penguin Publishing Group, a division of Penguin Random House LLC. Direct inquiries to Sarah Laskin at slaskin@penguinrandomhouse.com.